BELOW
THE
SURFACE

BELOW THE SURFACE

By
Kevin Firth

Strategic Book Publishing and Rights Co.

© 2015 by Kevin Firth All rights reserved.

No part of this book may be reproduced or transmitted in any form or by any means, graphic, electronic, or mechanical, including photocopying, recording, taping, or by any information storage retrieval system, without the permission, in writing, of the publisher. For more information, send an email to support@sbpra.net, Attention Subsidiary Rights Department.

Strategic Book Publishing and Rights Co.
USA | Singapore
www.sbpra.com

For information about special discounts for bulk purchases, please contact Strategic Book Publishing and Rights Co. Special Sales, at bookorder@sbpra.net

ISBN: 978-1-68181-017-1

Book Design by Julius Kiskis

22 21 22 20 19 18 17 16 15   1 2 3 4 5

DEDICATION

I dedicate this book to
my daughter, Michaella (Kila), and my son, Dominic.
May your days be filled with love and happiness.

 # CONTENTS

Acknowledgments xi
1. Below the Surface 1
2. Where It All Started 3
3. Meet the Family 8
4. Mum and Dad's Separation 26
5. Blackburn 28
6. Recruitment 30
7. Ribble Bus to Haslingden 32
8. Walking to the Train 35
9. Navy Boot Camp 37
10. Sea Training 51
11. *HMS Zulu* 60
12. Gibraltar 69
13. Malta 72
14. Naples 76
15. Durban and the Fabulous Shakas 78
16. Sinking of the Good Ship *Zulu* 87
17. The Beira Bucket 94
18. Bahrain, the Armpit 97
19. Bugis Street, Singapore 99
20. Hong Kong 101
21. Returning to the UK 109

22. *HMS Sultan* Engineering School	113
23. Diving Course	114
24. Marilyn	124
25. *HMS Brereton*	128
26. Bahrain Again	132
27. G and T is Good for Me	152
28. Returning to UK on the *Brereton*	160
29. New Skipper Aboard	168
30. Secret Wedding	174
31. *HMS Lincoln*	176
32. The Druggy	193
33. Spud Fight at the OK Corral	198
34. Marilyn's Intro to Red	201
35. De-Mobbing	203
36. We're Having A Baby	209
37. Our Very Own House	215
38. Feeling Restless	217
39. Biscuit Reappears	225
40. Sedco 707	229
41. Me and My Big Mouth	238
42. Fort William	251
43. An Unfortunate Accident	260

CONTENTS

44. The First Commercial Deep Bell Dive 265
45. Construction 269
46. *Ocean Kokuei* 272
47. My Crack at the Big Time 287
48. Diving Supervisor 292
49. Dad Leaves Us 294
50. There Has to Be More 301
51. Balder Davis 306
52. Canadian Immigration 310
53. The Big Move 316
54. *Zapata Ugland* 326
55. Mantis Duplus Subs 334
56. A Surprise Visit 340
57. *Bowdrill One* and *Two* 342
58. Raising and Sinking the *Ocean Ranger* 345
59. Hangover at Eight Hundred Feet 348
60. My Kids 353
61. My Transgressions 357
62. *Ocean Ranger* Seabed Clearance 359
63. Oops! 373
64. Is This Really Happening? 377
65. The Final Curtain Call 382

ACKNOWLEDGMENTS

I would like to thank my dear wife, Joan, for her patience and understanding during the long periods of time I have taken to write this. I would also like to thank Sherry Coman, (B.A.) *English Literature and Film,* who not only gave me confidence to put this story into print but was invaluable in helping me dig a little deeper.

CHAPTER 1
Below the Surface

Walking, walking, walking – it seems like such a long way today. How many times have I walked this route into town? Hundreds maybe, who knows! Today it is with a considerable load on my mind, like a huge weight hulking down on my young shoulders. After today, my life completely changes. This unknown journey ahead scares the heeber jeepers out of me.

Just try to concentrate on all the good things that may come out of this, Kevin, then maybe we'll get through this, I keep reminding myself. *Well, here's one good thought: I guess I'll never have to walk this road again, that's for sure. That is, if I have the guts!*

I'm not even sixteen yet. I've been living in a torment of a home with nightmarish middle-of-the-night experiences, wondering if Mum and Dad have done harm to each other. It's a regular occurrence, to be suddenly awakened in the dead of night by screams and thuds that seem to make my heart skip a beat. Many times, I found myself laying in the cold, inky dark, shivering in fear, listening quite intently, trying to pick up the seriousness of the engagement downstairs. Somehow, through this hideous situation, I also tried in vain to console my little sister, who at times was almost convulsive with her own fear. Sometimes the arguments rose to such a crescendo that we wondered if Mum would actually make it through the night.

Finally, after years of this abuse, I lost all semblance of restraint and beat my father to a pulp. Blinded with an uncontrollable temper and in one mind-numbing moment, I found myself with flaying fists beating and kicking him. I soon realized that the high-pitched screaming I heard was, in fact, my own voice as I experienced a total and unequivocal loss of control. Through my tears, I saw his vacant, expressionless face staring up at me amidst the tirade of blows he was accepting without a fight, surrounded by blood and mayhem. Seemingly moments later, I was running until my heart felt like it would explode in my chest, hoping that somehow I could escape from all of this madness. Then came the cold, empty, and helpless feeling I had thereafter, not knowing what to do or where to go.

I also remember sitting in a bus shelter; I had hitchhiked to the seaside resort of Blackpool. I was cold and wet. It had rained all night and I was miles away from home. Lonely and with a peculiar weakness in my legs, my mind full of very dark thoughts, it was probably the first time in my young life that I had contemplated saying goodbye to everyone.

Sad and unbelievable as it was, this episode was to repeat itself more than once. There were other similar times my siblings and I had to endure. My older brother and sister, twins, had left home at a very early age to remove themselves from this carnage, and in doing so, they left my sister and me to face the music alone! All of these experiences inevitably put an old head on these young shoulders.

We had moved to Blackburn in 1964 and had been there for the last couple of years. This town had been a busy hub during the industrial revolution in the northwest of England. It was typical of the many other industrial towns, except much larger. The numerous tall, coal-blackened chimneys still belched soot-laden smoke that towered high above the many grimy, rusty slate roofs. We lived beside a steel foundry that never seemed to stop. Day and night we heard the clatter of recycled steel being cut, bent, and thrown into carts. The view through my bedroom window was of a steel rail gantry that continually and very noisily unloaded carts of rusty metal to be smelted. There was a fine powdered layer of rust over our whole street and surrounding area. Mum had given up trying to clean our back windows, and of course we couldn't afford a window cleaner.

At the end of our street were the gasworks: monolithic monstrosities that took a close second to the chimneys in depressing any spirit you might have woken up with. The huge circular, grey, rusting steel contraptions, probably sixty feet high by maybe the same in width, mysteriously rose and lowered with the amount of gas they held in their foul bellies. This gas had been manufactured by burning the huge mounds of coal that seemed to be scattered hither and thither everywhere. This probably explained one of the reasons for those towering blackened stone stacks that over the years had painted just about everything in sight a dirty, sooty black.

Have I mentioned the smell yet? On my early morning half-hour walk into the town bus station, I had to pass a miserable excuse for a river. I tried on many occasions to see how long I could hold my breath while passing the effluent stink. Depending on which way the wind was blowing, I sometimes had to speed up the pace to a full-blown run in order to get the hell on the upwind side. To add to that industrious melee, the town also has one of the largest beer brewing facilities in the northwest, probably in the whole of England. On a good day, probably only the remains of the beer makings – used stale hops and barley –

went into the river, but the chemicals and ooze from other factories nearby rarely took a break. Tie that in with the local glue factory that used dead animals in their illustrious tacky recipe, add a few leftover dead animals, and then mix in a few old beds and car parts. It made for a repulsive early morning start, should your eyes reluctantly wander over to see where the sickening, stomach-churning stench was coming from.

Did I paint a gloomy enough picture? You bet your ass.

CHAPTER 2
Where It All Started
4 Back Ormerod Street, Rawtenstall

One of my earliest memories was being quietly shoved out of the kitchen window by my older brother Ronnie and his twin sister Rita to run to the police station. The coal chute grate from the street into our dismally dark coal cellar had been fixed closed by our dad to stop our escape. We had previously scrabbled up the coal pile, sometimes in the dark, and then quietly lifted the heavy grate to peep out to find our dad waiting for us. He would then escort us back into the house by the scruff of the neck.

I was just seven years old, but I will always remember seeing my little sister Freda's terrified eyes thinking that Mum wasn't going to make it through the night. The numerous times I managed to escape, I only made it to the police station once. Dad always seemed to have a knack of finding all my hiding places on the way, even in his drunken stupor.

I should probably mention here that Mum and Dad are both deaf. They both lost their hearing at a very early age, but because they had been born with hearing, they had already learned the basics of using their voice. Dad could hear a tiny bit. He liked to listen to music on a set of beat-up earphones he had put together himself. Although Mum and Dad messed up the pronunciation of a few words, which we then sadly learned, they could at least talk to us. For reasons only they could know (probably embarrassment at not knowing what they sounded like), they never used their voices to anyone but us kids. To communicate with our parents, we had learned from an early age to exaggerate our lips and basically charade. We rarely ever had to use sign language.

At that time, we lived in half a terraced house on Ormerod Street in Rawtenstall, referred to as a 'back-to-back' in those days. Rawtenstall was one of the few busy industrial towns in the Rossendale Valley in bleak, rainy Lancashire. If you can imagine a long row of terraced houses (Coronation Street style), then split them into two, back-to-back, then you've got the idea. To get to our half we had to go through a small, dark *ginnel* (tunnel), then onto a narrow concrete balcony that led to all the other 'back' houses. On the back of the house we were actually three floors up, because the street was built onto the side of a steep hill. There were rusty iron spiked railings all along the balcony, a mere excuse for safety.

Inside our house on the main floor was a living room and a small kitchen with a door down to a dark, dingy coal cellar. From the living room, which had the only coal fire that heated the whole house, there was a small curtain that opened to the stairs that led to the two upstairs bedrooms. At the back of the right-facing bedroom there was another curtain that then led up another set of stairs to the attic. At the landing on the top of the first set of stairs, between the two bedroom doors, there was a privacy curtain that covered a small area with a 'potty,' the only toilet facility within the house. If you had the unfortunate chore to empty this potty, you had to go outside along the balcony and down two flights of stairs to the outside toilet under the balcony, hoping dearly that you would not meet anybody on the way. The outside 'Tippler Toilet,' as it was known in it its infamous day, was basically a very deep hole with a raised wooden toilet seat attached to it. For a small child going to the toilet, it could be a scary event; one only had to count the seemingly many seconds to hear the faint *plop* to realize just how deep the thing was.

We never really stayed in a house for more than a couple of years. Almost like gypsies, we seemed to be constantly on the move from distraught neighbours or the failure to pay the rent. In later years, I believe it was mostly Mum's quest to move away from our dad, which always seemed to be high on the list of her reasons. It didn't work! He was always a thorn in her side.

CHAPTER 3
Meet The Family
Ronnie

Ronnie and I slept in the attic with a whole bunch of bike parts and other assorted junk. We had a roof window that we occasionally opened and climbed out of to take leisurely strolls, or to sunbathe in the rare hot days of summer. On our back side of the steep, broken, slated roof (which if you have been counting was actually six floors up), if either one of us had fallen, before we had hit the cobblestoned street below, we would probably have been impaled by the spear-like bars on the balcony fence. Dad knew we did this. I wouldn't say he encouraged it, but in his and our daredevil way, unimaginably it just seemed like the okay thing to do. In fact, when a slate needed to be repaired, we actually helped our dad, although he did tie me, the tot, to the chimney with just enough rope that I wouldn't fall off the edge.

Ronnie, even at fourteen, was always the ultimate daredevil. He could walk right down to the edge all matter of fact, then turn and give me his big wide grin. I was always the brother in training. I had to be trained and then tested to ensure I was 'Firth enough.' Much to my chagrin, to get me over my fear of heights at seven years old, he would hold my feet and dangle me over the edge of roofs and cliffs, with me screaming and pleading for him to bring me back.

Another sad lament I might have let slip once was that I was scared of ghosts. Ronnie's way of getting me over that petty fear was to lower me into a pauper's open grave and then leave me there! He taught me how to wrestle – I have a missing tooth to prove it – and through his fine tutelage I eventually overcame being bullied at school. Yep, at about age eleven I didn't need my daily hit. He also taught me how to make gas bombs, which I will not go into here except to say that I always seemed to be the one lighting the flame!

'Ronnie, I'm scared,' I'd utter.

'Go on, light the damn thing, ya big softy, then run like a bugger. I'll be here waiting for you,' he'd say.

BOOM! The tin lid was launched into the heavens, probably one of the reasons that I've always been a good runner.

Through sheer boredom one day we made a huge catapult from bike inner tubes that we fixed to each side of the attic window. Finding a nice-sized nut, we both stretched the tubes as far as we possibly could, then let fly. We watched eagerly as the nut flew over the church, then the car park, then the road and the river, to wonderfully come crashing down on the cotton factory's glass roof. Oh what excitement! I think we both did a jig or two in sheer excitement, and then went looking for an even bigger missile and added more inner tubes. This was going to be the cat's whiskers. We both stretched back those inner tubes to the other side of the attic, scrambling over much rubbish en route, then let fly once more. Ah, ecstasy! However, our aim was not as accurate as the first projectile, and said nut bounced off the side of the window frame, ricocheted off several walls, and came to rest on poor Ronnie's nose, thanks to which he has a scar today, together with another scar that I accidentally made while shoveling snow.

Ronnie, the handsome daredevil, was in all honesty, and still is, my number one hero. Much later in my early, difficult teens, like a father figure I sadly never had, he showed me the way. Girls were always a challenge, and thinking that I was the original ugly duckling, I was extremely shy around them. Ronnie was the opposite; he was a complete natural around the opposite sex. From time to time he brought home his latest conquest, which was usually some blonde-haired goddess that I would immediately fall in love with. They would pat my head and say, 'Oh, what a nice little boy.' I would immediately go scarlet red and scurry off amidst a dizzying bouquet of her perfume. For the next week or so I would wake up from sensual dreams wondering why my underpants were wet! He gave me the necessary confidence, and like a captain of his ship, he always steered me in the right direction.

In the late 1950s he was a 'teddy boy.' The mods and rockers seemed to come much later. His hair was greased back in the latest Tony Curtis style, complete with the DA (duck's ass) at the back. A mixture of sugar and water fixed it in place, and nothing short of a gale force wind could disrupt it. He had the winklepicker shoes with the impossibly pointed toes, the tightest pants ever, and usually a white T-shirt. That is, of course, when he was out dancing with the stunningly beautiful red head, his twin sister Rita.

Rita

She would be wearing a dress with what seemed a hundred crinoline petticoats underneath to hoop the skirt, together with the white, high heel winklepicker shoes. Her hair was always dazzlingly ginger red. She had the looks of a young film star and I'm sure she was the desire of every male. What a pair they looked! I think Grandma had helped to pay for them to go to dancing lessons. Needless to say, they knew all the steps and looked out for each other when fights started out in the local Astoria Dance Hall.

On Friday nights, little Freda, Mum, and I would clear away the furniture to the edge of our usually untidy living room, and put away all the guinea pigs, rabbits, and tortoises in their seldom-used cages. Freda and I would play with the big old radio and try to find some suitable rock 'n' roll music. We would then anxiously await the homecoming of the twins. Dad was usually out, and by then paralytic drunk, having spent the best part of the last week's wages on booze. The door would suddenly come crashing open, and two very excited red-faced teenagers would set the usually gloomy room alight! Almost like a circus act complete with brightly coloured attire, Ronnie would fling Rita over his head and then under his legs with the precision of an acrobat. The music would be blasting out; we were never very good neighbours. Time after time they would spin and swirl like whirling dervishes. Rita's dress would be just a blur, fanning out from side to side. Most of the time she almost looked like she was defying gravity.

Although Mum could not hear a thing, she could feel a beat, and this was like manna from heaven to her and our eyes. She screamed like a banshee every time Rita was flung over or under. After what seemed like hours we eventually all laid back, totally exhausted at the thrill we had just witnessed. It was a feast for my soul. I didn't want to blink, for fear I might miss something. They both shone like the very stars in the sky, completely unaware of their surroundings. It seemed that this is what they both lived for. To this day when I see them jiving, I always feel this surge of emotion coming up from a deep place within me, and inexplicably, tears of sheer happiness just take over my being. I have absolutely no control over it. If there are highlights in what seemed a miserable part of my life, this has to be numero uno.

Before Ronnie and I moved to the attic, we shared one of the second-floor bedrooms with Rita. Ronnie and I were in a bed together, and Rita was across the room in another. Freda still slept with Mum. Rita was always the boss: what time we went to bed, what time the lights went out, what time we got up, even why I hadn't cleaned behind my ears, all big sister Rita's decisions. Big Ronnie knew all too well who the real boss was, and he toed the line.

Rita was also the one who read us stories from her Enid Blyton books, wonderful stories about wishing chairs, magic, and adventure. I would waft along with her expressive voice and become part of the story itself, wishing for it to never end. It could transport me to another place, a place of wonder away from this gloomy, damp bedroom with wallpaper peeling off the walls, away from the bedlam usually happening downstairs, and more importantly, away from my nightmares that usually ended with violent, convulsive fits. Much to everyone's relief, the frightening convulsions stopped after a few years, but the nightmares stayed with me for a lot longer. Rita's stories gave me peace and tranquility, things that were desperately missing in those young years. In her way, she also gave all of us values in our appearance and general respect for our immediate surroundings.

Freda

As the twins were seven years my elder and Freda was four years younger, I think Freda and I looked out for each other most of the time, especially a few years later when the twins left home. They had both married by the time they reached eighteen, and taking themselves out of the madness, they were trying to make a normal life for themselves. That would make me eleven and Freda seven, and as Mum sometimes slept into the afternoon, we were basically left to ourselves. We had many concoctions to cook for ourselves. The basic ingredients always consisted of one or two of the following: toast, jam, eggs, bacon, sausage, and beans. Beans on toast was the hot favourite and quickest, followed by a healthy serving of Birds Custard. On those rare days when Mum was up, cooking was never one of her favourite chores, so we inevitably looked after ourselves anyway. Before Freda could even see the top of the counter, I had her buttering toast or making herself a jam butty (sandwich). I don't ever remember being hungry. There was always something in to eat. By today's standards it probably wasn't healthy or very nutritious, but it got us by.

When things became unbearable and our parents' arguments became explosive, I always tried to keep Freda out of the way. She would cry so hard at times I thought that something was going to happen and I would have no control over the outcome.

Mum had left the house one time after a long, maniacal argument that went into the middle of the night. We both went out to look for her at about three in the morning, only to find her sitting on a rock in the local rubbish dump. She was completely delirious and couldn't even speak, which made Freda go into a total hysteria. We thought Mum had finally lost her mind! At eleven years old, I had to escort them both home, put them to bed, and try and reason what to do next. Mercifully, over the next twenty-four hours Mum slowly recovered.

Needless to say, we didn't spend too much time at school in those days. Time after time the school board sent out the 'hooky man,' a scary red-faced chap that, if he caught you, forced you to go to school. We would hit the floor like a pair of seasoned soldiers, crawl upstairs, then peep through the bedroom curtains and stay deadly quiet to his calls through the letterbox. 'I know you're in there. Come to the door right away or we will send the police.'

At one point, after only spending less than sixty days in school in one year, we were about to be taken from our mother and put into care. I think this was one of the scariest times of our youthful lives. Amazingly, our first thought was who would protect Mum! We would be lost forever. To be taken from our mum would be a catastrophe neither of us could endure. Providence came our way and we were put on probation, as it were, and as long as we went to school and the police weren't called as often, they would leave us be.

To say we had a different upbringing would be an understatement! What seemed perfectly normal in those days makes me seriously wonder now why none of us have had serious adult problems. I'd like to think we have all seen the worst of it, and it has inevitably made us stronger adults knowing that we could face just about anything. In older, different stages of my life, I have been able to withstand what I think are very demanding, difficult, and sometimes dangerous tasks. I'm not saying that I'm tougher than the next guy, but it always seemed I had something to prove, so I actually looked for the more demanding and somewhat dangerous job. For a while, though, during difficult times in my first marriage, I thought I was developing a reckless attitude toward my own life, almost in a masochistic kind of way, as if I wished for the worst to actually happen!

One fact, however, has remained – it has been difficult for all four of us kids to stay in a marriage. We've all been divorced, some of us even twice. I nicknamed it the Firth Curse.

Mum

Besides being deaf, Mum was also a bit different in other ways too. She was not what I would call a tidy lady – clean, but not tidy. Our house was always a bit cluttered and untidy. On Monday, wash day, it was all I could do to just not be there. Piles of clothes, from God only knows where, appeared in the tiny kitchen. They were put into a dolly tub, which was a large zinc, ribbed barrel about thirty inches tall by almost two feet in circumference. This was filled with hot water, usually from the kettle, a gas geyser, or on the rare occasion when we lived in a house that had a back water boiler to our coal fire. If I hadn't already escaped, it was my job to use the posser – this kind of looked like a large toilet plunger, except the plunger part was made of copper.

So, after much complaining that my arm was about to drop off, I would posser away at the dirty laundry that may have sat there for a day or two soaking. Mum would then wring out the clothes over the ceramic sink or use a hand-operated mechanical wringer called a mangle. Dad once brought home an old electronic mangle. He probably stole it or found it in a junkyard, as he probably couldn't stand washday any more than us. He had an uncanny knack of being able to fix things he had absolutely no idea about. Anyway, Mum loved this thing until it almost dragged her through the wringer. Her complete arm went through it before she managed to stop the infernal machine. Her arm was black and blue for weeks. So back to the posser we all went.

Mum and our pets

We have all inherited an unusual love for pets. From my earliest memories, we always had a menagerie of animals living with us – and I mean actually living with us. Mum didn't like them being caged up, so we lived with guinea pigs, rabbits, pet mice, tortoises, dogs, cats, and budgies running around the living room. That was our entertainment; we couldn't afford TV. Mum would scream with laughter when a rabbit, so pleased at its freedom, would jump and click its heels.

Freda and I woke Mum up one morning to a brand new litter of tiny baby white mice. Mum didn't like mornings. Her day usually started at around twelve, but lasted until around four in the morning. In my eagerness to show her the ten little mice, I accidentally tipped the whole box into the bed with her. I don't think I ever saw my mum move so quick, and we never did find all the mice!

In our very different upbringing, what we missed in material and obvious other needs we made up with lots of affection and profound love. She had such a caring and loving way about her. In her world, animals were meant to be loved and cared for. They also had feelings that needed to be nourished. I don't think she was really a religious person. A spiritual person? Most definitely yes! Her thoughts were that these animals were put here for a deeper reason we all have difficulty understanding. When you hold or stroke an animal and it responds with a purr, a lick, or a knocking noise (as do guinea pigs), that warm, tingly feeling of contentment you receive can be rewarding, and in some cases very healing. Inexplicably, she seemed to know these things, and in her way wanted us to understand.

We visited Bellevue Zoo in Manchester on occasion. Our all-time favourite by far was to see the monkeys. By this time, being embarrassed with our parents, outside the home was kind of 'Okay, it's going to happen, so we might just as well live with it.' Mum would, as usual, scream with laughter at the monkey antics, sometimes embarrassingly wetting herself to boot. People would form a circle around us wondering what all the fuss was about. We had by now given up caring and had joined her in hysterical laughter.

I sometimes came home to find her weeping like a baby because she had read in the newspaper or saw on TV, when we had one, some awful cruelty toward an animal. It would just tear her apart. It was so alien to her that someone could do that to an innocent, defenseless animal. Through her, we all learned a beautiful lesson for which I will always be grateful. For every animal we share our lives with, if we open up and return the same unconditional love as it gives us, it will inevitably grow its own very special and distinct character, to the point, I believe, it will be hard to reason that there is not some subliminal, otherworldly connection going on. I am so content to have been given that precious gift of love from Mum, and all the pets too, who live with me.

Mum the artist

My mum was also a very natural artist. Sadly, she never used it professionally, despite all of my prodding. From an early age she sat and drew for us. She was a caricaturist mostly, in that she could see a face, and with just a few lines and in a matter of seconds, you would see that person's full character appear before your eyes. She worked mostly with pencil and crayon until I introduced her to paints and brush when I was taking art at school.

Years later, I came home on leave from the Navy to find all these wonderful paintings – but she had painted them directly onto the wall! She would change them on a daily basis to suit her moods. The paintings usually consisted of a cottage on a hillside. It would have fields of flowers that might be changed into a lake on occasion, but always with beautiful purple sunsets. The laneways to and from the cottage would also change on a daily basis.

All across the top of the room were individual paintings on old paper of us kids and whomever we might be with at the time. I always knew when one of us was in trouble by scanning to see if our picture was still up. We had a system that we would call each other if one of the pictures were down. 'Ronnie, you had better go visit Mum – your picture is down!' Uh-oh!

I suggested that she use separate paper, which she did. However, the thought of spending money on proper paper was just too much. She used the back of old wallpaper. Oh, and the brushes ended up in the bin. She had found that it was far easier for her to just use her fingers.

I was going through a teenage-lonely phase at one time in my adolescence. I didn't have any friends in Blackburn and I just sat in my bedroom on the bottom part of a metal bunk bed playing my guitar. Mum sensed this. I returned home from school one evening to find a beautiful and very voluptuous mermaid had been painted onto the wall. It was as if my bed continued into the wall, and there she was lying beside me, a blonde, blue-eyed beauty, partly topless and beckoning me with her eyes. Such was our life with our different, but wonderful, mother.

It is so easy to look back now and wonder why we weren't looked after better, taken away from the carnage that we had to endure. As I am writing this, I can understand the reader asking the obvious question, 'Well, if she loved you so much, why didn't she protect you better?' Circumstance. That is the only answer I can come up with. Of course, it's not a viable excuse when you think of all the damage and pain that it caused. Maybe it was because they were two deaf people with everything going against them and were being treated like imbeciles. Or maybe it was bad health and then addiction with all its ensuing problems.

We may have missed out on a lot of things that a child should normally have to grow into a healthy adult, but we always had her very special love. I cannot think of a time when she wasn't looking out for me, whether I was on the other side of the world or deep under the North Sea. I always knew she was there, right there, beside my heart – as she still is to this very day.

Dad

We despised our dad for many years because of all the torment and nightmares that lasted for half a lifetime, the lost childhood of memories we've all tried to forget. We all have our pet hates for one thing or another that he did during his alcoholic binges. For a time we just wanted him to disappear. He was everything one could easily despise. He could do the most dastardly thing, and the next moment when the police arrived he would put on the wounded angel look. *I'm handicapped. I work too hard, had a little bit to drink. I'm so sooorrry. It won't happen again. Whimper, whimper, few crocodile tears, whimper, whimper.* He could have won an Oscar with his heart-wrenching performances. The police would inevitably go away with tears in their eyes. It wasn't often that his act wouldn't work, but when it didn't they'd take him out back and rough him up some. However, then he couldn't work for a few days.

We came home from school one sunny afternoon to a trail of blood leading through the ginnel into our house that was literally full of police. Mum had been taken completely over the edge in our absence and, in a rare act of violence on her part, she had smacked him over the head with a high heeled shoe. He was in hospital for a day or so before he booked himself out. He was always pretty much indestructible.

I had loosened the wheels on his bike one day after a really bad night. I couldn't have been more than eight years old at the time. He came off the bike face first into the road. What a mess he looked. All along he knew it was me. However, he rarely laid a hand on any of us kids. Sure, we got the leather belt a few times, but he was stone cold sober and knew exactly what he was doing, and we had generally deserved it on the rare occasion it happened.

Ronnie and I received the belt once from Mum because we

had completely wrecked a bed. She really laid into us, no messin', way worse than Dad ever did.

She actually threw a porcelain teapot of scalding hot tea at Ronnie once. I remember it like it was one of those slow motion movie clips. I was lying in bed waiting for Ronnie to come home; we slept together. I heard Mum screaming at him downstairs. At fifteen years old, he had gotten caught smoking. All of a sudden he was running up the stairs, ten to the dozen. He leaped sideways into the bedroom, closely followed by a now airborne teapot. It missed him by inches and hit the wall above the potty. The curtains were open at the time, and it smashed into a thousand pieces. The stain was on the wall until we moved from that house. I don't know how Ronnie missed the dreaded leather belt that night.

The belt used to hang above the fire on the chimneybreast. It was an intimidating, thick leather belt with a big brass buckle. When we kids got out of line, all Dad had to do was point at the belt. Or, if it wasn't in his line of sight, he would point at the front of his boot, as in, 'I'm going to kick you right up the arse if you don't cut it out, right now.'

I had seen photographs of our dad in his younger years with the baby twins. He was a tall, healthy young man with handsome Errol Flynn looks. He looked to have everything going for himself. I guess that was before the evil totally possessed him. It was cleverly disguised in the beer he consumed at the local pub.

Every Christmas morning Mum would try her best to have as many toys and chocolates as they could afford laid out on each side of the settee for Freda and me. I always loved to cycle, and every bike I rode was usually one that I had inevitably put together myself from all the bits and pieces that Dad had brought home. I would sometimes wait for weeks for a wheel or a pedal that Dad might scrounge from God knows where. This one Christmas I woke to a brand new shiny bike. I was ecstatic. I took it out for a spin and it was nothing short of wonderful – it even had brakes! When I returned home, a huge argument had brewed, ruining the whole Christmas, and the shiny bike went out with my dad to be returned from whence it came.

Looking back, I often wonder exactly why and when he became the demon that I knew him to be in those early years. I guess losing your hearing would be bad enough to deal with in that period of time. Deaf and dumb people, as they used to be called, were kind of lumped into the category of being almost mentally handicapped, I suppose because of the dumb connotation. He was anything but dumb. I had witnessed with my own eyes how he could fix just about anything. He was able, with the most basic of tools, to build things with his bare hands. He had been born with an innate and mysterious know-how. It still haunts me as to why he did not fall into a more rewarding job. Every job that he ever had was usually the most meaningless, dirty, and foul work that was available in any of the factories throughout the valley.

For a while he was a fire beater in a cotton factory. His job was to stoke the furnace with shovels full of coal twelve hours a day, which would then produce steam to supply the weaving machinery. Mum and I visited sometimes to take his lunch if he'd forgotten it. I could not believe the conditions he had to work in, day in, day out, stripped to the waist in a meager attempt to withstand the heat, black from head to toe with the coal dust.

He told us he was always treated like an idiot because of his deafness, the fulcrum of everyone's cruel jokes and scorn. He would then poignantly say to us, 'But I know,' tapping his head with his forefinger and giving a sly, knowing wink.

Another wonderful job he had was as a sweeper in a cotton factory blower filtration system. When the blower was on, it basically vacuumed the factory of the loose cotton dust that everyone breathed which caused all kinds of respiratory problems. Did they even spare an occasional thought for the poor bloke who subsisted *inside* the fan room sweeping the dust off the filtration grills with no protective mask whatsoever? He couldn't even exit the room unless the fan was stopped, as the door was vacuumed shut. He had acquired this job simply because no one else would do it, and the noise in that room was also deafening.

Through all of this, he smoked roll-up cigarettes that he would sometimes poach from other unsuspecting ashtrays. Not surprisingly, he had asthma in a bad way. He used a small hand pump that would deliver the medicine into his lungs to allow him to breathe. In later life the medicine was outlawed because it was causing serious bone loss. It basically turned his bones into rubber. He developed a large hump on his back and shrank considerably in height as the years went by. When he lived with us, his early morning ritual was to have a few strong tobacco roll-ups before seemingly coughing up his raspy, liquid-filled lungs.

This was his lot in life! When he and our mother were eventually divorced, we went to see him in his hovel of a home. He had cleverly rerouted the electric meter that usually took shilling coins. He was now illegally on free electricity. The gas meter that usually took three-penny pieces had also been disconnected and now sat menacingly on his kitchen table. He had re-routed and piped in the gas for free. He was eventually caught and had to appear in court. He put on one of his more stellar performances and was surprisingly allowed to go scot-free, grinning to us with a sly wink, tapping his head and miming, I know.

Grandma Hill

I had spent a lot of time with Grandma and Pop. They lived out in Stockport where most of our known relatives were from, and Oldham where Mum grew up. We always looked forward to seeing Grandma and Pop. Freda and I spent most of our summer holidays with them, usually one of us at a time. Grandma filled us with all her delicious home cooked meals. We were never really hungry at home, but our meals obviously weren't very nutritious. I remember having to go to a clinic once a week for sunray treatment. I think it was after a bad bout of yellow jaundice that had left me weak and malnourished. Mum gave us yucky cod liver oil tablets and a spoonful of malt, which I didn't mind. At one point, Mum even made us carry a little bag of herbs on a string around our neck, which was a little embarrassing at school.

At Grandma's, everything was clean and tidy. We had to get up early in the morning, which we weren't used to with living on Mum's crazy schedule, and we even had breakfast, an unusual and rare meal for us.

Gran would go to work and Pop would keep me busy with card games and stories from his past. Occasionally I did some gardening in their small backyard. Pop never set foot outside the house for some mysterious reason, so occasionally I would walk down to the local bakery to pick up our lunch. It was a special treat to pick up freshly baked, scrumptious meat pies, with a custard pie for desert. Sometimes he would show me how to cook something.

There was a small park where I spent some time on my own. There never were too many kids around. We had a meal at teatime when Grandma came home at about 5:30, and even a supper before going to bed. The house was always warm and comfortable, and I could sleep soundly with no fear of nightly fiascos. I loved spending time there. I always felt safe and relaxed.

On the rare occurrence that Uncle Fred, my other hero, came home, I was always in awe. He was a big man, over six feet tall, with a deep, gravelly voice. He worked as a mechanical engineer for a company that built diesel generators, and he was sent all over the world, spending two to three years in the Persian Gulf, Pakistan, and Canada. It was his and our Auntie Ena's house that Gran and Pop stayed in during their substantial travels. They had two children: David, who had joined the RAF, and Henry, who was a year or so older than me. Henry and I were pretty good friends and spent some time together.

Auntie Ena was quite strict and kept her boys on their toes. So when on those rare occurrences that I spent time with them, I was also kept in place. I actually enjoyed being part of their family. I didn't mind the strictness in return for the feeling of bettering myself. They could afford to put their kids through private school, and I thought they were destined for higher places.

I followed Uncle Fred like a shadow. When he walked down the street in his light tropical suits, he took giant strides. To me, he was the archetypal John Wayne. Every time I spotted a plane flying high above the clouds, I automatically thought of Uncle Fred and all the adventures and places my imagination could possibly muster. Yep, it was hero worship all the way. I never thought in a million years I would ever be in a position to follow in his big footsteps.

When Grandma came to our house all hell broke loose. She was like a Tasmanian red devil zipping around the house cleaning and tidying, constantly giving Mum sheer hell at her untidiness, and saying things like, 'Why weren't you wearing your hat when you went out?' Mum would look at us kids and roll her eyes in mock amusement. Our mother was the complete opposite of her own mother. Grandma could cook a meal for seven, including dessert, with half a dozen assorted vegetables, all on a tiny four-burner gas stove. There would be pans on top of pans, and everything would be ready and perfectly cooked on time. She was a truly amazing woman and loved every one of us dearly.

I remember telling her from a very early age that I was going to be a lumberjack in Canada. Where I had gotten that from nobody knows, but she always reminded me of it while I was growing up. I once gave her a penny that I had found and told her that one day I was going to take her out. To the day she left us, she had that penny in her purse. She also sits beside my mum, especially in times of fear and sorrow, deep within my heart.

CHAPTER 4
Mum and Dad's Separation

Eventually Mum and Dad separated, which basically meant nothing. We could lock all the doors and windows, and somehow he would figure a way of getting in. He climbed up a lamppost, shimmied across live wires, and somehow found his way into a locked bedroom window one night, much to our total amazement. I can still see him now. We had kicked him out of the dog's house that he had been sleeping in, in the backyard. And there in front of all the neighbours, he would casually walk down the street with his rolled up mattress on his shoulder, only to return the following night.

We lived on Warburton Street at the bottom of Grane Road in Haslingden. There was an old coal station beside our house where in the not-too-distant past steam trains stocked up with coal. A lot of spent coke, as they called it, littered the train tracks for miles around this station. Dad would force me to go with him in the dead of night to pick up this coke, and even coal when we found it, for our winter heating. How many times did I remove Dad from the track of incoming trains? He couldn't hear them coming! When the pickings became thin we hit the local coal yard. It didn't take too long before the owner, a school friend's dad to boot, found out and eventually caught us red-handed helping ourselves to the coal in his yard. It was pitch dark as the bright flashlight caught us in the act. We both separated and ran off. I found a small hidey-hole beside a dilapidated garage, and thought for a few precious moments that I had got away, only to be dragged out by the scruff of the neck minutes later. Among many other embarrassing obscenities, I was now also labeled a coal thief at school.

Shortly after that episode we moved yet again, this time completely out of the valley to the large town of Blackburn. It seemed we moved every couple of years, basically trying to move away from Dad. He very quickly found us and eventually squirmed his way back in.

CHAPTER 5
Blackburn

I hated Blackburn. The only good thing I found of interest was the running track at Witton Park. There were also some wonderful walks around the hills of Pleasington that looked away from grimy old Blackburn toward Clitheroe over farms and moorland. Jake, my trusty German shepherd, was always by my side on those walks.

All of the houses we had lived in up to that time were in Rossendale Valley. The valley itself had factories and street houses, but you didn't have to walk too far before you were up in the fair hills and dales around the valley. In the seemingly few sunny days of summer, we took long walks with our dogs into the hills, sometimes swimming in the reservoirs. In Blackburn, we lived in the center of a very busy industrial town, much larger than any we had ever known previously. It was quite a distance to walk before you found anything that closely resembled fields and trees. I also didn't know a soul, let alone have a friend in that town.

It was going to be my last year of school. At fourteen, I wanted to stay and complete my last year of school in Haslingden. I had done a complete 180, and was now actually enjoying school. All of my friends were here, and there were a few thoughtful teachers who thought I had a little more to offer. I didn't want to leave and start afresh at some strange school where I didn't know anyone, so I persuaded my mum to allow me to travel back and forth from Blackburn to Haslingden – no trivial feat in the days of slow moving buses over moorland roads.

CHAPTER 6

Recruitment

Apart from the usual upheavals at home, this was probably my busiest and happiest time during my youth. Alan Bird and I were toying with the idea of the Merchant Navy after we had sat through a recruitment talk given by an impeccably uniformed officer one afternoon. He must have been good, because he had us hooked in the first five minutes. We both shook hands and decided there and then that the navy was for us.

Toward the end of the year we went to the recruitment office just a-raring to go. The uniform of the chap that met us was very similar to the one we remembered. He sat us down and said, 'Oh no, you don't want the Merchant Navy, son, join the Royal instead.'

So, without any more ado, we signed up for the Royal Navy. It wasn't as easy to get Mum to agree to sign the papers allowing me. She eventually conceded after much pestering. In my young mind, it was either that or the cotton factory, or even the dreaded coal pit. Ronnie had worked down the coal mines for a few years. I had memories of him coming home black from head to toe. To get down the side cut mine, they had to put individual trollies on tracks and kneel or lay on their stomachs. The roof of the tunnel was so shallow in places that he would catch his back on the sharp rocks. I remember his screams as Mum tried to clean his scarred back with a scrubbing brush.

Freda was on my mind, even though Dad was slowing down a bit and Mum now had a boyfriend who was large, and pretty scary to boot. Freda had also buckled down and was doing really well at school in Blackburn.

At the time, I thought my schooling was coming to an end. Coming away with some academic qualifications was not likely to happen in my foreseeable future. Freda was a different story. I was hoping that she could stay at school a little longer and get the qualifications that had eluded the rest of us.

I don't think our family was much different from many others so close after the Second World War, especially in the north of England. We had been brought up to believe, from the rest of our family and our grandmother, that when you left school you went to work and gave your entire pay packet to your mum and dad. You got your spending money and thought yourself lucky. Even when you got married you still had to coffer up and help Mum and Dad. Ronnie and Rita did this for only a short while before they realized this was not the deal in this day and age, and got themselves married off quickly. Dad's thought was, 'Hey, I've worked my ass off for you guys, now it's your turn to pay back.'

I can speak like this now, but for the longest time that is what we believed. In not doing what was expected, you were turning your back on your whole family, in particular your mum and dad. Perplexing stories were bandied around the family of cousin such and such who was glorified and would most definitely go to heaven because he coughed up his pay packet every week and never wanted for a thing except his mother's kind love. So the plan forming in my youthful mind was sending my navy pay packet home – well, at least until Freda finished school. Then we would take it as it came.

CHAPTER 7
Ribble Bus to Haslingden

For over a year after we moved from the somewhat beautiful town of Haslingden, I had to take the long route to school every day. The first bus out was the one I had to take for the forty-minute trip at the unwelcoming hour of 5:30 in the morning. I willingly endured this.

Once the red Ribble double-decker bus slowly topped the hill, left the grey and yellow haze of darkened Blackburn behind, it headed over the tranquil moorland of the Grane and a unique transformation would take place in me, like the shedding of a second skin. I was flooded with warm memories of many hikes over those ever-present hills that surrounded the scenic valley of Rossendale, leaving hills and moors dotted with grey sheep and mile after mile of blackened stone Roman walls. Nothing was excluded from the soot. I thought of the clear reservoirs, the pine forests, and the inviting hills; long, hot summer days swimming in the reservoir with my dog, Jake; some very rare days with Mum and Freda and our other dog, Meano, camping out for the day beside the water. Hey! Sometimes we even took our pet guinea pigs, Charlie and Tiny. Yes, Haslingden was full of warm memories. It was one of the many places we had lived, but for me it was the only home we ever had with some happiness and friends.

I completed at least two paper route rounds before school, three if my good friend, Bernard 'Biscuit' McVittie, slept in, which was quite a regular occurrence. I truly loved my bike and riding around the hills and dales of this small town. Delivering papers was my little piece of heaven.

School was also getting interesting since a few teachers had taken notice of a couple of other attributes I might be able to offer the world. You see, in earlier years I had spent minimal time at school, possibly due to our bizarre family life and, of course, my fear of unkind kids who mocked our poor attire.

As Mum and Dad were deaf, I guess some words we used were kind of mixed up and sounded strange. Put the two together and you end up being the center of attraction for bullies and the like. Generally, the schooling most of us rough kids received was basically to prep inadequately educated kids from poor families as fodder for the cotton factories and coal pits that littered the valley and surrounding areas. We had an inexcusable teacher, whom I will never forget, inform us, 'You should not set your sights too high. Settle for a meaningful laborious job more fitting for your station in life.' How's that for a real morale booster?

What I thought was to be my final year at school changed when I was surprisingly asked to stay on for another year and try for some qualifications. I had designed and built, with the help of the music teacher and the woodwork class, an eight-string dulcimer with frets. I had drawings and sculptures showing all over the school from the art class. I would be guaranteed at least two GCE qualifications. Other teachers in the school thought that would not be all I would come away with if I stayed.

Having already signed on to join the Royal Navy, I reluctantly quit school and worked with my brother Ronnie polishing stainless steel sinks at a factory nearby waiting for the navy call-up papers to arrive. Three months later, after much deliberate thought, I decided to go back to school and try for the qualifications. My new goal was to try and catch up with what the other smarter kids had been learning for four years in just nine months. At this time in my life I was bound and determined to do something better with my life. The Navy still seemed to be the answer I was looking for, but I thought having a few qualifications would certainly help.

CHAPTER 8
Walking to the Train

All the mixed thoughts and the sheer sadness I felt filled my brain like I was going to bust apart at the seams. As I walked that long road, tears welled up in my eyes. Trying to be strong, my strangely weakened legs pleaded with me to just turn around. It seemed like ages had passed, but in reality it had been only minutes since I'd turned the corner at the end of our street and looked back one lingering last time to the two tiny figures still waving, tears streaming down their faces, sodden handkerchiefs in hand. That would leave an indelible imprint in my brain forever. Feelings of shirking responsibility haunted my every step, pulling me back like an invisible magnet. It was so unbearably hard. Who would take care of Freda if she cried? And would Dad keep his promise and not come back? What would I do if I needed that caring hand of my sweet mother to say everything is okay?

'Just put one foot in front of the other, Kevin,' something deep inside told me. 'You know this is right. Everything is going to change from this day forth. There is a huge adventure ahead if you can just keep walking.'

Eventually, boarding the train brought a little relief. I had no control in turning around the train. However, the urge to jump off at the many stations on the way was overbearing. I was traveling from Blackburn to Plymouth, which is in the southwest of England. It could have been the other end of the world for me, as I had never set foot outside of Lancashire.

Keeping track of the train and station changes from the itinerary the navy had mailed and going over the call-up papers kept me busy and concerned enough to lessen the trips to the bathroom for uncontrolled weeping episodes. By the time I arrived in Plymouth many hours later, I was in a little better shape. Strangely enough, the station seemed full of young boys all around my age, complete with matching red, bloodshot eyes with the same what-do-we-do-now expressions on their faces.

CHAPTER 9
Navy Boot Camp

Petty Officer Marine Engineer McDougal, or POME McDougal to his hierarchal equals and above, met us at the station. He would be our main instructor throughout basic training. To us miniscule maggots it was 'Petty Officer three bags full, and don't speak until spoken to or you'll get me boot up yer arse, laddy.' POME McDougal was a Scot and very proud of it. And having been in the navy for about 300 years, the accent had waned enough to be only just intelligible. God help you if you didn't understand the last order. I think I spent the first six weeks of boot camp continuously running around and around the immense parade ground for one punishable offence or another.

They sure kept us busy, which in retrospect was the best thing they could have done. At the end of the first week we were all given the opportunity to either sign on for twelve years (nine years of service and three in the reserve), or leave with our tails between our legs and scurry off home. It wasn't until we had signed on that we learned, 'Oh, by the way, your time doesn't actually start until you are classed as men – that would be eighteen.'

I should probably add here that once signed, even at the tender age of fifteen, there was no escape, excepting possible medical discharge, and to get that you would have to literally have 'custard pie for brains,' or, of course, be gay, which at the time was a big no-no in any of the armed forces. To go AWOL was extremely silly, as you would most definitely be caught and then thrown into the dreaded navy detention quarters. I also learned while I was serving my time that, in fact, many young criminal teens were given the choice of a juvenile detention center or – yes, you guessed it – Her Majesty's Royal Navy. And they said the press gangs of the old Royal Navy were no longer used – hmm, I wonder! I believe much later, in the 1980s, the sign-on rules were thankfully eased with options for leaving the navy if so desired.

In the second week we received our kit. I had never had so many clothes – well, that weren't somebody else's castoffs, that is. Two pair of pajamas! What the hell do I do with these and why would anyone want two pair? We were issued the most uncomfortable serge underwear imaginable that came down to your knees. I think they must have been made out of sixty grade sandpaper! Later, I found them to be commonly known as 'pusser's patent passion killers' – pusser being one of the many slang names used for the navy.

We were shown how to sew name tags on just about everything, and iron and fold everything to exact specifications. POME McDougal came around with his measuring tape on kit inspection day, and if it wasn't folded to within specs, plus or minus three-thousandths of an inch (slight exaggeration), then in the garbage can it went. All clothes were washed by hand, commonly termed 'dhobying,' with the same carbolic soap you used for washing and showering and, of course, hair shampoo. Did you ever wonder why so many former sailors are bald?

I made friends with Brian Reid during the first week, and we vowed we would both stick it out and sign on together. He was from Aberdeen, Scotland, and we struck up a very strong friendship that would last our duration in the 'Andrew,' another slang name for the navy.

One very hot afternoon, after missing at least three right turns and putting the complete platoon into total confusion, I was shamefully ordered to run the parade ground continuously with my right hand stuck proudly in the air repeatedly shouting on the top of my voice, 'I wank with my right hand. I wank with my right hand,' much to the chagrin of a WREN officer also putting her girls through their steps close by.

I was one of the markers, meaning the tallest boy at the right end of the middle row of three. The tallest boy in the platoon by far was in the front row, in front of me. He was somewhat unkindly nicknamed Clockwork Frankenstein, due to the surprising resemblance he had with the afore-mentioned superstar, right down to the large protruding forehead. To say he was an odd sort of out-of-place boy would be an understatement. The *clockwork* title came from the fact that he just could not get the hang of swinging his arms in what would be for most people the natural way, hand opposite to the leading leg. To actually see someone walking – nay, marching – swinging his arms in this very unnatural kind of clockwork manner and being deadly serious about it made it very hard not to bring about even the most minimal snicker. Even the tiniest, teeny weenie chortle was punishable by at least death on an official, shiny-black Royal Navy parade ground.

Let me explain; I have been plagued, yes plagued, all of my life. It seems that at the most serious episodes of my life, being scolded, for instance, by headmasters or wives, officers or bosses, I inanely, and usually unwisely, find something funny about the grave situation I am in, thereby bringing on uncontrollable fits of laughter. This has the adverse effect of turning a scolder insanely angry, almost to the point of spitting blood and contemplating murder.

'Firth, I know that was you! Ten laps of the parade ground. GO!' It wasn't that I could not tell my left turn from my right. However, between trying to keep in step and swing my arms the correct way, thus not putting the whole platoon into clockwork mode, while also trying to conceal my plagued laughter, made for few points with POME McDougal.

As much as Clockwork Frankenstein seemed to inadvertently get me into trouble on a daily basis, I was his only friend. Remembering myself being the target of seemingly everyone's jibes in younger days, I watched over Colin, alias C. Frankenstein. I even tutored him on the delicate matter of how to put a mirror finish on his boot toe, which seemed to get big points with the fearsome McDougal.

The process was a long, highly complicated, and secret affair passed on through generations of marching GI Moonies. Start with melting vast amounts of shoe polish onto one's boot toe with a cigarette lighter, rub over with a hot spoon, and then lace with gargantuan amounts of spit. Then commence rubbing with aching finger and rag into the depths of the night. Colin, being the way he was, had a great deal of difficulty with this seemingly safe procedure. When I eventually thought he was making some headway, to everyone's astonishment he frantically exited the mess hall screaming with a boot in one hand and one of his trouser legs both engulfed in raging flames. Through my tutelage, he had successfully cremated one of his boots and a pair of navy-issue, number eight work pants, and narrowly escaped first degree burns. I did still watch over him, and on several occasions removed him from harm's way, but decided to give him a wide berth.

The day that he inadvertently stabbed himself with an SLR rifle bayonet was indeed sad, to say the least. We had all progressed to the final captain's parade all dressed up in our new number one suit, white gaiters and belt, boots like shiny black glass, and bayonets on our crisp, clean SLR rifles. The parade ground was full of new and older platoons, but today it was our platoon's final passing out parade. We had spent the last two weeks learning all the rudiments of marching and coming to attention with the rifle. To explain: the butt of the rifle is on the ground, your right hand thrust out at a thirty degree angle clutching the rifle nozzle just ahead of the bayonet. This is 'at easy.' To go to attention, you smartly closed your legs (from being apart), and at the same time pulled the rifle toward your body so it now pointed directly up, meaning that the bayonet was quite close to your shoulder.

In Colin's eagerness to show what he was made of, he came to attention directly in front of all the brass *HMS Raleigh* could muster – captains, admirals, you name it – and astonishingly managed to stab himself in the armpit with the blunt side of the blade. Realizing what he had done, and probably feeling the hot blood run down his arm staining his beautifully ironed white front, after a short delay and with the utmost of composure still standing to attention, he fainted and fell to the ground face first.

Six weeks under our belts

After the six weeks of boot camp we all had to choose our classification. I had decided on marine engineer mechanic, in hopes of gaining some kind of useful trade. Fortunately, my close friend Brian also joined the same classification, which meant we would both be doing training together for the remaining nine weeks, coincidentally at *HMS Raleigh*.

We were all now granted our first two weeks leave and given free return train tickets to go home. How I had looked forward to this moment! The six weeks at the time seemed like forever, but now looking back at all that we had achieved, the friends and camaraderie, looking out for each other and the laughs, it wasn't that long at all. Even McDougal seemed like an old sheepdog looking after his herd. He had actually been caught red-handed smiling with pride when we passed the parade of colours. There were rumors that some of the lads were not coming back; even Brian threatened the same. To my knowledge everyone returned, even though some went on to other camps for different trades.

Our first leave

I stepped off the train in Blackburn on a beautiful sunny day, which was quite rare in Lancashire, wearing my new immaculately pressed number one navy-issue suit, complete with bell bottoms, jersey, and white front. Not forgetting the jersey, collars, silk, rope lanyard, and all the rest of the paraphernalia that make up the complicated affair of the Royal Navy uniform, I must have looked a proud sight, all suntanned and as fit as a butcher's dog from my many tours of said parade ground.

Mum, Freda, and, surprisingly, a teary-eyed Dad were there to meet me. Everything was so complete and life was good. After being paraded up and down our street a dozen or so times arm in arm with my mum just as proud as a peacock, tipping my hat to all and sundry – oh, I can play the part when I want to – we eventually came to our house. The door was decorated with a larger-than-life painting of a smiling sailor, hat cocked in jovial form. This was of me! As much as I complained in the years to come, she steadfastly refused to ever remove it.

Bernard 'Biscuit' McVittie

I visited with my long-time friend Biscuit in Haslingden, all suited up, probably to show off a little. I also had other ulterior reasons. I had my beady little eye on Susan, Biscuit's younger sister. I was disappointed to find out that she was now seeing my other long-time friend, Alan 'Birdie' Bird. He had signed up in the navy a few months before me and had come home on leave to beat me to the lovely Susan. Damn that Birdie!

Mrs. Mac, 'Elsie,' Biscuit's mum, whom I had spent almost as much time with as my own mum in the latter years, was ecstatic, oohing and ahhing in her charming Geordie accent. 'Away now, look at the man all spiffy in his sailor suit.' She, like my own mother, had struggled all her life to single-handedly bring up her three kids. The similarities didn't quite end there either. Both women were quite eccentric in their own ways, which seemed to get worse with age – in an odd sort of way, I am quite proud to say.

Biscuit had been working in a cotton factory at the bottom of Grane Road. He seemed to have a grey, waxen look about him, almost as though the life was slowly being sucked out of him. I guess seeing me and Birdie all spiffy and full of spit and polish was just too much for him. He held on for a while and then decided to join up too.

The navy was now looking for personnel to train as clearance divers, which would be on a par with the famous US Navy Seals we constantly hear about. The attrition rate to succeed the strenuous course was quite high. For the few who made it through, they would more than likely be part of a bomb disposal team. The Suez Canal, having been laid with underwater mines during the many hostilities, needed to be cleared.

Biscuit's life, similar to mine, would be forever changed. He could never foresee the many adventures he was about to embark on as he went from working a cotton loom in a dreary old factory to dismantling complicated underwater bombs in the Middle East.

When I look back now at those events almost fifty years ago,

I am absolutely mystified at all the turns and coincidences life's road takes you on. 'Life's wibbly-wobbly way,' as another friend of mine used to say. Biscuit, my childhood friend, would also never know how important he would become in my life later.

Marine Engineer Mechanic

Mum alluded to me one evening about how my sister Freda had missed me, to the point of dreaming that she could hear me playing my old guitar in my bedroom as I had done locked away many lonely evenings in the past. I hadn't realized how much I had meant to her. I promised myself that night that no matter what happened in my life that I must be there for her and always keep my little sister safe.

I decided to take my guitar back to the navy, as I had promised to teach my new friend Brian how to play. Going back to *Raleigh* was a breeze now that I was a sailor of the seven seas! With much more confidence and a huge willingness to learn, marine engineering school went well. The fact that I was a decent cross-country runner didn't go amiss either. I had broken all records at school for cross country, and in the previous couple of years had joined the Blackburn Harriers, the town athletics team, to run at most of the big races all over Lancashire. Put me on one of the muddiest, dirtiest courses and I would always come back with flying colours. However, if things were too dry and neat, I struggled to attain a decent placing. I was useless at football and cricket, which at any English school is not a good thing, but I certainly made up for it in athletics. The physical training instructors (PTIs) at the base thought they had died and gone to heaven when I whipped all the other training camps in the southwest. I could do no wrong. While the rest of my class was busy doing work detail, cleaning garbage and being galley slaves, I was out taking new recruits on very scenic cross-country running courses.

The southwest of England is a very beautiful part of the world. For once in my life I felt good about myself and was enjoying every minute. Sports day was my finale. I ran and won three races – the 400 yards, the 800 yards, and I broke the course record in the mile – and finally threw the javelin twice as far as my nearest competitor, also breaking the record. However, the gunnery instructors (GIs) were at a loss.

Everyone hated assault courses – but not me! I actually enjoyed them. During break I would go and do it again. It wasn't just to show off. Swinging from tree to tree, climbing rope ladders, and sliding through mud – wow, give me some more!

I got in royal shit one day and was made to run the parade ground until dusk because I had gone off on my own on the assault course and nobody knew where I was. I think the dressing down I received was way worse than the parade ground run.

Clockwork GI

I was summoned to the Chief GI's office. He was the ugliest and meanest of them all. His nickname on base was *Clockwork*, but not for the same reason as the now-departed Colin. In the fifteen weeks of training nobody had ever seen him not marching. It was an offence not to march whenever you were on the parade ground. I had found that out on many earlier misfortunes. This guy, with his little riding crop tightly tucked under his arm, marched to breakfast and marched to the washroom! We all wondered if he marched when he was making love to his wife. *Present arms! Hup, two, three. Hup, two, three. Keep in step! Hup, two, three.*

I was surrounded. Clockwork sat behind his dark, wooden, creaking desk, all adorned with ancient navy brass artifacts, and pictures of him on the wall eating dead, burned recruits. There must have been half a dozen other petty officer GIs present, all shouting different orders at me at the same time. I didn't know whether to stand to attention, salute, or just give way and shit my pants and get things over with. They were all around me like vultures waiting to peck out my eyes. The volume was excruciating. Then, all of a sudden, a scary silence fell on the room. The baby GIs all took one marched step backwards. Where did the signal come from? Was it the twitching scar on Clockwork's right cheek?

After a long silence, and obviously wanting to show his cohorts how these things should be handled, he swiftly rose from his creaking swivel chair and noisily marched around his desk. He came to attention, smashing his steel-studded boots down fractions of an inch from the front of mine. We were now nose to nose. My sphincter muscle was weakening. Through the avalanche of words now being propelled at me, most of which were indecipherable, all I could do was resist the urge to blink as the little droplets of spittle came my way. The tiny blue veins in his large, red, cratered nose seemed to have some kind of pattern that headed in the direction of the large blobs of hair on his cheeks, as was the fashion for mean-looking GIs.

Oh, I could feel the giggle plague mustering deep inside of me. *God, please not now!* I thought. My right eye started to twitch, making its way down to my cheek. Saved by the bell! Miraculously, it was the tea bell. Yes, folks, everything stops for tea, even in the British Navy. This is, of course, top secret and I will inevitably be shackled and put behind bars in a dirty naval dungeon to rot for the rest of my days for letting this out. If the Russians ever discovered this during the Cold War it would have been curtains for us Brits. Very simply put, attack around four in the afternoon and you've got it made. There will be no one manning the guns; the missile bays will be vacant – it's tea time!

I was dismissed and, of course, allowed to have tea. I mean it's sacrilege not to, right? I then spent the evening until the sun fell below the fair hills in the west running around and around the now very-familiar parade ground, my rifle at half-mast to the occasional bellow from somewhere in the void of a hangar. 'Firth, get that rifle up!'

Things I learned:

1. Never be at the front or the back of a queue (queuing is a national pastime in Britain). Somewhere around the middle is a good place to be.

2. Coming in first is not good – the team, platoon, or crew always come first.

3. There are those, usually in positions of control, that are there solely to crack you; this is what they live for. Once you understand this, it becomes a game. The task takes second place. You can push yourself a lot further if you know that it just comes down to a duel of spirits.

4. *Illegitimi non carborundum* (Don't let the bastards grind you down; similar to above rule).

5. If someone is getting up your nose, do not be courageous. Just be patient. Somebody else will do him in sooner or later, and then *you* don't have to carry the can.

6. This is a scary one. Never fear bullies. Stand up to them and be real weird about it. Example: 'Okay, buddy, you can beat the living shit out of me right now, but sooner or later you're going to have to go to sleep. I have a fire brick in my locker with your name on it.' It helps also if you can conjure up real wild eyes – you know, *Texas Chainsaw Massacre*-type eyes – while you're saying this. It usually works a treat.

6b. Most bullies are, at heart, usually big softies and a tad thick. If you can win them over and make friends they make great guard dogs. *'I bet my bully can whip your bully.'* You can have inter-mess bully contests, inter-ship, and sometimes even inter-navy contests.

7. This is probably close to the above rule. If you are unlucky enough to end up in the middle of a mass fight and you can't use your running skills to get the hell out, find the nearest table and hide until all is abated. This is not cowardice, though it might look kind of sissyish. However, if the idiots of the world want to get into it for some stupid reason, just let them go for it!

8. Again, this is probably on the same important subject. This I learned from a black belt PTI when I was undergoing un-armed combat training. If you're in a position as above and you haven't found a suitable hidey hole, and a big gorilla has you by the throat and you have no were to go, he is in the process of sorting you out. Do the following:

a. Find his nuts.

b. Preferably with both hands, start to twist.

c. Very important – do not let go! Usually by about the third 360-degree twist he will stop.

9. Never leave your locker door open or valuables lying around. You are almost as much to blame as the person who steals. Temptation is a powerful fault that we are all born with.

NAAFI *(Navy, Army, and Air Force Institutes)* Dance

The last nine weeks of training we were allowed into the NAAFI Saturday night dances on the base. Hey, this is where the WRENS (Women's Royal Naval Service) also trained. I was still a little shy around girls and still thought of myself as being the ugly duckling, even though I tried to be more like my hero, big brother Ronnie, who had the gift of the gab when it came to the opposite sex. He had put me in much better shape. Being older than me, he was more a father than a brother. Lord only knows where I would be without his careful shaping and molding, not to mention his love.

A navy base is like a little city; garbage collection, galley slaves, and cleaners were all navy under-training personnel. Gossip spread like wildfire – lesbianism in the WRENS quarters, homosexual encounters in the men's mess room – all mostly a figment of someone's overactive imagination. A young recruit, I remember, was caught stealing. It wasn't bad enough that he was dishonourably discharged and paraded in front of the whole base as an example. The flak that he received from just about everyone was incredible.

Pervert

A pervert? Not me! The WRENS beat at me mercilessly with their heavy handbags, tripping over themselves to get a good swing at me. Will I ever live this down? I will be the laughingstock of the whole base. Worse, I may be labeled a pervert! Oh God, why me?

We were all having a good time and goading each other to go and ask out the cute WRENS across the dance floor. For the most part, they totally ignored the upstart new recruits who were stupidly grinning and waving as if they had just been let loose from the local loony bin. It was a particularly busy night. The rock band was putting out some mean tunes. Some of the older hands were up just a-hoppin' and a-boppin'. I needed to find a bathroom, and as it was my first time in the dance hall, I was unfamiliar with the setup. I found a not-too-well-lit corridor, and there at the end was the bathroom. As I was pretty much bustin' by now, having been looking everywhere and too shy to ask, I rushed over and opened the door. Inside the small room there was only one cubicle with a toilet.

I quickly stepped in and went about my business. Moments

passed, and I started to wonder why there weren't any urinals in the room. A tiny but inescapable worry began to emerge deep at the back of my skull. This transformed into panic and terror when I heard the outer door open and high-heeled shoes enter the room. 'What have I done? You stupid idiot!' I repeated over and over under my breath. 'Okay, I'll wait it out. Maybe she'll get fed up and leave.'

The door opens again, with the sound of more high heels. *Oh, my God.* Now one of them is telling the other, 'She's been in there forever,' meaning me, of course. Before very long, there must have been five of them squashed in the little room. One of them knocked on the door and said, 'Are you okay, dear? We can call the duty WREN officer if you like.'

What was I to do? Flashing through my brain were scenes of me being dishonourably discharged for being a pervert. Oh God! I stuck it out for what seemed like an eternity, sweat dripping from my forehead. By now the bathroom was chocker block, with a lineup outside the outer room. One WREN was on the way to the officer of the day.

'Okay, Kevin, it's time,' I said, cursing under my breath. I squared myself away, put on my very best I-don't-know-what-all-the-fuss-is-about face, opened the door to blood curdling screams and yelling, and calmly walked out. Needless to say I wasn't brandished a pervert, but in the fifteen weeks on base I never did get so much as a dance or a smile from any of the WRENS – I was a marked man!

CHAPTER 10
Sea Training

During the last few weeks of training we were all sent away to join *HMS Ulster* for our actual sea training course. She was a type 15 anti-submarine frigate, 363 feet long with a displacement of 2,091 tons, and a normal crew compliment of roughly 180 men. The ship was docked at the busy dockyard in Plymouth.

Just out of refit with a brand new skipper whose last commission was on fast, small, very maneuverable patrol boats, the *Ulster* was a bit of an antique, but it served its purpose at the time as a training vessel. All ships coming out of refit have to carry out sea trials, usually out of Portland, before they are considered seaworthy.

We were all pretty excited. POME McDougal had the hardest time keeping us all in one place. We were like lambs to the slaughter! The mess deck we were allotted became a very crowded place, especially when we were shown how to hang our hammocks. The hammocks had to be stowed away every morning in proper navy fashion to allow access to and movement in the mess. Hammocks had to be stowed in this seemingly complicated manner, as they also became flotation devices should we ever need them!

The ship had not been at sea for more than a few hours before ninety percent of us were stricken with seasickness. For anyone who has not experienced this little treat, it is probably one of the worst feelings imaginable. Your only objective is to try and find a hole to crawl into and die.

To leave harbour, POME McDougal had put Brian and me in the tiller flat to watch over the machinery of the rudder controls. Apart from being in the very stern of the ship, it also accentuated all the heaving and pitching, and was quite hot and sticky, not to mention having the strong smell of hydraulic oil and grease. I thought this would be something we had to get used to pretty quickly, and McDougal had put us there for that very purpose. All of our pleadings from below the deck hatch fell on very stony ground. McDougal was a hard man.

'Git duwn thar, an dinne cum up an tell a tell ya tae,' he said in his now-familiar, outer-Hebridean Scottish brogue. Even Brian, a fellow Scot, couldn't budge him. So this was what our lives were going to be for the next twelve years. After an hour we were allowed to crawl out, when another unlucky pair was thrown down into the now well-puked dungeon. The cold sea air tasted so good!

'Go and get some scran (food in navy tongue) afore yer next shift lads,' McDougal told us. Not feeling remotely like eating after the numerous upchucks down below, he explained, 'Go an' get some ship's biscuits. It'll put a linin' on yer belly an' help with yer sicknesses, lads.'

As Brian was in a little better shape than I was, I followed him across the quarter deck into Burma Way, the ship's main passageway. This old boat was bouncing around like a cork, and it wasn't helped very much by a hell-bent skipper still thinking he was on fast patrol boats (FTBs). Some of the turns made it feel as if we were going to completely roll over. It was all you could do to stay upright. The bedlam that we saw as we neared the galley was unimaginable. There before our eyes was lunch for roughly 200 men sloshing around on the deck amidst serving pans and trays. Dinner rolls were bouncing off the bulkheads. Two of our classmates assigned to the galley were attempting to clean up the chaos amidst being sick and occasionally falling over into that yucky broth and sliding into chairs and tables like skittles. It was not a pretty sight!

Finding the container with the ship's biscuits took a little time. We had decided not to ask the rather exasperated chef, who looked like he was ready to do serious harm with the large knife he was brandishing. Ship's biscuits are a miserable excuse for food. Not only do you need teeth like sharpened chisels to bite through them, they are completely tasteless and immediately dry up any vestiges of moisture in your mouth. Even trying to talk after consuming one of these delights takes a lot of concentration. Do they help with seasickness? No!

In the afternoon, still feeling dreadfully sick, I was told to go up onto the bridge wings and paint the starboard handrail supports. Eventually, after finding this part of the ship after much of a to-do, I commenced painting. Maybe if I worked hard and concentrated the sickness would go away. An older able seaman had given me this gem. No, that didn't work either! At one point I held it in as long as I possibly could, then, in a pointless effort to subdue the oncoming gush, I erroneously placed my hand over my mouth. This is commonly termed a five-finger spread in navy talk. To roughly explain the physics of a five-finger spread: $a + y + b = x2$, where a = puke, y = size of hand, b = heaving of said ship, and $x2$ = distance. You are, in fact, creating five separate vortexes of highly propelled . . . well, should we say "substance" that will travel twice the distance, not taking into account the spread.

Now, had I been on the port side, which on that day would

have been out of the wind (leeward), there would have been no problem. Not my luck! In my inexperience on these matters, not only did I receive a face full of my departed puke, a rather startled lieutenant on his way to the bridge also caught some. For the next thirty minutes I was disciplined by one very annoyed lieutenant and the chief stoker on the intricacies of puking, or for that matter doing whatever, over the side. Golden rule: never into the wind!

A long weight

I tried to befriend an able seaman who was painting the port rails. I asked him if he had any other ideas to rid myself of this torment. All I received back was a brusque, 'Get back to work, shithead.' Ten minutes later he came over and ordered me to go to the paint locker and pick up a long weight to help tighten up the guard rail wires.

Firstly, I asked, 'Where is the paint locker? And what is a long weight?'

'The paint locker on any naval ship is the most forward lowest compartment, you grease monkey dummy,' he abruptly replied, amongst other insults on my parentage. 'Talk to the seaman in the paint locker. He'll get you the weight.'

Down into the bowels of the ship I went, down and down, finally finding the tiny paint locker. There was a lineup of a few of my classmates there already. I eventually made my way to the front and asked the ordinary seaman for the tool. 'Okay,' he said, 'hang on there and I'll be right with you.'

This part of the ship was just awful when the bow surged up over the waves. It felt like your legs were like lead, your knees buckling under the weight. Then when the bow came down and eventually crashed into the sea, you experienced weightlessness. Just a slight jump and you could actually become airborne. The smell of paint and this roller coaster ride was not faring too well with my stomach. The cold sweat and dizziness was more than I could bear. After a very long time I reminded the OS about my long weight. He grinned at me and said, 'I think you've waited long enough, don't you?' Bastards!

Sleeping in the hammock took a little getting used to. Rigging it and then trying not to get too close to your nearest neighbour was the objective. Once a hammock swing commences, as was brought about by our illustrious captain, the pendulous action of thirty or so swinging hammocks in a not altogether rhythmic pattern creates havoc. Crashing into each other makes for a rather sleepless night. The only saving grace was that the hammocks counteracted some of the heaving and swell of the ship. We all had to quickly get used to the idea of being squashed into these small mess decks, not unlike sardines.

Down below

For the latter part of sea training, we were set up into duty watches. This meant we were now included in the ship's watch-keeping roll. I was assigned to the boiler room on one middle shift (midnight to 4 a.m.). I had been instructed earlier on how to enter the boiler room hatch. This was a double hatch lock system; close one door before opening the other. The air pressure inside the boiler room was slightly higher than the ambient pressure of the rest of the ship. Climbing down the metal ladders into the heat and deafening noise was like going down into hell. There, perched before the oil furnace to the massive boiler strewn with gauges, were the two stokers on watch, punching furnace fuel oil sprayers on demand from the ship's control room. Through the sight glass you could see the cauldron of flame inside the furnace. Should anyone come through the hatch and forget to close the outer door, the flames from the sprayers could back flash into the stokers' faces. This is not what I imagined I would be doing for the next, how many years?

Having finished my shift and completing all kinds of unimaginable tasks given by the leading hand, I did receive a kind of "Hey, I did it" feeling. I wondered what the people back home would think of all this. Would they even believe me? It was a feeling of being thrust into a completely different world where incredible situations occur that you just have to find your way of handling.

I instinctively knew I had to watch my back. I learned very quickly that there was nobody looking out for me. My mother's constant warning, 'Look before you leap,' was always there in the forefront of my mind. Inevitably, experience sharpened my senses, and with a bit of luck, I thought I might come out of that and many of life's other moments unscathed.

I had only just started my journey and already I knew there were changes in me that I could not refute, including the inner excitement I felt having conquered a fear or difficult task. I constantly compared what I was experiencing to that of my fellow compatriots I grew up with. It was my gauge to keep pushing me ahead.

I was starting to feel a burning desire, maybe because of my meagre start in life to be someone, to accomplish something special, to raise my head above the weeds. So far in my life I had been made to feel inconsequential. Sure, I had the love of my family, but why did I have this sadness in my heart? Whenever I felt love I seemed to know sooner or later there would be torment and shame, then the building blocks would eventually tumble to leave me in a place where I hated being.

Portsmouth, my second home

After what seemed like a lifetime, the ship finally went into port. Portsmouth was probably one of the busiest and most famous navy ports in Britain at the time. *HMS Victory,* Admiral Nelson's flagship, was still there under constant refit. Brian and I had what was popularly termed 'Cinderella leave'; we had to be back on board no later than midnight! All this freedom was intoxicating, to say the least. The many accomplishments we had both survived over the last weeks of our adolescent lives were thankfully behind us. We hit the tiles with a passion and with confidence abound. We quite fortunately met up with two local girls, Angela and Rosemary, at a fair ground.

I must take this time to explain a misnomer. The saying that a sailor has a girl in every port is not quite factual. Most ladies from large seaports are usually not that willing to date sailors, for various reasons explained below:

1. Mother will beat her brains out if she finds out, wanting better for her daughter.
2. To be seen with a sailor is common and trashy to other locals.
3. He usually has pals hanging around who also hit on her when the main guy is not looking.
4. One day he's here and then he's gone, usually for a long time.
5. Once bitten, twice shy.

Even when camouflaged in civilian clothes, these local women could spot a sailor at a glance. I was never quite sure what they picked up on – the short hair, the overabundance of aftershave (to mask the odor of fuel oil), or the frothing at the mouth and the wild stare after not seeing the opposite sex in such a long time. It was uncanny how some girls could just cut you short. 'You sailor, get out of my face right now. Go!'

My first love

Well, I guess Lady Luck was with us today. These two very pretty ladies were all we could have hoped for. Angela was the older of the two sisters at nineteen. So I, not being sixteen yet, thought I was doing pretty well. Over the next few hours we got to know each other and seemed to hit it off. I was in complete heaven, and midnight was coming on very fast. The sultry kisses she gave me at the dockyard gates just about sent me over the top.

Over the next weeks I could not get the lovely Angela out of my brain, which made the final part of sea training bearable. To our absolute astonishment, Angela and Rosemary made their way to Plymouth during our final weeks of training. This was love; call it what you like, puppy love or whatever. She was everything I had dreamed about and more. She was a lot more experienced than me, the shy, bungling, and very unsure of himself kind of kid. With a great deal of patience, she steered me always in the right direction. All the attention, not to mention the passion, just made me dizzy. I was hers to do with as she pleased.

She later reluctantly confessed that she was married to a sailor, also a stoker. He was a petty officer. I felt almost destroyed by this bombshell. She later separated, and for a few years we had an exciting relationship, except for numerous breakups due mainly from being apart.

Angela taught me so much in those earlier years. One thing that I shall always remember her for is that she lived for the moment. Don't worry about tomorrow, or even yesterday. Live it the best you can with all the passion you can muster right now!

Brian married his Rosemary two years later, but marriage eluded our relationship. As much as Angela could inspire me, there was no in between. It was either amazing love or excruciating, painful, heart-crashing breakups.

Expedition training

Expedition training was our last trial to finish off our navy instruction before we would all be drafted to our first actual operating ship, usually for two and a half years. We were given instruction on how to read maps, compass readings, and average hiking speeds. We were then taken out to Dartmoor, made up into teams, and dropped off at different locations and told to report to a certain location on the map before a certain time. We camped out overnight, and at first light set off on our orders. Although we were all in pretty good shape by now, by the time we had progressed to the location at the end of the day, some of the lads were being carried. In my team, we only had one lad that I and one other took turns carrying. I enjoyed every minute and would have gone back to do it again.

CHAPTER 11
HMS Zulu

After fifteen weeks of naval training we were all excited and ready to join our allotted ships. Brian was drafted before me to *HMS Arethusa*. It was a sad farewell when he left. After all we had gone through together, it was like losing a newfound brother. As usual, my mother made sense out of it all, in a three-page letter explaining in her way that life is full of meeting new friends and losing old friends. The real life friends you will have for life. Wherever they are in the world, they will watch out for you, and you for them. *They* are the ones to be treasured.

Meeting the ship

Petty Officer McDougal gave me the draft chit that said when and where I was to join the relatively new frigate *HMS Zulu*. McDougal had become almost like a father figure in the last weeks of training, even inviting the remaining few of us to his married quarters house to meet his wife and family.

The railway tickets showed I was to travel via London and Edinburgh to meet the ship in Rosyth dockyard, which was just finalizing a major refit. So, with a huge kit bag in tow and all kinds of other paraphernalia, I headed out on my next big adventure.

Sleep eluded me on the overnighter to Edinburgh, with its

uncomfortable, packed, and tobacco smoke-filled compartments, my head propped up against the gyrating window. Little did I know how many of these train trips I would have to endure, squashed into corridors and the like, in future years.

My head was a buzz of thoughts. Where was the ship going? What kind of ship would it be? Would I eventually set foot on a foreign land? No one in my family, apart from my other hero, the rarely seen Uncle Fred, had ever been abroad. I don't think my mother or father had ever been out of Lancashire! How long would it be before I saw my sweetheart Angela again? Would I receive any leave in the not-too-distant future to go home again?

I arrived in Edinburgh station in the early hours of the morning. I was totally lost, wandering around the platforms with all my gear anchored to my various appendages. I made the mistake of asking a ticket clerk where I could find the train connection to Dunfermaline. He might as well have replied in archaic Hebrew. Between the 'och ayes' and the 'nooos,' the rest was a gibberish tongue unknown to me. However, I did take note of the various directions his bony little finger was pointing me in. How I eventually made it to the ship remains a mystery. Finding an appendage free to salute the officer of the day from the gangway was a challenge.

The ship looked like nothing I had ever seen before. Everything about it just gleamed. Having just completed an extensive refit with a fresh paint job and shiny polished brass work that must have used up literally gallons of Brasso, I was impressed!

HMS Zulu was a relatively new Tribal class general-purpose frigate with a displacement of 2,300 tons and it measured 360 feet in length. It had some pretty fancy new upgrades, and had just been fitted with a state-of-the-art Seacat missile launch pad. It was propelled by a mixture of steam and gas turbines. It even had a gas turbine generator, which rarely worked, and sent one chief artificer almost to a mental home. It seemed some of the equipment was so new it was still in the experimental stage. It had computer-controlled twin 4.5-inch gun turrets fore and aft, amongst various other armaments. It also had a Westland Wasp helicopter. Wow, what had I done to deserve this?

The able seaman on gangway duty escorted me down below and showed me the stokers' mess. As it was still in the early hours of the morning, for the most part everyone was sleeping. The only illumination in the main passageway and in the mess itself were red night-lights that produced a hi-tech but eerie red glow. As tired as I certainly was, the excitement of all this sent shivers down my spine. I found an empty bunk and tried ineffectively to sleep for the few hours before the wakeup call.

I overheard one of the petty officers say I was a keen baby stoker full of piss and vinegar. I had made a promise to myself to learn as much as I could and eventually try for petty officer mechanician, which would give me a trade. I had found out along the way that my classification, marine engineer mechanic, would not qualify as a trade. Even if I made it to Chief MEM, which usually took twenty-six years of service, it still would not be of any use outside of the navy. Although the title sounded technical, we were basically machine watch keepers, ensuring all machinery was serviced and running correctly. If the machine needed to be taken apart and fixed, that was the job of an artificer, usually a petty officer or chief who had served two years or so in a naval engineering college. A new classification had recently come about where talented, leading MEMs that had passed certain exams could qualify for the two years of naval college later in their careers and then become petty officer mechanicians, a trade similar to artificer.

When I wasn't down below doing whatever was asked of me besides the duty watches and being a total pest asking countless questions of the POs and chiefs, I was in a quiet corner of the mess studying and passing every auxiliary watch keeping certificate way ahead of any of my shipmates. This had the adverse effect of making me not very popular with the rest of the more senior juniors who had been on board longer than I had. Never being too fussed about being popular and usually being a loner, this was okay with me. I had my guitar, my study books, and my pencil drawings of old, weathered, steaming boots, which the 'father' of the mess (the oldest stoker, probably thirty-five years old) took a fancy to. He had them framed and hung on the bulkheads. Brother Ronnie still has one of these drawings to this day.

First run ashore

My first run ashore with the older stokers, which was more of a 'you will come ashore with us tonight' kind of a deal, proved to be a real eye-opener. This happened to be our last night. The ship was heading out the following morning for sea training. In the next few months we would eventually head out to the Persian Gulf. There were around thirty-five stokers in our mess, consisting of eight juniors, including myself, and various levels of marine engineer mechanics, the real name for stokers. My arm badge showed a single propeller; I would later earn a star above the propeller denoting I had passed certain exams. Once I was classed as a man above eighteen and had passed more exams, I could become a leading hand, a killick, and would have a single anchor above the propeller. It was the equivalent of being a corporal in the army. It surprised me that some men in their thirties and older had never even reached leading hand. They were the lifers. It was my opinion that they would be totally lost in civilian life. They seemed to have no goals or dreams, and usually hit the first pub ashore, not venturing any further no matter what interesting port we were visiting.

We all hit 'Maggie's Pub' (Saint Margaret's Lounge and Fine Dining) in Dunfermaline almost at the same time as the seamen's mess and various other reprobates of the remaining mess decks. Within a very short time things started to get out of line. It seemed our theme song, 'Zulu Warrior,' known throughout the fleet, was quite popular amongst the ladies. It was partly because the song was about someone usually under much influence who detached himself of his attire. They would then dance on the tables and bar completely naked, with much beer being thrown in their general direction.

I highly suggest you sing this behind closed doors, just in case it has the same hypnotic effect I have seen with my own eyes. The song goes as follows:

Zulu Warrior

Hold 'em down, you Zulu warrior
Hold 'em down, you Zulu chief, chief, chief, chief
Hold 'em down, you Zulu warrior
Hold 'em down, you Zulu chief, chief, chief, chief

I got a zumba zumba zumba
I got a zumba zumba zumba zee
I got a zumba zumba zumba
I got a zumba zumba zumba zee

Repeat those simple words over and over to the beat of many glasses on tables, and usually someone will eventually take off their clothes. It never fails.

On this particular evening, much to the chagrin of the owner, the ladies present were one at a time being turned upside down, dresses flowing above their heads, and having much beer poured into their undergarments – strangely enough, with little if no complaints! However, the owner and lady guests had by now managed to separate most of the ship's crew of their hard-earned pay packet handed out that very day.

The following morning I awoke to find a complete plastic wall from the St. Margaret's Lounge covering one of our bulkheads, complete with fixtures, Scottish highland paintings, lamps, and a clock. I never figured out how they had managed to get this wall into a taxi then through very strict dockyard security – this was a nuclear dockyard when all was said and done – then bypass the officer of the day on the gangway, down our small hatchway and ladders, and into the mess. When the ship returned eighteen months later the police were waiting on the dock. With three large policemen and all the help they could muster, we could not get that wall back through the hatch without cutting it in two.

Pricky Price

Inasmuch as the ship was new, clean, and efficient, it was not a happy ship; in particular, the stokers' mess seemed to be a particularly unhappy place. Among others, 'Pricky' Price wanted out of the navy so bad he went 'on the trot' (AWOL) three separate times, a highly punishable offence. The second time he came back he had a tattoo on his forehead that read 'I hate the fuckin navy.' The navy, determined to crack Pricky, forced him to have a skin graft, and then sent him to DQ (detention quarters or navy prison) for forty-five days. This was a place harsher than your worst nightmare. The garbage cans were the most highly polished ones you would ever set eyes on. Men were made to stand out in the freezing snow naked until they dropped. Cruelty was number one! Short of extreme torture, they tried just about everything else. Thankfully, a national TV crew somehow managed to get some footage and the place was immediately closed down. We heard many a sad story from the men who had gone through this torture camp set up to crack the so-called hard nuts. It was another huge embarrassment for the Royal Navy at the time.

When he came back the second time he had changed from a talkative, friendly fellow into a caged animal who talked to no one, excepting perhaps an occasional snarl. It was months before he became his usual friendly sort. He was older than me by a few years, and always seemed ready to give a helping hand and a joke to bring up your spirits when things were down. He disappeared again, this time for good. We unbelievably received a postcard from him in Yugoslavia. Maybe this was a ploy to get them off his tail. Who knows? Wherever he is now, good luck, mate!

The angry, big slob

We had a big slob of a guy on board, a Geordie (from the northeast of England, in particular Newcastle). He would go ashore and get completely lambasted, then come back on board and beat the snot out of everybody, including juniors way younger than himself. Many was the night I was woken with screams and smashes, flesh being beaten with large, lumbering blows, sudden reminders of home. It was an unwritten rule to report this. How many people actually fall down the ladders? Does the sickbay tech really believe this?

The junior area of the mess deck was a narrow, partitioned corridor with lockers on one side and two tiers of bunks on the other. The top bunk was hitched up or rolled back during the day to allow for seating on the bottom bunk. It was named uncouthly as 'gobbler's gulch.' The father of the mess was an ancient man – almost forty. He had the farthest bunk at the end of the corridor to keep an eye on us juniors. We had been at sea for a few weeks when the father noticed that one of the rather untalkative juniors had been reading the same comic for over a week. When he decided to take a closer look, he realized the comic was actually upside down! Shortly thereafter, the junior was sent via the ship's chopper to the navy's funny farm.

His replacement was also a quiet guy, a few years older than me. He was given the bunk below mine. Our bunks were at the entrance to the gulch. He hadn't been on board more than a few weeks when the big slob came back from a heavy drinking session ashore, determined to knock the pulp out of someone. The new guy was his second of the night. It was horrific. Even two of the older guys could not stop him. His big fat fists were hammering down mercilessly, and through his drunken, slobbering curses, I could hear the new guy pleading with him to stop. It was all I could do to just scurry down into my blankets and pray I wouldn't be on his dance list tonight. Eventually he tired and staggered, with help, back to his bunk. The new guy was taken care of and cleaned up. All evidence of the bloodied sheets were taken to the laundry.

I eventually fell into a discordant sleep, listening to his painful sobbing, but was woken in the early hours of the morning to screams and a sickly smushing and pounding sound. The new guy had quietly removed his metal bunk bar, a metal U-shaped pipe with flat ends that slotted into the side of the bunk to stop you falling out in rough weather. He casually, but very intentionally, walked to the slob's bunk and beat him over the head with the bar. The slob was so badly injured he was flown back to England to hospital. The new guy was sent on to who knows where. We never saw or heard from either of them again. The new guy had inadvertently done us all a big favour.

It seemed morale was quite low during my time on the *Zulu*, in particular in the stokers' mess. At one point, over half of the personnel were on some sort of punishment. I remember all personnel in the stokers' mess having been suspended of leave, being paraded up to the quarterdeck in our number one suits to be reprimanded by a very angry and rather snotty engineer officer. This was the day after we had left the wall (harbour) in Naples during a huge NATO exercise. Everyone was there, with the German, Italian, French, and American navies showing off all their shiny brass – their big guns and fancy armaments.

Along the busy jetty appeared a very ratty looking sailor running to try and catch his ship as it untied. He was half-dressed, holding up his pants, having been previously detached of his money belt. He was obviously still very drunk, even though it was eight o'clock in the morning. He was waving frantically at our ship; the skipper was totally ignoring him. 'Nope, he's not one of ours.' We, the stokers, obviously recognized him, as we stood to attention on the quarterdeck all shining and smart in our number ones, with the rest of the ship's company all smartly saluting the side. He was one of our leading MEMs, but probably about to lose his hook (anchor) very shortly. The chief was trying to keep us quiet, but there was a lot of sniggering and the odd 'Good on ya, mate! Was she worth it?' The engineer officer was dispatched to the quarterdeck. He was pissed. This was probably the closest he had ever come to a possible mutiny.

CHAPTER 12
Gibraltar

The ship spent several months around the UK. We had completed sea trials off Portland and visited what seemed my second home, Portsmouth, many times.

Angela and I became pretty much inseparable. Whether it was love or lust, either way she knew she had me hook, line, and sinker. I was smitten. This beautiful brunette with the painted lips and long legs knew pretty much everything one needed to know about the act of sex – and I was her humble but very willing pupil. From the moment we set eyes on one another until the sad leaving, we were constantly making love in some form or other. This experienced lady wanted nothing more than to teach me all the moves!

Young Love

Cold-hearted woman she did me wrong
It was a cold-hearted woman who took my heart
They called it puppy love, then I'm just a dog because
Cold-hearted woman she sure took my heart.

Young love, straight outta the box

Young boy, far from home
He gotta broken heart from runnin' away
She casts her spell, he's blinded by lust, he got
He got no chance
He's drownin' in her

Because
Young love, straight outta the box

She was an angel, in fact that was her name
She had jet-black hair and ruby-red lips
Let me tell you now she was so fine, she had
She had this young boy all tied up in knots

Because
Young love, straight outta the box

Now here's a moral, ain't no mistake
You handle fire, you're gonna get burned
Stay away from divine ruby lips
'Cos fall in the hole, you might never get out

Because
Young love straight outta the box.
—K. Firth, September 2009

Gibraltar was the first place I had ever set foot on a foreign land. I was still only sixteen. The thrill of stepping off that gangway has stayed with me all through the years. From that moment on I was truly hooked. I knew I would not be completely happy until I had seen it all, every nook and cranny of this wonderful world we live on. The different aromas and feel of a place, the different languages, it was all just *different*.

I was never too fussed with towns and cities, and generally tried to get up into the hills. I was always pretty much on my own. Most of the lads preferred the night life.

In Gibraltar I hiked to the top of the rock and was thrilled to see the cheeky Barbary macaque monkeys that scampered around completely free. Like Mum, I could sit for hours just watching their antics. Tourists would drive up the road, which didn't quite make it to top of the rock, and stop to see the monkeys, which were often cheeky enough to climb into the cars through the windows, raid whatever they could carry, and then zip out the opposite window.

I sat on the wall that probably had an eighty-foot vertical drop on the opposite side, and tried for hours to make friends with one of those critters. Eventually, a lone monkey edged closer and closer. I had my hand outstretched. He was so cute. I was imagining what my mum would be like had she seen me. He was almost talking to me with his eyes and brow. When he got within touching distance he held out his hand too. I reached out, and in a split second he had bit my finger and leapt over the side of the cliff. I could hardly believe the agility as he bounced off the cliff here and there and then into a nearby tree. He looked up as though to say to me, 'Ha, ha! Got ya, numb knuckles.'

CHAPTER 13
Malta

We left Gibraltar and toured the Mediterranean, visiting Malta, Naples, and Pompeii and the Mount Vesuvius volcano.

Malta was a beautiful place, and as we were anchored off, we had to take liberty boats to go ashore. If you missed the liberty boat when returning to the ship, it was easy and pretty cheap to take a water taxi in the colourful gondola-type boats.

Valetta, the capital, was the nearest town to get to once ashore. In the hot afternoons it was unbelievably quiet, like a ghost town. Then, at five o' clock, it seemed that everyone just came out of the woodwork. The main street would be closed off to car traffic as pedestrians filled the streets. Restaurants, souvenir shops, and open cafés seemed to appear from nowhere. Adding to the hustle and bustle were people going to church, the Maltese generally being quite religious people. However, at the far end of the main street it was a far different story. If you ventured down any of the narrow walkways and steps going toward the sea, you stepped into a totally different nether world! It seemed every other door was a small dingy bar or nightclub. Multitudes of sailors oozed out from either side of the narrow street, which in some places was less than ten feet apart. This whole area of usually dark and mysterious streets was surreptitiously called 'The Gut.'

Malta was an important ally during the Second World War and was strategically placed in the Mediterranean. Ever since then it had been an important place of call for American and British warships patrolling the Mediterranean during the Cold War. There had even been a British naval base there at one time.

Massive American aircraft carriers would arrive, and literally thousands of men after long spells at sea would be ashore looking for women and booze – not necessarily in that order. The prices for everything from taxis to beer increased overnight. Supply and demand was what it was all about. The American navy personnel were paid well compared to us Brits. Inasmuch as we loved our American neighbours and felt a strong kinship, Lord help the bar owner who happened to have both. It would be almost guaranteed that before the night was out, much glass and many heads would be broken. If the Aussie, or for that matter the Kiwi (New Zealand), navy were in, then don't even bother going ashore.

The few women that were in the bars were basically buy-me-drink girls. They would come and sit with you, or bring you to the bar where you could buy them a drink, which was obviously coloured water or cold tea. She would secretively be given a token for every drink, and at the end of the night she would conveniently cash in her tokens.

One of the other juniors and I had been talked into going ashore with the older lads. Neither one of us actually drank alcohol yet, which was unusual even at our age. We just sat listening to the music and watching the live show take place as the men steadily became drunker and more stupid by the minute. We just couldn't figure out why you would pay the earth for coloured water.

One of the lads at the bar had his wallet stolen by a couple of the working girls, obviously a tag team, and a bit of a kafuffle was beginning to get out of hand. Although the local police rarely came into the Gut, tonight they had been called and were in business to crack heads. Two of them came into the bar, and with no questions asked, commenced swinging their heavy truncheons into all and sundry. In a matter of seconds the whole bar looked like a battle zone. Chairs, tables, and glasses were flying everywhere. Some of our shipmates were trying to get to the lad who had had his wallet stolen. He was buried in the center of the melee and was by now unconscious and still taking many beats to the head. One of the older lads shrieked to us to 'Get the hell outta here as fast as you can.'

This was all happening very close to the door. We squeezed through the door and I was trying to get the other kid, who was scared shitless by now, to get moving. I looked down the street and saw six more of the police running toward us, screaming and waving their truncheons. We set off running, and three of the six chased us. They were not interested in the bar fight, which had now expanded into the street. I was ahead of the game, but my buddy was just not running fast enough and kept stopping as though he was going to explain to these nice police that we really hadn't done anything, so could they please leave us alone. They easily caught him. He was a small-framed fifteen-year-old boy and they were three grown men with truncheons. They rapidly beat him down to his knees onto the hard cobblestone road. He then curled up in a tight ball, trying in vain to protect himself with his hands on his head. All three of them laid into him with such a force I was surprised when they eventually lost interest and left him be that he was actually still alive.

When I was sure they had departed, I returned to pick him up and virtually carried him back to the liberty boat. He was beaten black and blue, with blood coming from seemingly every orifice. When the medic on board finally finished with him, I helped him limp down to the mess and helped him into his bunk. He cried like a baby all night, asking for his mother.

After that, I didn't venture too many times down to the Gut. Instead, I enjoyed taking the local buses on hair-raising drives across the island. The buses had so many crosses and religious dangly bits hanging down from the windows I was surprised they could actually see through them! Every now and again, after a dangerous turn or screech of tires, the driver would cross himself and sometimes turn around with a reckless, relief-like expression.

I met a beautiful young lady on one of these excursions and was on a date in a small restaurant where we were having coffee. Across from us were two American navy chiefs who kept glancing in our direction. The next thing I knew, the chiefs had bought us both a meal. One of them came past me on his way out, said, 'You guys look so happy together,' and left. She always had to be home early. We had a couple of well-behaved dates and then I had to leave. She wrote me quite a few letters, but eventually we lost touch.

A few years later I had heard that a Royal Marine had been killed in the Gut. There were many violent repercussions thereafter until the admiralty had to put a stop to it. I believe the Gut was cleaned up considerably and is probably now a tourist destination.

Chapter 14
Naples

I met Brian, who was still serving on *HMS Arethusa,* when our ships were in Naples. Both ships, and many others, were there on NATO exercises. We had a pleasant run ashore together where he told me about his marriage proposal to Rosemary, which would sadly change her surname from Rose Budd to Reid. I had received my first Dear John letter from Angela only months after leaving the UK. I had taken it pretty badly at the time, but I was hoping once I returned to Portsmouth we might make up again.

We visited Izmir in Turkey and parts of Greece during many exercises, but I thought it was mainly to show our naval presence. We were in the thick of the Cold War with Russia, so we were being constantly followed by various Russian surveillance ships. There was a lot of silliness going on. A Russian warship that had been following us for weeks and generally wreaking havoc during our sometimes dangerous exercises had broken down, much to our glee. We were exercising with oil tankers to refuel at sea (RAS). This is where flexible pipelines were run from our beam to the tanker while both ships were steaming ahead. Sometimes we would even pass personnel back and forth along various wires and ropes. This Russian chump attempted to come in between us, which was not only very dangerous, but a bit silly. We came up alongside the broken down warship to much agitation on deck as secret stuff was being covered with canvas sheets. This ship looked like it had just come out of a serious refit a bit too early. It hadn't even been painted yet. Lord only knows what conditions the poor buggers had down below decks. Anyway, just for the hell of it we bombarded them with potatoes, as is the norm at sea.

CHAPTER 15
Durban and the Fabulous Shakas

I don't know how the band started. Sam, our easy-going black singer who was an ordinary seaman on board, seemed to me to be the mainstay. The radio operator had an electric guitar, but couldn't play it worth a shit. He also had a bass guitar, which he could play only slightly better. I took over as lead guitar player and learned a few tunes from a corporal from the band of one of the Marine detachments. The ship's cook was our drummer. April Ashley was his name, believe it or not, to which he took much ribbing. However, he was pretty keen with a carving knife also, so ribbing was at one's own risk.

We called ourselves the Fabulous Shakas, which was the name of a famous tribal Zulu chief. At sea we became quite popular, setting up our various bits and pieces on deck and going through our Beatles, Otis Redding, and soul music. Our usual finale was Eric Clapton's 'Sunshine of Your Love,' where we would go off into a wild feedback-wailing climax akin to Jimi Hendrix.

We had practiced and practiced, and were ready to perform ashore. South Africa would be our next shore visit and it looked very promising. The beautiful city of Durban was the first port of call. However, two days prior to our arrival the skipper had us in his office, minus Sam. He gave us the bad news that we would not be allowed to perform together, as apartheid was at its height. Whites were not allowed to mix with blacks. Sam would not even be allowed to come ashore with us. Sam and I were the best of friends. He had a Cockney accent, and I was sure he sounded more British than me. I wasn't going to take this lying down. He wasn't even allowed in the same bar as us!

I met him one afternoon walking out of the dockyard, and was upset when he tried to ignore me. When I stopped him and protested, he told me it was for my own good. Later that day, I met some people in a music store where I had just purchased an acoustic guitar. I had also arranged a gig at a private party. I told Sam about it. At first he flatly refused, but after much pleading on my part he eventually gave in. The late 1960s was an era when soul music reigned. Our hottest numbers were Wilson Pickett's 'Midnight Hour' and Smokey Robinson's 'My Girl.' We set up and performed for this private party of about sixty white people. When Sam came out front and strutted his stuff like we had never seen him before, it was totally unbelievable. There wasn't a female there who would not have jumped his black bones! He just poured it on thick and greasy, gyrating and hitting those notes like a professional. When we finished and half the women were frothing at the mouth to meet him, he didn't even say goodbye, but left immediately. I think he got the better of South Africa.

We played in Mombasa in Kenya a few weeks later, and here again he was hot, hot, hot. This place was the complete opposite, a totally black audience right in the thick of soul music. Other local bands came to see him perform and we did our best to keep the backing music up to his par. We played in Karachi, Pakistan, then it was on to Singapore and various other places.

Wherever you are now, Sam, I hope you tried the music

business.

With those gratifying ventures into different forms of music, I was already starting to realize what a strong pull it had on me. I particularly loved to experiment with my acoustic guitar, even putting some words to the different chords I was finding. I could be hundreds of miles out to sea playing my guitar in a quiet, dark corner of the ship. Sometimes I felt almost like I was being transported to a wonderful place where any demons that might have been bothering me were completely washed away. Hours later I would return to the hustle and bustle of the mess deck energized and strangely fulfilled.

We didn't have TV on board. Sometimes as a special treat we might have radio piped into the mess, and other times maybe a movie in the main mess hall where the ship's company normally had meals. The occasional newspaper would circulate the ship, so keeping up with what was going on in the world was sketchy at best.

The Vietnam War was being fought, and we wondered how long it would be before we might be dragged into the fray. I had met two US soldiers ashore who had both been shot. One had his arm in a sling and showed us his scars. They had just come out of hospital and were waiting for a flight back home. I knew this could very well happen to me; I was in the armed forces, when all was said and done. It didn't take too much imagination to realize that I might one day be in a position to have to kill someone. Whenever those thoughts came to me, my conscience always came into play. What if that person had done me or my family no wrong and I was being told to kill him just to obey orders? Or worse, would I run like a coward if he had a gun pointing in my direction?

Bob Dylan came to my rescue! To be more exact, the sixties peace movement did. I was deeply inspired by the sincere words and captivating, simple music. How one person with one guitar could inform and entertain a whole generation about what was really going on! I found I couldn't get enough of this kind of music. It sure wasn't mainstream, but it kindled a fire in me. I started to lose interest in the band, and I was eventually replaced by a new lead guitarist who also played a blues harmonica. I loved to listen to him playing the harp, so I bought one and learned to play myself.

Here is one of the first songs I wrote. It was a protest song. I was starting to realize my pacifist thinking.

In My Life

One night as I slept, I had a nightmare
I remember it well
I had visions of my life
And the world as we progress

In my life (repeat 3X)

In the morning of my life, I saw many things
That frightened me,
Like man killing man for more land, more power
Rights, democracy, christianity, and colour

In my life (repeat 3X)

In the noon of my life came more hate, more wars
Science developed weapons that could kill
Even more and faster
We defended our lands with computers
That were fed to attack our enemies

In my life (repeat 3X)

In the eve of my life we succeeded in our efforts
To kill each and every one, destroy one and all
The sights that I see, they bring tears to my eyes
Burned bodies, houses ruined, fields and trees,
   they're all gone
Like the charred piece of oak tree that I played on as a boy
But me, I'm still living; tell me what went wrong

In my life (repeat 4X)

—K. Firth, circa 1967

The real Zulu warriors

The main notice board in Burma Way, just outside the galley, was where the lads posted their Dear John letters, quite a common occurrence once the ship had been away from home port for a few months. Other hardened sailors would sometimes write callous but very funny comments on the letters. There was also the contest for the ugliest girl. To qualify you had to have a picture of the woeful female sitting on your knee snogging! Such is life at sea! Other general information was also displayed.

Coming into Durban, there were numerous interesting invites to stay with rich white couples. Sometimes invites came for two, four, or six sailors to some farm or business, or even a full-fledged safari hunt. Reading the fine print, it was usually to meet their whiter than white daughters! Young, purebred, and white Brits, it seemed, were quite an item.

I signed on to visit the Zulu National Park. Apparently, everyone on board wanted to go, so it was decided to put all the names into a hat. I was one of the lucky forty or so picked to go. There were a few officers, including the captain, the first lieutenant, and some chiefs and POs also picked to go.

Our dress going ashore, if not in a British Commonwealth country, was our navy uniform. In hot countries we wore our standard issue tropical gear, which consisted of white shorts, white front (a starched cotton square-neck T-shirt with a blue strip around the wide collar), long white socks (sometimes blue), and white blanco shoes or sandals – and of course, finished off with the flat, white hat with the name of your ship around the front of the brim. If you can imagine for a moment what a sight we must have made, turning up looking like Mister Clean. For officers attending a cocktail party or other fancy functions, with all the gold braid it worked quite well. Generally speaking, enlisted men ashore tended to hit the darker side of town. In that situation, we really stuck out like the proverbial sore thumb.

The coach pulled up alongside the ship beside our gangway on the dock and we were all loaded on. The drive up to the top of the tabletop mountain was brilliant. Even the soil was different, being a dark red, unlike the stuff we were used to back home. Eventually we drove through a gateway. This was Zululand, a municipality within the province of Natal. We were told by the guide that very few non-Zulus were allowed here, but as we were on *HMS Zulu* it seemed very fitting.

All around us were peaceful, pasture-green hillsides. The Zulus, who were predominant in South Africa, were third-class citizens during apartheid, as it was during our visit. We pulled into a fenced area. On the other side of a barbed wire fence, there were more black people in very scant clothing than I had ever seen. Some women had no tops. There were official looking black, khaki-clad guards with whips keeping the hordes of people away from the fence. We were all feeling a bit tense leaving the protection of the coach and being told to stay on the inside of the fenced passageway that had been hastily built for us. On either side, the guards were cracking their whips to keep the people away from us. The officers were in their sparkling white tropical attire, as were we. We couldn't have felt more different than if we were visiting Martians.

We were then corralled into another fenced area with a long wooden bench for us to sit on. In front of us there was no fence, just a field probably a bit bigger than an English football field, again all completely fenced. The outside was lined with masses of the Zulu people. To our left was a makeshift podium and a small seating area for a few other civilian white people plus our guide. There wasn't too much conversation going on between any of us, as we were a bit dumbfounded with all of this and a tad nervous. The announcer got up to the podium and spoke in an African language first and then in English.

It was explained to us that we had been invited to the annual Zulu dance competition. We wouldn't be voting, but any applause by us would be duly recorded. I was thinking 'This can't be "*come dancing*"'. I really didn't expect a couple to arrive in this field with the man dressed in top hat and tails. Maybe we had lost something in translation.

After a sudden long silence, we felt a slight vibration coming from under our feet, and at the far end of the field there was a commotion as part of the fence was opened to allow around fifty Zulu warriors in full battle dress into the field. They had a low bass chant that coincided with feet being heavily stamped into the dusty ground, which felt hostile and very disconcerting. Slowly and in step, three rows of warriors went from one side of the field to the other, but all the time edging closer as the vibrations and chants got louder and louder.

Halfway down the field toward us, we now started to make out through the dust cloud that was being formed what they were wearing. I think the first thing we all noticed were the short spears (*iklwa*) they carried behind their cowhide shields (*isihlangu*). At a certain point they stopped and hit the backs of their shields with a knob-like cudgel (*iwisa*). Even at this distance the sound was unbelievably loud. The bench we were sitting on shuddered, as we were all startled at the same time. Closer and closer they came. Although we were sitting in the hot midday sun, I don't think the beads of sweat I noticed forming on most brows were completely due to the heat.

All through this wild procession there were two battle-clad warriors with different headdresses adorned with horns whipping around the well-formed tribe, charging hither and thither like wild animals. I had remembered watching the movie *Zulu* years earlier when the Brits took on the Zulus at Rorke's Drift. Eleven Victoria Crosses were handed out for bravery after the bloody battle. Almost 4,000 Zulu warriors were involved. It was hard to believe how so few soldiers could have kept their cool after the psychological bombardment they must have received. I was getting a little taste of that right now.

As these thoughts passed through my imagination, I was looking around at what seemed hundreds, if not thousands, of wild-looking Zulu people that totally surrounded us. I compared it to this little bench of clean, white-clad, seemingly baby-faced Brits. What chance would we have if things turned nasty? The few guys with whips wouldn't last very long, that's for sure!

At around eighty or so feet from us everything stopped and there was an intimidating silence. Even the many Zulu spectators were silent. The only thing heard was the clicking of grasshoppers and, of course, the creaking wooden bench. At some indistinct signal, the whole tribe of these wild and furious-looking warriors charged. The chant was replaced by a blood-curdling scream and the beating of shields. The hair on the back of my neck felt like tiny, sharp darts.

If we had all stood up at that very moment in time, the suction that had been created by the many constricting anal muscles would have probably lifted the heavy wooden bench right off the ground. They thankfully stopped about five feet from our noses, with the fiercest of looks in their eyes and the short spears ready to plunge. We were all taken completely by surprise.

When I could turn my head I noticed I wasn't the only one with the nervous, oh-now-wasn't-that-nice look on my face. There was now thunderous applause from everyone, and the tribe broke away to be corralled into an exit in the fence. This was repeated three more times. The foot stamping and general routine changed ever so slightly, but now we all knew what to expect, so it didn't really have the same feel to it. We were now nonchalantly almost swaggering. 'Ah, I wasn't scared – really!'

CHAPTER 16
Sinking of the Good Ship *Zulu*

Our watch-keeping system at sea was quite hardy and usually kept us busy and tired. Just about everyone on board belonged to either the port or starboard watches. For example, the port watch took the afternoon (1200 to 1600), the first (2000 to midnight), and the morning (0400 to 0800). The starboard would be the opposite shift: the "dogs" (1600 to 2000), the middle (midnight to 0400), and the forenoon (0800 to 1200). You then got twelve hours off watch while the second port and second starboard shifts took over. This was a four-watch system.

Every forenoon, whether you were on shift or not, you still had to turn to (work). Sometimes the dogs were split – the first dog from 1600 to 1800, and the second dog from 1800 to 2000 – so that meals could be had. There were different variations of this, depending on how many men were on board.

I had spent the first six months keeping watch in the hot boiler room, which was mostly automatically run from the main control room above. My tasks were basically taking readings of the many gauges, and the oil and water levels of the auxiliary machinery that supplied the massive boiler, plus a huge and very noisy superheated steam generator. I was on my own for the whole watch, unless it was a forenoon. There was cleaning, oil changes, painting, or whatever else they could find to keep me busy, and of course awake. It was a serious, punishable offence to be found sleeping.

I had surpassed all the required auxiliary watch certificates for the many machines in the boiler room, so I advanced to the main engine room. This had two massive super-heated steam turbines and a state-of-the-art gas turbine that served as the ship's main propulsion. We also made our own drinking water from the sea through a rather temperamental steam-powered evaporator. To leave this machine unattended for just a few minutes would be a disaster, as the seawater would overflow and end up in the ship's fresh water tanks. At sea there was always a wee taste of salt in our fresh water because of this. There were many other machines that needed regular maintenance, so a four-hour watch usually went very quickly.

We were alongside the wall in Durban for a couple of weeks, so the boiler would be shut down, and of course the propulsion turbines would be allowed to slowly cool and eventually run down. The ship was on shore-supplied water but on our own electrical power, which was supplied from the diesel generator in the engine room.

We had been at sea for many weeks so it was time to catch up with many scheduled maintenance projects. It was, as usual, a working forenoon, so everyone was busy with one task or another. The chief stoker had reluctantly given me the task of cleaning some of the sea strainers in the engine room. I had asked for something interesting to do, and was very keen to impress on my new duty part of ship. I could have taken all day to finish this, but again, I wanted to show how super-efficient I was and have it completed sooner.

Pretty much every engine on board, including the two large

turbines, had some form of seawater cooling. Basically, there was an opening in the ship's hull where seawater flowed via a shutoff valve, then a seawater strainer, another shutoff valve downstream of the strainer, and then on to the machine and back out to sea via another shutoff valve on the hull. Pretty basic stuff, really; however, all of these valves are below the deck plates in the bilges. The bilge was a very busy place, just a labyrinth mixture of lines and valves. You had to slither through all the disgusting mess down there and trace the lines to the valve you wanted to close. A good MEM knew where every valve was hidden and the easiest route to get to it. The deck seamen had many insulting nicknames for us stokers, one of them being bilge rats.

I had successfully cleaned quite a few of the sea strainers and was getting very confident. I had noticed a huge strainer that consisted of a plate maybe fourteen inches square. It had the usual four slip bolts with wing nuts that were removed to take the plate off. Inside, there would be a smelly metal filter full of seaweed and gunk that had to be removed and hosed clean. With the valves closed on either side of the strainer body, it would stop any seawater from flowing back up the pipe. Although the chief had mentioned I could leave these, I was being beckoned by my zeal to impress. I was deep in the bilges, and at this point my head was at the level of the bottom of the turbine deck plates. Five feet above that was another set of deck plates, the main engine room deck. The top of the engine room, reached via a metal ladder, where the hatch was to the main control room, was about another twenty feet.

I commenced loosening each of the butterfly nuts one at a time. I immediately noticed a small amount of water coming through the rubber seal. Ah, no problem! *It's just what is in the line,* I thought. *I'm an old hat at this now.* All of a sudden, *bang!* The plate was literally shot off the top of the strainer body. There before my shocked eyes was a solid wall of water. It had knocked two levels of deck plates off to the other side of the engine room and was now hitting the ceiling of the engine room probably twenty-five feet above me. *Oh my God,* I thought. *I am in deep, deep shit now.* I was looking at the large valves along the pipeline that I knew I had closed. This defied logic. I was doomed!

I ran up into the control room through the loud din being produced by this massive fountain of water. It could be heard quite clearly above the noise of the diesel generator. Oh no, there was no one in the control room! I ran into Burma Way, asking anybody if they had seen the chief. People seemed to want to have idle conversation with me.

'No, no,' I said, 'where is the fuckin' chief?'

I zipped across to the workshop. *Oh, thank God he's here!* He was in conversation with a PO. I was thinking, *I don't want him to panic, so I had better not seem too anxious.* I sauntered over to him nonchalantly.

'Ahem, Chief?' I said with the utmost composure.

'What is it, Firth? Can't you see I'm talking?' he replied angrily.

'Oh, sorry, Chief, but there's something . . .' I was pointing toward the door.

'Firth, would you shut up and wait? I'll be with you in a minute,' he said, now even angrier.

'But Chief, could you . . .' I tried to say.

'Firth, I'm not going to tell you again,' he abruptly interrupted.

I took the plunge and raised my voice. 'Chief! There really is something I have to show you!'

He somehow acknowledged the fearful look in my eyes and slowly walked out of the workshop. He seemed to want to chat with everyone on the way, but I was now kind of shouldering him forward. 'Firth, what the fuck is wrong with you? I'm going to kick your ass if you don't stop messing around,' he said, now quite red in the face.

Eventually I got him to the hatchway from the control room into the engine room. I slid down the ladder handrail and stood on the top deck plates. Three feet to my left was a scary, solid column of water. He was half in the hatchway still talking to someone in the control room. Under my breath I was pleading, 'Come on, Chief!'

He leisurely came down through the hatchway and very quickly noticed the column of water as he was coming down the ladder. His face, which was normally quite red, very quickly turned an awful colour of white the closer he came to the deck. He looked at me and said, 'What the fuck have you done, Firth?' 'I was blithering about valves and really dark down in the bilges, Chief,' I said as he was flipping his lid. He literally flew back up to the control room and screamed orders at various people.

It seemed that in minutes the engineer officer, a two-and-half-ring lieutenant commander, was in the bilge with the chief artificer. Half a dozen other people were sliding into all the nooks and crannies trying to solve the catastrophe. By now the water was five or six feet deep, almost covering the bilges in the engine room. It didn't take a genius to know that if we did not find the problem soon . . . well, it just wasn't worth thinking about! I was reminded that if the water level increased to eventually close down the generator in the engine room, we would have no electrical power to pump out the water. The only other diesel generator on board was down for service.

The chief, who was quite portly, had found the plate and was trying to sit on it while the engineer officer was straining to clip up the slide bolts, which was impossible and only succeeded in launching the chief through the deck plates. Every now and then the chief's bloodshot eyes met mine and he looked like he wanted to hang me from the nearest yardarm.

Having spent many hours in the various ship's bilges, I suppose with all the brass that was down there I was probably more familiar with these pipes and valves than they were. I was up to my waist in the oily bilge water, frantically looking at all the pipes and wondering where I had gone wrong. Through the dark, oily gloom, I noticed there was a T-junction along the large pipe supplying the main steam turbine condenser. In my enthusiasm to please, I hadn't noticed there was a crossover valve going to the other turbine strainer. Of course! An emergency crossover valve! I literally swam over to the large valve and commenced to close it. The chief thankfully ceased to comically hover over the supercharged fountain as the engineering officer quickly fastened the bolts over the strainer plate.

The water in the bilge was almost up to my shoulders. Everyone departed the engine room muttering profanities and bestowing me their vile, disappointed looks. The last one out was the chief. 'Firth, clean up this mess and then muster outside the engineering officer's wardroom,' he said with a mock sadness as he disappeared up the ladders.

It took me a couple of hours to pump out the water and clean up the mess as best I could, feeling like a total idiot, thinking what a stupid mistake I had made, and wondering what punishment would be given for my folly. In my keenness to convince my superiors that I was worthy, I had inadvertently blown it. All the work I had done in the months since I came on board to prove myself was now wasted. I had single-handedly almost sunk this modern warship in Durban Harbour!

My next move was probably just as stupid. I was filthy dirty, dripping oil and bilge water from my sodden overalls. I had never been in the wardroom. I opened a door to a gleamingly polished passageway. There were shiny mahogany and highly polished brass handles everywhere I looked. I proceeded to wander up and down looking for the engineer officers' quarters. I eventually came to an open door that had a brilliant white curtain pulled across the opening. I peeped through to see the engineer officer somberly looking at a piece of paper on his desk. I very lightly tapped on the door.

'Come in, Firth,' he said rather gruffly.

I stepped through the doorway onto his beautiful light-coloured carpet. He took one staggering look at me and screamed, 'Get out!'

I stepped back in astonishment. I was aghast to see that I had succeeded in putting two very oily boot marks on his carpet. The curtain was also covered in black oil, and as I looked down the passageway, I had probably caused at least two days' worth of cleaning for the wardroom stewards.

I was stood in the hallway to attention, peering through his half-open curtain for what seemed an eternity, wishing that the earth would just open up and swallow me whole. He had his head in his hands, seemingly struggling with some inner question, and staring at this drawing on his desk, all the while with a look of complete disbelief on his face.

After a lingering silence he said, 'Firth, I thought you were intelligent.'

I just wanted to find a hole and bury myself. What possessed me to go that one step further? He showed me the drawing he had made of the strainer assembly and plate and said, 'I can understand that you missed the emergency valve, but why would you loosen off one bolt at a time? If you had simply loosened them all, bit by bit, the plate would eventually push up against the wing nuts showing you there was a problem that you could have rectified without risking SINKING THE DAMN SHIP!'

CHAPTER 17
The Beira Bucket

Most of the other juniors, a title given to anyone under seventeen, went ashore together. With some coercion, we sometimes went with the older ratings to be 'shown the ropes.' Usually, a typical run ashore with the older lads was to the first pub outside the dockyard gates. That seemed to be what most of them ever saw.

I had made a vow to myself not to touch the evil booze, or even smoke, lest I turn out like my ill-fated dad. That lasted until I was almost twenty. Sometimes, this difference from the norm put me in the oddball bracket, but being a bit of a loner, it was okay with me. I was only sixteen, but looking a lot older got me into a lot of places. In most ports of call I was either hiking up the local mountains or catching buses and trains to get me off the beaten track to experience something different.

Keeping fit on board was difficult. The heavy watch-keeping duties that we had left only enough time to catch up with sleep during your off time. Trips at sea sometimes lasted for months, especially during the long, boring Beira patrols off eastern Africa during the oil embargo. The idea was to stop oil tankers entering the Mozambique port of Beira, the main oil terminus for oil into Southern Rhodesia, preventing any oil destined for there from being docked.

For many years during the embargo two British warships constantly patrolled a small stretch of water alternately day in and day out for months on end. Occasionally to stop the crew going stark staring mad, the two ships would meet beam to beam and either have a potato fight, much to the captain and the chief cook's chagrin, or have various silly contests. Lord only knows what the British taxpayers would think of this had it got into the tabloids. Some of the antics included Royal Navy personnel dressed up as women during an Easter bonnet parade, or the monthly kite flying contest. The latter was taken very, very seriously. Some of the most time consuming, highly engineered, and very costly monstrosities were let loose into the heavens, only to come to a rather quick and watery grave. Many tots of rum were lost to the other ships amongst all the enraged protests of 'Ya cheatin' bastards' and other such grievances.

The Beira bucket contest was the ultimate in foolishness that transpired out of sheer mind-boggling boredom. The holder of the bucket, i.e. the winning ship, would invite the other ships' contestants on board for an afternoon of well-prepared events. It commenced with a rather violent version of deck hockey, which would usually end in carnage and much spilling of blood. This would keep the various ships' medics busy for the next fortnight or two mending limbs. Countless duct tape pucks, plus the odd appendage or two, would end up in Davie Jones's Locker (the bottom of the sea, for you land lubbers).

The final contest of this bizarre foray was a race through and around the ship, engaging in many booby traps and bad play on the way. Commencing at the farthest aft position, the quarter deck, the contestant would fill the now rather holed and bruised Beira bucket from a large forty-five gallon drum of water. The race would start and the contestant would follow the well-marked route in and out of various compartments, up and down ladders, through hatchways, etc. They would traverse as best they could, and finally end up on the fo'c'sle (forecastle), the farthest part of the ship forward. The sad remains in the bucket would be poured into an empty forty-five gallon drum conveniently placed there. The contestant would run back the shortest way possible, again being hassled by many poor sportsmen and nasty booby traps en route. He would return to the quarterdeck to hand over the bucket relay fashion to the next teammate. The bucket would be recharged and repeated; this would go on for a predetermined period of time, at the end of which the water contents of the drum on the fo'c'sle would be accurately measured.

This beaten up bucket was passed from ship to ship over the many years that the embargo lasted and is now in the Royal Navy Museum in Portsmouth to this day. It is decorated with ship names and crests. It has been said that it represents 'the ultimate futility of all political aspirations in Africa.'[1]

Other days various contests would be judged, including the card games and the famous Navy 'Uckers Game,' which deserves another chapter but we'll omit for now. Only the ship's grand masters of the game would be allowed in to play.

The beauty contest and the Easter bonnet parade were very popular. How they ever came up with the protrusions, wigs, and attire is beyond imagination. Weeks later, however, the officers' wardroom would notice missing tablecloths and mop heads, and the mechanics' workshop would be missing tubing, cups, and grease nipples. Enormous amounts of canvas, parachute chord, paint, and all kinds of things would be missing from the quartermaster store.

---

[1] http://www.openwriting.com/archives/2008/12/the_beira_bucke_1.php

CHAPTER 18
Bahrain, the Armpit

Bahrain had to be the armpit of the world, from my point of view. During the few visits, generally to fuel and water the ship and spend a few days of R&R, we were met with a stiflingly hot and unfriendly place. Outside of the small dock area and a short taxi drive into Manama, it wasn't anything to write home about. The many poor people living in sand-driven tin shacks, being passed by shiny new Mercedes and Rolls-Royce cars with the standard creepy black-tinted windows, just gave you a taste of the greed and hostility there.

Our only hangout was a small café that sold chocolate drinks. Walking through this town, with many unkind looks from many men actually holding hands, was weird, as was seeing the clusters of black-cloaked women with leather *niqabs* covering their faces turning their heads and cowering. We had been warned that even staring at them could land you in the local jail, eating rice and being raped from asshole to breakfast time. No sir, not for me. Let's get right the hell out of this nightmare!

I remember looking over the side of our shiny new frigate complete with air conditioning (when it worked, that is) and feeling particularly sorry for the guys on the minesweeper squadron that were based there. God, how did they manage? A tour of duty on a navy ship was usually two and a half years or thereabouts. Out here they probably got to fly home for leave once per year. I can't imagine being broiled alive day in day out, with no women and no booze. At the time the latter didn't interest me, but the establishments sometimes were interesting to see and a place to meet the opposite sex.

Going to sea on a minesweeper, which was made completely of wood (for obvious reasons), and being tossed around like a cork didn't seem like where I would ever want to be. Hmm, you can probably guess what's coming . . .

Toward the end of the usual two and a half year tour on a ship, you are asked to fill in a request for what type of ship or area of the world you would like to go. So, filling out the request, I put a big X on the Middle East. *No thank you on that!* Far East or Caribbean? *Yeah, that sounds like a plan. Big ol' tick on that one.* Small ships? Minesweepers? *Hmm . . . no thank you!* Aircraft carrier? *Hmm . . . sounds like a floating parade ground to me. Nope, give that one a big X. Frigates? Destroyers? Yeah, give those a tick or two. That'll give me lots of space.*

Okay, now I firmly believe that the guys down in the drafting department had a sense of humour, and it must have just tickled them pink to send me back to Bahrain – again. And yes, on the damned sweeper squadron, the last place in the world I ever wanted to end up. We'll leave *HMS Brereton* for another chapter and get on with the Zulu crusade.

CHAPTER 19
Bugis Street, Singapore

After the first three months of the Beira patrol it was time for 'a jolly,' so off we went to Singapore. Wow, now that was something to write home about! Well, not *all* the details. I'm sure Mum would not have approved.

As I was now the grand old age of sixteen, six of us from the stokers' mess were now nervously venturing up the infamous Bugis Street. We had been warned about the Red Light, No-Go District, which was probably one of the most ridiculous things the navy ever did. We had been shown movies about catching various horrible diseases where your pecker just ends up rotting and dropping off. Plus there was the espionage stuff – 'The Russians are everywhere. You'll get caught on film having it off with some Singaporean maiden.' If 'it' just happens to be a man, then the Russians will blackmail you into telling them the secret recipe for a pint of pusser's lime juice, which has been known to take the paint off a gun turret at forty-five yards.

Well, what are ya gonna do when curiosity gets the better of you? Of course you're going to head on down and see for yourself what all the fuss is about, right? So you go on down there thinking that you're the only one to *brave it*, only to find half of the ship's crew also there braving it! As long as you can stay clear of the military police, it was usually no harm done.

Bugis Street was a colourful labyrinth of passageways and side streets, with masses of people going about their business, chairs and tables scattered everywhere, and kids trying to persuade you to sit. The clatter and smoke of cooking woks were everywhere, holding mysterious concoctions, the aroma of which just drew you in like a moth to light. There were buy-me-a-drink girls just ready to pounce as soon as you sat. Pimps, male and female, usually the taxi or rickshaw drivers, offered you everything under the sun like a waiter with a menu.

Okay, I'll have a starter of blue movies followed by two pieces of white trash. Then a sex show with three women and a dwarf followed by . . . Hmm, how's the black meat tonight? Rare? Hmm, no, I like mine well done, thanks. Oh, a side order of fellatio and cunnilingus for dessert, thank you. Wine, sir? Oh, yes please, I like them to whine.

Singapore at the time was famous for its 'catamites' or 'kyties' – basically transvestites, men dressed as women mostly having had the *chop* (sex change). The adage at the time was if you found yourself with a really attractive female, it was most probably a man! There were many stories of guys getting drunk and ending up with one of these, only to find a bolt and two nuts after getting amorous, sobering one up very quickly, and running to the nearest washroom to puke and severely wash his hands. The whole atmosphere had a kind of circus feel to it. Every freak and vice was there for the take, or on the take for that matter. In the various visits I made over my naval career, I never actually made it to the end of the street. To this day, I believe there was no end, as there is no end to depravity. I can see how one could sink to the lowest of depravity, sometimes never to return.

CHAPTER 20

Hong Kong
The Dance of the Flaming Assholes

Returning back to the mind-numbing, sweltering heat of the Beira patrol was indeed sobering. Being a bit of a 'keep fit' nut, one of the seamen and I went ashore wherever we could to find interesting places to run cross-country. My partner later won the mile distance championship of the whole navy. We had been dropped off at an isolated bay in front of a huge, rocky, steep hillside. We had challenged the ship that we could make it over the mountain into the bay on the other side before the ship could make it there. When the ship made it into the very hot bay, they found us both languishing in the clear, tropical waters.

'Where was you?' we shouted from the beach.

We did a few forays into different parts of the Middle and Far East in the eleven months away from the UK, venturing as far east as Yokohama, Japan; what was known as Bombay, now Mumbai; Ceylon, now known as Sri Lanka; and Karachi in Pakistan, but mostly places around the Persian Gulf.

We visited Hong Kong more than once, going alongside at the British base of *HMS Tamar*. I had been on a training run with the Marine detachment on board, attempting a relay race up one of the famous steep peaks. I trained with them regularly whenever we were in port. It also usually got me out of working down below for a morning. A couple of the lads had asked me to join them ashore later.

Just outside the docks was the village of Wanchai, where I was introduced to – wait for it – the dance of the flaming assholes. I had decided to meet the lads in a bar in Wanchai to waste a few hours before checking out a nightclub I had heard of. It was kind of a long bar, with a door in at one side, and a door out at the other. Many naval personnel, Marines included, were as usual drinking their way to oblivion.

In the late sixties streaking became quite famous thanks to one lone streaker who made fame by being filmed on British national TV running across the field stark naked during a football match. This started a rush of copycats throughout the UK. Well, the navy lads, not ones to be outdone, as usual decided to go one step further.

The door of the bar burst open. A totally naked sailor, complete with a newspaper tightly curled into a funnel shape, the tight end rammed up his bum, the other end aflame, ran onto the bar at one end. Drinks and food were kicked all over the place. The angry kitchen and bar staff armed with carving knives was chasing him, a little too close for comfort. He barely managed to reach the other end of the bar and get out of the door where he went into a waiting cab, winning who knows what kind of bet. It was probably the funniest prank I had ever seen. There must have been sixty or seventy people in that bar, mostly servicemen. I don't think anyone was able to stand for at least ten minutes, tears of laughter streaming down our faces.

Maria de la Teo

I met Maria in the nightclub that very same night. She was a petite and quite pretty Chinese girl about the same age as me. I had heard that the club had good music and was a suitable place to meet girls. However, servicemen were not allowed. I was in civilian clothes, and even though I had short hair, I still managed to convince the bouncer that I was a civvy. It was probably the fact that I was alone that made the difference. I was feeling a bit out of place, being much taller than the average Chinese person. I did eventually notice a few other Caucasian people once my eyes got used to the low lighting, so I was starting to feel a little more comfortable.

She called me to her table, asking for Roland. It was pretty dark and the music was loud. When she realized I wasn't this Roland guy, she got a bit disinterested. However, as the evening progressed we got to know each other a bit more. She was easy to talk to, as her English was perfect. She obviously had an excellent education. We had a few slow dances together as we both tried to feel for ulterior intentions. She must have been wondering what I was doing in Hong Kong if I was not in one of the armed forces, whose members were usually and quite obviously just looking for quick sex. I would be lying if I were to admit that sex was not on my mind.

I was also thinking about her Roland pick-up line. Could she be 'on the game?' Would she conveniently bring price into the next conversation? It was normal for any guy to be aware of these things after being in the Far East, or any other busy port in the world for that matter. Over the few hours that we talked, I soon realized she was just a sweet girl trying probably a little too hard to convince me of her virtue, which made me feel a little guilty for my previous doubts.

Even at the tender age of seventeen I had tried the pay-for-sex game and had found it quite unsatisfying. I couldn't get over my guilt of using a woman in that way. I needed to feel a woman respond in the same way the whole love act made me feel. I was very surprised, and still had some niggling reservations, when she invited me back to her place. *Oh*, I thought, *I just might get lucky tonight.*

She was obviously Chinese, but she had a long Portuguese name. In the taxi she seemed to develop a nervous, far-fetched chatter. She boasted that her father was the Portuguese ambassador to Hong Kong, that she lived in a luxury apartment, and that her brother had a fantastic yellow sports car. The more she seemed to boast, the more I was starting to have reservations. I decided to go along with things, even though my newly developed self-protection seventh sense was starting to itch big time.

The cab eventually pulled up to a beautiful skyscraper. There in the lower garage, she quickly pointed out a beautiful yellow sports car.

'Wow,' I said, trying to show enthusiasm, but I was really thinking, *Why is she bullshitting me?* My hackles were starting to raise. Something was not right about this situation.

We entered the very classy building and the doorman knowingly nodded to her. We then stepped into a stylish elevator. I was trying hard to show a lackadaisical attitude to all of this, but deep down I was getting very nervous. My willy was quietly saying to me, '*See were this has got you? And I'm going to get you into a whole lot more trouble!*'

We were almost to the top of the building when the elevator door opened directly into the most elaborately furnished room I had ever seen. My heart was now pumping, and I was starting to get the jitters. Way across the other side of this massive room sat a short, portly guy watching his TV. He just happened to be – yes, you guessed it – the Portuguese ambassador to Hong Kong! His wife was a beautiful and serene Chinese lady. He graciously stood, waiting to greet me into his home. I stumbled across the huge room, embarrassingly tripping over the carpet en route, and like a clown I stuttered and stammered my name. With a very relaxing and kind smile, and in perfect English, he later invited me to Sunday dinner.

I arrived later that week in my best bib and tucker, determined not to make such a fool of myself as I felt I had done on our first meeting. I sat at their elaborate table, which had three levels of swiveled layers at the center. There was an amazing assortment of foods that I had never even seen, let alone tasted. There were even three different choices of rice! A maid was handing out little bowls and chopsticks. I had eaten Chinese food since joining the navy, especially since we had been visiting the Far East, but never with chopsticks. I waited until last to fill up my bowl from the amazing items on display swiveling around the table. I tried my best with the damn fangled chopsticks, but I was obviously struggling and feeling a little embarrassed. Most of my choices ended up on the table and not in my bowl. Dad then said something in whatever language, and the maid came scurrying in with a large spoon! With my red face and careful smiles all around the table, I thanked her dad and proceeded to eat every morsel.

After dinner I played some music with his playboy son, who later wanted to give me some marijuana, but that's another story.

The ship visited Hong Kong quite a few times during the year. We even had a mini refit and sprayed for cockroaches, as the ship was infested. I gave blood regularly and received soft drinks in return; the rest of the lads got beer. We anchored off during Red China Day during some violent demonstrations, but apart from that it was such a friendly and adventurous place.

Maria and I got quite close over the months that I knew her, even though sex was off limits since she was very Catholic. Her dad was very approving and seemed to like me. For a year or so after we had left to return to the UK, she wrote me almost every day, a godsend when you had been at sea for weeks, if not months, on end. When the ship got mail there was usually a pile of letters for me that caused a wee bit of jealousy with my shipmates.

She told me that her dad owned a casino in Macao and a hydrofoil boat service back and forth to the island. If I ever decided to quit the navy, I would have a job and would never have to look for money. I was seventeen and not quite ready for marriage, even though my older siblings had married not long after that age.

Life is full of almost unbelievable coincidences.

A couple of years later after the many letters had ceased, partly because of my lack of replying, I was drafted to a base in the UK that shall remain nameless, as the Navy would probably have my nuts for garters. It was the only shore base I ever had in my eight years of service, and it consisted of a relatively small, unassuming office building with lots of security, which was part of my job. There was more navy brass in there than you could shake a hairy stick at. I had control of the main electronic doorway. Captains and the occasional admiral came to this door, and if they weren't carrying their ID they didn't get in. It was part of my job to buzz whoever they were coming to see to allow them entry and escort them directly to that same officer inside the building. Unbelievably, I had access to secret files that I had to pass on from one office to the next. Did I read any? Well, I'll leave that to your imagination.

At lunchtime, I was relieved and usually went across the road to play basketball with the radio operators and writers who worked inside the hill! Occasionally I was invited down below for coffee. The whole hillside was riddled with literally miles of underground passageways. Along these subterranean passageways there were three tiers of hitched-up bunk beds, with hundreds if not thousands of beds.

During one of my lunchtime visits I had got to know a few of the lads and commenced to tell my tale about the lovely Maria. To my astonishment and chagrin, one of the lads piped up, 'Wot a load o' shit, mate. I 'eard that one before.'

Totally shocked and bit embarrassed, I said, 'Oh yeah? And who told you, ya big shit?'

He replied, 'A radio op called Roland.' It seemed he wasn't on duty at that time.

The plot thickens, I thought.

Over the next few weeks I put the word out that I wanted to speak to this Roland guy. Eventually I met him, and sure as hell, as you have probably guessed by now, I was dumbfounded by the incredible coincidence that he was, in fact, the same Roland she had mistaken me for that night in the club. He didn't seem as surprised as I certainly was. He went on to tell me how *his wife* had 'fessed up before they were married about our relationship. They were now living in married quarters not too far from the base.

A few days passed and he sent me a message that he and Maria would like me to come to their house for dinner. 'Okay,' I said, still not completely believing this could possibly be true and that we were talking about the same Maria. This couldn't possibly be the same Maria de la Tao.

Maria explained that after I had failed to reply to her many letters to me, Roland had shown up in Hong Kong. He was now serving on another ship than the one previous. They had gotten back together, and this time decided to marry. He had brought her to the UK to live in naval married quarters. Roland told me that he was buying himself out of the navy and would be out in the next few months. He proceeded to tell me her father had given him a job with his hydrofoil service and he would probably land himself a plumb job, if not eventually running one of his casinos.

Maria was happy to see me, and further explained that she

wanted to be sure that any feelings for me were indeed history. We left on good terms and promised to stay in contact, but I never heard from them again.

Who knows what road I would have travelled had I made other decisions in life!

CHAPTER 21
Returning to the UK
Welcome home

Everyone on board ship seemed to be looking forward to returning to England after eleven months away. The ship's crew excitedly sailed into Portsmouth Harbour to a jetty full of wives and family greeting their long-awaited loved ones.

Feeling a bit miffed and left out, as the ship was now crawling with family, wives, and girlfriends, it seemed no one had made the effort to see me. I had received yet another Dear John letter from Angela months prior to returning and she was living in Hull, Yorkshire, having gone back with her husband.

From a shoreside telephone kiosk I called my brother Ronnie and informed him when I would be coming home on leave. Weeks later I caught the train going north via London and arrived in Preston, which is about twelve miles from Blackburn. I would arrive in the early hours of the morning, so I had decided I would probably hitchhike the remaining distance.

As the train pulled into Preston to a very quiet and deserted platform, I readied myself for a long, cold walk. I had travelled in uniform, knowing from my limited experience that it was the best way to hitch a ride. My white hat was secured to my navy issue 'hold all' bag, facing out so that the drivers of the cars would easily see me. I headed down the long train platform toward the exit. I noticed a commotion in the distance, but couldn't quite make it out. As I came closer to the exit, I could make out people with a banner and wondered to myself, *What could they be fussing about at this time of night?* As I walked closer I could read the banner; it said 'WELCOME HOME OUR KEVIN.'

My whole family was there to greet me. Ronnie picked me up and just spun me around. I was totally and unequivocally overwhelmed. Never before, or after for that matter, have I been welcomed home with such gusto and love.

Leaving the *Zulu*

For the remaining time I spent on the ship when it wasn't in refit, we pretty much stayed in the waters around the UK. We took part in extensive exercises with NATO in convoys off Scapa Flow in the Orkney Islands in northern Scotland. It certainly gave you a feel for what the courageous sailors must have gone through during the Second World War.

On a rare, one-day shore leave, some of the off-watch lads were ferried ashore for an inter-ship football match. We had been at sea for many weeks, and we were ready to stretch our legs. The old MOD (Ministry of Defense) base was strewn with rusting wreckage and dilapidated buildings, an ominous reminder of wartime England.

I snuck away and hiked over the desolate moorland. To be away from the hustle and bustle of ship life, even if for just a few hours, was wonderful. I climbed to the top of a large hill and sat taking in the beautiful view. There were rabbits everywhere, and in the distance I could see a small village. I decided to hike down and check it out. By the time I had arrived at the tiny fishing village, I realized it might be difficult to return in time for the curfew.

I eventually found a telephone kiosk and started looking in the telephone directory for a taxi service. I couldn't believe how many pages of the quite thin directory were named *Firth*. I knew my surname wasn't a common name. I had only met one other person in the navy with the same surname, and here was a book full of them! So I figured us Firths must have originally come from the islands off northern Scotland. I knew the name Firth was a term for an estuary or sea inlet, or arm of the sea. In Scandinavia it would be a fjord. Examples would be the Firth of Forth and Moray Firth. There are many to be seen on any map of Scotland, which probably explains why tears involuntarily run from my eyes whenever I hear a set of bagpipes being played.

Leaving *HMS Zulu* after two and a half years wasn't hard to do. In fact, I remember the day I left, turning around on the jetty and giving her the big finger. As much as I thoroughly enjoyed the places we visited, dealing with some of the officers was hard work. It always seemed to be such a drudge to move forward and up the advancement ladder. I worked so hard to learn my job. I had also taken some correspondence courses in math and science. I literally volunteered for everything. I had grown considerably in the last two and a half years. I had been a rather gullible junior stoker, and I was now an experienced hand who pretty much knew every machine on board confidently.

I had gained a star above my propeller badge to denote first class MEM, and I was way ahead of any of the other MEMs my age. The only thing holding me back from becoming a leading hand was my age. All this, and it seemed my only stumbling block was dealing with some of the snot-nosed officers. They seemed to go out of their way to make me feel like I was just dirt under their fingernails.

My mother country of England has always had a strict class system. Call it my touchy working-class background if you like, but it just seemed to me that it wasn't what you knew or the quality of your work. It came down to who you were related to and what part of the town or the country you were from that got you ahead. I hated that system then as much as I do now. From this early in my life, I was starting to realize how unfair that system was and how I wasn't put here to blindly take orders. Respect, in my mind, always had to be earned. When I saw an officer not much older than myself, he was just a man. He might have had a better education, he might be able to talk without one of the many colourful accents of the British Isles, and may have sadly inherited the grating *la di da* accent of the upper class. He might have never got his hands dirty or even seen poverty, but to me he was just a man, end of story, and he had absolutely no right to insult or degrade me. Without valid reason, he certainly had no right to alter my already limited freedom or reduce what meagre pay I should receive.

I would be the first one to agree that discipline in the armed forces, particularly on the battlefield, was paramount. But there are much smarter ways to deal with grown men to attain that same discipline: one word – respect! This was 1968, not the sad period when sailors were flogged on the main mast. In my mind, the Royal Navy was very slow in catching up with the times.

CHAPTER 22
HMS Sultan
Engineering School

As I was now qualified for steam ships, I decided I would like to make a change and go for diesels, figuring that it might come in handy when I eventually ended up back in civvie street. I was accepted at an ICE (internal combustion engine) course at *HMS Sultan* Engineering Training Base in Portsmouth. The final exam was a breeze, so I went on and sat for the acting leading hand exam, which meant I had to do a full boiler clean. My next draft was the shore base mentioned earlier, where I took time off for a couple of days to perform a very dirty boiler clean on the aircraft carrier *HMS Hermes*.

Weeks later I was standing to attention receiving my hook from an engineering captain. I was now acting local, leading marine engineer first class. The captain congratulated me on being the youngest leading hand in the navy at the time. I was seventeen and would have to be eighteen before the acting local was removed and I received the additional pay.

I volunteered for a ship's diving course, as it interested me, and it also paid six shillings per day more in 'danger pay.'

CHAPTER 23
Diving Course
First week

I travelled down to Plymouth to attend the six-week ship's diver course. I was given a rather silly psychological assessment and then got the green light. The first day of classroom went well, but after the second day when we experienced our first actual diving, I was starting to think that I might have bitten off more than I could chew. What had possessed me to take this course in the middle of winter in the first place was beyond me.

I should probably explain before we go much further that the diving profession in the Royal Navy goes back many years to some possibly reckless men, but heroes all the same. These very brave volunteers will forever have their names engraved in the annals of time. We all know who the first man on the moon was, but very few of us know who the first man to put footprints on the seabed was, 535 feet down. Petty Officer Wilfred Bollard had been using what would be now classed as very primitive and extremely heavy gear. At those extreme depths, experimental mixtures of helium and oxygen gases had to be tested. A few divers never made it back to tell the tale; some did but found themselves in wheelchairs for rest of their lives.

Most of the first experimental deep sea dives from 500 feet

and deeper were completed by the British Royal Navy as early as 1948. On October 12, 1956, Boatswain George Wookey dived to a record depth of 600 feet. Between the US and British navies, complicated diving decompression tables were being devised to allow the working divers to surface and hopefully not develop the bends.

At a water depth of thirty-three feet, the pressure on your body has doubled. At 330 feet it is ten times the pressure, 150 pounds per every square inch of your body! For a diver at that same depth, he has to internally equalize that pressure in order not to be crushed by the tons of pressure acting on his body. So, ten times the pressure of breathing gas has to be supplied through his, suitably named, umbilical hose from the surface.

At roughly 150 feet, most divers get nitrogen narcosis, nicknamed *the narcs*, or as the famous Jacques Cousteau coined it, the rapture of the deep, a very euphoric or scary, sometimes hallucinogenic, drunken feeling. Many divers have succumbed to this feeling, putting their lives in danger; some, sadly, didn't make it back to the surface alive.

At 270 feet, if you were breathing air (21 percent O^2 and 79 percent N^2), not only would you be narked out of your friggin' head, but you would also be breathing the equivalent of over 250 percent oxygen. At this point, your lungs would be literally burning up by the second, and you would be ready for a major convulsion. Basically, air is poisonous at those depths, so it's time to bend over as far as you can go and kiss your ass goodbye. I have experienced a chamber bounce dive to 300 feet on air and can personally vouch for the euphoric high, from what little memory I had of it!

Therefore, we used helium instead of nitrogen, which is also an inert gas. It does not have the adverse effect of nitrogen. And lowering the amount of oxygen in the mix as the depth is increased seemed to do the trick. The diving tables used during these extreme dives to bring these men back from the depths safely had been invented by a few very smart doctors and scientists, and probably a few not-so-smart risk takers.

Having now got the guy down there in one piece breathing a mix that would not kill him or send him totally bonkers, to bring him back to the surface safely, the inert gases running through his bloodstream had to be diffused out. If he came to the surface quickly with all that helium in his lungs, he might float on up into the sky like one of those dirigible balloons. Sorry, I couldn't help myself! He would have to stop his ascent from time to time to allow the soluble helium in his bloodstream enough time to diffuse and gas out through his lungs. Once he was close to the surface, he may then breathe pure oxygen to help purge the inert gasses out of his system.

The navy had a whole branch called clearance divers. They, like the submariners branch, were in a different kind of navy, it seemed to me. Officers were usually a respected and well-earned part of the team. Clearance divers were trained to take apart bombs or use explosives to safely dispose of them. If you have ever met a bomb disposal person, they tend to be a little different, and usually get a lot of slack when it comes to soldier discipline. However, you won't find anyone who is disciplined to the ninth degree when it comes to safety and getting the job done.

I had found my job! This was me through and through. I now wanted so bad to change branches. We weren't using hard hat diving, the big brass headgear usually known as the MK-5 that you see in the old movies. This was the modern navy, and it had just been mothballed – thank God! We used the Swimmers Air Breathing Apparatus (SABA), which consisted of a full face mask that was supplied adequate air pressure via corrugated hoses from the second and first stage regulators attached to a twin set of air bottles, known as the set. The set was fitted with an equalization lever to allow air from one bottle to cascade into the second; on the second equalization, it was time to surface. It's pretty much what you would see today's divers using, only with a twin set of bottles.

We were also introduced to Surface Demand Diving Equipment (SDDE), which I would become very familiar with many years later. This was basically a hose to the surface, the umbilical that supplied you with air. There was also a small bottle that was the emergency bailout bottle, in case the umbilical air was interrupted. The suit (rubber bag) was a dry suit, in that you wore an under suit of woolen underclothes (woolly bear), and then squeezed your whole body through the neck of the dry suit. There were tight rubber seals on your wrists that you squeezed your hands through. Once you were in, you put a neck ring over your head, then a neck ring seal under the neck part of the suit. Then a clamp was firmly fastened to supposedly stop any water ingress. Yeah right! If you were to go deep underwater this way, the suit would eventually crush you. So, a small suit inflation air bottle was attached so you could equalize the pressure at depth. To remove that air pressure in the suit during your ascent back to the surface, you held your arms above your head and pulled out the rubber cuffs around your wrists, usually allowing water into the suit!

Okay, so thirteen of us had done the first day of classwork, and we were now dressed in and had removed the slippery ice from the dock. We had been taught to memorize a signaling system of pulls and bells. A rope attached to a strap, called a Sam Browne, on our suit was very important. The other end was firmly held by the tender on the dock; it was our lifeline. Pulling the rope or ringing it like a bell, for example, we could tell the tender, 'Pull me up slowly,' or in fact send somebody down because

'I am stuck and unable to surface.'

We were not allowed fins, only big, heavy lead boots. Fins and neoprene hoods were only for the successful trainees who made it to the second week! Gloves were also nonexistent throughout the course.

We were put into pairs, one person on deck with the lifeline tending while the other was the diver. Our first task was clearing one's own mask of freezing-cold seawater. A simple enough sounding task, I thought. In the very first hour, eight of the class were dismissed, having been failed by the very nasty clearance diver leading hands (second dickies), who seemed to relish failing the recruits.

It was my turn. I was feeling very awkward clunking across the slippery dock in a baggy rubber suit, weight belt, and lead boots, complete with a really heavy set on my back and levers and ropes hanging off every appendage. *Surely, if I let go of the ladder I'm going to sink like the proverbial stone!* I thought. What happened to the daydream of me, the super-duper aquanaut in a slinky wetsuit, wowing the girls?

I had already made a couple of misdemeanors that had angered the chief. 'Do not ever call them bottles or tanks,' the chief shouted. 'Tanks is wots on Salisbury Plain, lad' (referring to the army tank training ground). 'This is your *set*, an' while wur at it, those ain't flippers either. That's wot dolphins 'ave. Those is *fins!*'

Down the steel ladders I went as the suit shrunk to my body. My hands immediately started to go numb when they hit the freezing seawater. Then I felt a stream of water going down the back of my not-very-good neck seal. I also felt my left leg slowly filling up with the freezing water as I miserably discovered that I must have a hole there.

I had my safety line clenched tightly in my fist, I thought, as my hand was now totally numb. The second dickie was screaming at me. 'Get down there, ya chicken piece of shit, and fill up yer mask.'

Oh my God, the cold water hit my forehead, and for a second or two I was almost blinded with pain. I just bit down hard on the mouthpiece (tit) and tried to grin and bear it. *Okay, fill up the mask.* What little part of my body not freezing wet was now there with the rest of my body. *Okay, remember what I was told. Hand on top of the mask, lean back, then blow out and pull up on the bottom part of the mask.* One move and I had removed about two-thirds of the water. I received four pulls on the rope. *Oh yeah, the signal for come up.* I started to come up, but then received a very sharp tug that almost pulled me off the ladder. *Ah shit! I have to give one pull to agree to come up.*

I broke surface to the screaming second dickey. 'Get back down there and do it again. Remove all the water or yer walkin'. Oh, and make one more mistake with the signals and you're also walkin', got it?' A few more insults on my parentage, then I felt his boot on my head pushing me down into the cold gloom.

Needless to say, the second time around I made doubly sure there was no water in my mask before breaking surface. These guys were just fuckin' *mean*!

Five of us made it through the first day and were feeling pretty proud of ourselves. Little did we know what was ahead.

On day two we were given a large hammer, a mason chisel, and a small length of chain, and were introduced to the shot weight. This was a large circular concrete block attached to a thick rope that normally sat on bottom and acted as an anchor. The ladders attached to the dock stopped at about ten feet. So to reach the bottom at about thirty feet, you had to shimmy down the shot rope. By climbing this rope, it gave you a controlled decent and ascent.

At most times, this being a busy dockyard, it was a dirty

muddy gloom. At thirty feet it was difficult to see your hand in front of you, so you really didn't want to lose the shot weight rope. With lead boots on, you were basically at their mercy. Once on bottom you gave a series of lifeline bells and pulls to raise the shot out of the mud to be used as a workbench.

The task was to cut through a link of this heavy chain during your dive. That's not so easy when you can't see the chain in the first place, and you probably don't know if you hit your hand with the hammer, as after a few minutes they are numb from the cold. On top of all this, we were told to use control breathing to conserve the air. If you managed to stay down for an hour you got valuable points with the nasty men up top. Not a good idea, as the CO^2 builds up in your bloodstream and you end up with a nasty headache. Double points if you actually managed to cut through a link. God help you if you lost anything, which was very easy to do. Coming up minus one item cost you an exhausting mud run.

The mud run started by swimming across this sea inlet to where the tide had left deep, slushy mud with all the effluent one can imagine. You waded in the mud, trying in vain to run in the quagmire, and were sometimes up to your waist in it! The evil second dickies sometimes threw thunder-flash fireworks at you if you were not moving fast enough for their depraved pleasure. As with the previous in-training parade ground runs, I was soon quite familiar with mud runs during the course.

I kept reminding myself of the lessons I had learned earlier in my naval career. (Things I learned – #3: There are ones, usually in positions of control, that are there solely to crack you; this is what they live for. Once you understand this, it becomes a game. The task takes second place. You can push yourself a lot further if you know that it just comes down to a duel of spirits.)

The two second dickies on the jetty just seemed to have it in for me one way or the other. They wouldn't stop until I cracked. There were times I thought I might just as well quit, as they would get their own way sooner or later. But it just came down to a duel of wits and sheer will, and once I knew it was them or me, a kind of weird game, it gave me amazing strength to overcome.

First week . . . again!

We usually each completed two dives a day. By the end of the first week I was the only one remaining from the initial thirteen. I was feeling pretty good about myself, and the chief didn't seem as nasty. I was starting to think that I might actually get through this.

At the beginning of week two he ludicrously informed me that it was not possible to keep me on a course all on my own, so if I wanted to carry on, I would have to join this week's new course – and do the whole first week again!

This week's new class started with twenty-three. At the end of my now seven-week course, four of us passed. In my seventh week I caught a cold. The chief said if I couldn't dive (in other words, clear my ears), I was off the course. In my determination at that point, I was surprised I didn't do permanent damage. I pumped my ears, meaning I repeatedly went down to a point just before the pain was too excruciating to bear, then immediately went up a few feet. Eventually I felt a large pop. I was hoping I hadn't punctured my eardrum. I surfaced at the end of the dive with blood streaming from my nose and all sorts of colourful items swishing around in my mask.

Stepping off the *Belfast*

Part of the course included stepping off the forecastle of the massive *HMS Belfast* completely suited up. The only item we didn't have when jumping off into the void was the heavy breathing set or weight belt. However, we did have the bailout bottle, which was held in a Sam Browne belt attached across your waist. I am guessing we were about seventy or so feet up. Once we had straddled over the guard rail with wobbly nervous knees, the chief said in a stern voice, 'Do not look down. Look straight ahead across the harbour, take one step forward, march!'

After what seemed like a lifetime or two, you eventually hit the water. Very importantly: point your fins down. Above all, keep your legs crossed, put your left hand on the suit inflation bottle, and your right hand on the top of your snorkel mask. If any of those orders was not performed exactly, you either got seriously hurt or had to go do it again. If you looked down, you would inevitably hit the water face first, which is very painful. If you accidentally let go of the suit inflation bottle on hitting the water, it would swing up and wind you in the stomach – not good when the next breath you take is probably ten feet underwater. If you don't cross your legs, well, you end up with another pair of Adam's apples in your throat, and of course your fins end up around your thighs. If you were unfortunate enough to return to the surface with a fin, a mask, or a snorkel not correctly attached to your limb, you had to go do it again!

I think we lost three potential divers that day, not to mention the ones that got hurt. On my third attempt I lost both fins, but I made damn sure that before I reached the surface they were correctly attached.

Awkward

Getting in and out of the dry bag was a procedure really only possible with help. We practiced so many times during the course to get in and out of it as quickly as possible. At any time of day or night, if the word awkward was used, it meant you had four minutes to get completely dressed in it and get into the water.

At the bleak hour of 4 a.m., we were awoken with a loud thunder flash and a chief screaming, 'Awkward!' A thunder flash, we had learned, was a very loud firework usually used to signal divers below to return to the surface. In my mad rush to get dressed in, I had inadvertently forgotten to attach the screw cap onto the suit inflation line into my dry bag.

We were all floundering in the freezing cold water in the dead of night. I had very quickly realized my blooper and was surreptitiously holding my finger over the opening, trying in vain to halt the ingress of the icy cold water filling up my suit. A grinning nasty second dickey, as they were fondly called, noticed my calamity. Much to his torturous glee, he then made me stay there for over an hour, followed by a slick mud run as the night turned to a grey, misty, cold morning.

I received my well-earned gold diver's badge, which I proudly displayed on the cuff of my number one suit. As long as I put in a minimum of two hours per month underwater, I would keep my diver privilege of six shillings a day, which is now fifty pence, or the equivalent of roughly one US dollar. Bear in mind this was in the 1960s, not the thirties! I had learned that during any dive, the task itself was number one. You and your comfort came a very distant second. Safety was always of utmost necessity; only a fool takes chances. Always have a second, stand-by emergency way out and know it confidently; your life depends on it. There is a tried and tested adage that says 'Go beyond that or think you know better, and you'll end up with the rest of the fools – dead!'

There are bold divers and there are old divers, but there are no old bold divers!

CHAPTER 24
Marilyn

I met my wife to be on a leave from the navy in my hometown of Haslingden. My first blundering meeting was at a pub called the Bay Horse. She was with her sister, and just shone above all the other women there, a tall, gorgeous, blonde lady with a very pretty smile. My heart just flipped, and although she smiled at me a couple of times, it just seemed she was way above my station. *Give it up, Kevin, and don't even go there.*

Christmas was coming on shortly and I had been invited to a party on New Year's Eve. I had chased down Susan, Biscuit's sister, who was working at the Woolworths store in Rawtenstall. I asked her out, only to find I had been beaten to the post by Birdie, who was also serving in the navy. *Goddamn that Birdie!*

Again, life's wibbly-wobbly way stepped in. Just prior to the party I was walking down Grane Road to visit my old mate Biscuit and his mum. There, walking up the hill in the distance, was the mysterious, gorgeous blonde lady wheeling a pram! *Oh my God, what to do?* I had ample time to come up with something smart to say, and was practicing under my breath, but at the same time all kinds of things were going through my head. *What's with the pram? Is she already married? Will she just laugh at me?* Through all of this posturing, I had stupidly missed my chance. She had passed me by, but she still managed to give me her very cute smile as she passed.

I was so angry that I was going to go around the next corner and just beat the living shit out of me! Then, all at once, something inside allowed me to stop and turn around. She had done the same. We looked at each other, and even in the dark I could make out her beautiful face. I knew it was now or never. My mouth wanted to open, but absolutely nothing was in my head worthy of saying.

I cannot remember to this day who spoke first. I think I might have said something stupid like, 'Wasn't it you I saw in the pub last week?' *Duh! Of course it was, ya big dipshit!* I thought.

We had a very quick conversation, and somewhere in the midst of my mindless verbiage, I had somehow managed to invite her to the New Year's Eve party. To my total amazement, she actually accepted. Okay, Kevin, say no more unless you blow this, I hesitantly thought. I had never even asked if she was married or where the baby came from. I think I floated the rest of the walk down to Biscuit's house – this was love!

Although she was a year and a bit older than me, she had married early, as was the case for many young people in the valley, but it had not lasted long and she was now already divorced. Dominic, her child, was eleven months old. Although it was strange at first to be wheeling around a pram at nineteen, I knew that Marilyn came as a package. If I wanted to win her over, I had to buckle down and try to be a dad. Angela, my first love, also had a little boy, so it wasn't something I wasn't used to. However, I was still reeling from that affair, so I had a few hang ups to start with.

Marilyn lived on a street, unremarkably called Coronation Street, at the bottom of Grane Road that she rented with whatever social assistance and help from her parents she could muster. She'd had the courage to leave her cruel husband, and was bravely trying to make a life for herself and her son. Financially, she made do with what she received from the state and help from her elderly parents. She was a proud lady, as was her mother, and basically kept things to herself. She could handle pretty much every catastrophe that ever dared to come her way. Under her demure looks was a feisty don't-mess-with-me kind of woman. Lord help the person that ever tried to come between her and hers. Behind that pretty face and petite frame was a strong no-nonsense woman – enter at your own risk!

I tried to come home every weekend I was allowed during the one year I was at the base. I caught trains when I could afford it and hitchhiked when I couldn't. I sometimes shared the petrol costs with senior petty officers travelling north. Whatever way I could, I somehow made it home.

I was madly in love. Being with her and Dominic just felt right – it felt like home. I sometimes arrived home in the early hours of Saturday morning absolutely shattered, only then to have to try and put baby Dominic to sleep, who just happened to be hyperactive. After a week or so of Dominic's antics, Marilyn was always in worse shape than I was, despite all the travelling I had had to do. We were getting used to the dirty looks in public when we prodded poor Dominic to keep him awake, lest he have his two minutes of sleep, which was his need for the next twenty-four hours.

When I think of how she struggled in that house, I only had to look across the street to the Sharkeys' house to wonder how they made it through their days. Mr. and Mrs. Sharkey were from Ireland, as were a lot of people in Haslingden. They had twenty kids, but still welcomed home any person that they had met in the pub for a wee meal and a drink. They had big hearts and were loved by everyone. I got to know a couple of their sons my age pretty well. I was told that Mr. Sharkey was a tinker, in that he dealt with horses. His horses regularly trespassed on the land across the river. Many times he tried to sell me sovereign rings and the like that he told me had been handed down from his 'Dear muther, now sadly departed from dis fair land.' Once a week the bread van would arrive at their door, and a line of children formed from the back of the van into her house and deposited many loaves of bread to her tiny kitchen beyond.

Marilyn and Dominic managed to move to a much better council home closer to her mother up shoot. The shoot council estate was known as the Catholic end of town. They were still two-up and two-down houses, as they were called, but they were comfortable and clean.

I spent all of my leave with Marilyn, and saw very little of my own family. Our relationship, though rocky at times, still flourished. Little Dominic started to grow on me. Being a dad wasn't too bad. I was starting to get used to the idea. Then, just as life with her was getting comfortable and interesting, I received the dreaded draft chit:

> Make your way to RAF Brize Norton to fly to Singapore. You are to join the ship *HMS Brereton* then to sail to Bahrain to join the Ninth Squadron.

Oh my God, I thought, *I need this like a hole in the head, and Bahrain of all places! Been there, done it!*

We both said our fond farewells and promised we would wait this out and one day we would be together again. With absolutely no idea how long I would be out in that hell hole, I reluctantly departed once more.

CHAPTER 25

HMS Brereton
Terror barracks

I flew out to Singapore via a tiny airstrip in the middle of the Indian Ocean. It was a long flight strangely facing backwards on the RAF plane. I had met a couple of sailors during the flight that would be staying at 'Terror Barracks' like me, waiting for their ship to arrive. After the seventeen-hour flight pretty much everyone was tired. A small rickety local bus picked us up at the airport to transport us to the British military base beside the village of Sembawang. The ride through some of the small towns was a bit hair raising. The crazy driver seemed to spend most of the time hanging out of his window cussing the many yellow cabs and street vendors. At one point, he lost his rear view mirror to another truck very close by. We were all very relieved when we arrived at our destination.

Terror Barracks had an army detachment. The living quarters mostly surrounded the large parade ground. The barracks was just a small part of the sprawling naval dock area. It was late at night when I was billeted into my temporary sleeping accommodations by a rather tired quartermaster. Then I was sent in the general direction toward one of the large, square, block buildings.

The air was thick with humidity. I was soaked to the skin by now, and the strange jungle noises coming from the surrounding trees made me realize I was a long way from home. I eventually found the room, which was basically four walls with large square openings for windows. Inside there were a dozen or so beds with mosquito nets draped over them. A single ceiling fan struggled in a miserable attempt to move some air. I found my bed quietly, as everyone else was sleeping by now. I was tired and didn't want to look where the nearest toilet facilities were. I just stripped off and laid in the bunk. As much as I was dead tired, I got little sleep. The different noises, the humidity, and the strangeness of it all kept me awake. The only time I had ever slept like this was outside camping.

The following morning at breakfast I met a talkative Marine who was waiting for the commando carrier *HMS Bulwark*. He was such a character. He would drag me and any other reprobates he could muster and we would go and paint the town red. Singapore was a long taxi ride, but the shared cost between the four of us was affordable. We found hidey-hole bars and nightclubs in the most out of the way places. Sometimes we would just hang out in the bars in the village of Sembawang just outside the dockyard gates. Bob the Marine always seemed to be up to no good, and would usually get us into situations where we would rather not be.

There was a whole row of bars across the street from the dockyard entrance. Out front of these bars were many food vendors. The food always tasted so good, especially after a good run ashore. No one actually knew what kind of meat was being cleverly mixed into the large woks, but just watching these juggling magicians was a stage show that hypnotized. Surrounded with charcoal smoke and steam, the heavenly aroma found its way directly to your taste buds. At the end of the show he masterfully tipped the mysterious contents from the wok into a long, fat roll of bread, and then snapped two elastic bands around the whole thing and . . . voilà, one very tasty egg banjo. It would generally last you the long walk through the docks to your ship. And sometimes, if you were lucky, you might even find some leftovers on your pillow in the morning for breakfast. Yummy!

There were also small shops were you could buy almost anything. In the window of one such shop they displayed sex toys and enhancements, including little phials of pills with 'Stay Hard' or even 'Stay Awake' colourfully advertised on them. It was hard to bypass this busy area, leaving or returning. The clever entrepreneurs had no limits in finding ways of keeping you amused and spending!

At the far end of the street beside the bars were the very basic toilet facilities, which consisted of a row of small cubicles with no doors. Inside each cubicle was a black hole in the ground where underneath a stream flowed into a nearby storm drain. For a laugh one night, Bob managed to get his hands on a thunder flash. He waited until pretty much all of the cubicles were busy with not only sailors, but the buy-me-a-drink bar girls as well. He then dropped the thunder flash into the stream flowing into the latrines, which when exploded blew everything back up through the various holes, soaking the startled users with unmentionable artifacts. Everyone by now knew it was Bob, and as we were his run ashore buddies, we were also liable for a beating. We made a very hasty retreat to the safety of the guarded dockyard gates, then ran like buggery back to the barracks.

Our ships eventually arrived, one by one, over the next few weeks, and we each had to move on board. Because of the heat and humidity, most of the military was on what they called tropical routine, which meant work started at 0600 and finished at 1300. After that time, if you were not on duty watch you were allowed shore leave. It seemed that at 1301 every day Bob would be on board persuading me and whoever else to go ashore. We often stayed until the early hours of the following morning, sometimes only managing an hour or so of sleep before starting work.

Work for me was usually sitting in a dirty bilge with a chipping hammer, chipping away paint prior to painting – if I hadn't found a suitable hidey-hole to catch a few precious slumber moments, that is. I actually learned from an old hand how to almost nod off while aimlessly chipping away. Just making the chipping noise was enough to keep the PO on duty know you were actually working down below. If you had a real good buddy, he would use two chipping hammers at the same time while you slept, doing mini shifts between the two of you.

I don't know where Bob is today, but I hope he is not rotting away in some military prison, which I fully expected he would end up in.

We left Singapore shortly thereafter and headed to the dreaded Persian Gulf.

CHAPTER 26
Bahrain Again!

HMS *Brereton* was a Ton class minesweeper/hunter with a displacement of 440 tons and an overall length of 152 feet. Propulsion for the ship via the two shafts was from two very unusual and complicated Napier Deltic diesel engines that were basically designed more toward locomotives. With a full complement of thirty-eight men, this wasn't a big ship. It had a wooden hull for obvious reasons – magnetic mines and all! She was the flagship of the Ninth Minesweeper Squadron in the Persian Gulf. The ship had a team of clearance divers on board, of which I had earlier asked to change branches to. I had been informed previously that I had been refused because marine engineers in the navy at this time were harder to come by. *Nice one, Kevin. You asked for this, ya dumb shit!*

I was the leading MEM in a small mess of six stokers. Across the narrow corridor, Burma Way, was the chief and petty officers' mess next to the tiny galley. Below us down a hatchway was the main mess, where the rest of the crew, seamen, CDs, and radio ops lived.

The skipper was a full three-ringer, an elderly commander who was almost ready for retirement. Usually, the skipper of a sweeper was only a lieutenant. We were the flagship over two other sweepers stationed in this awful place, so we got the three-ringer! My immediate thoughts were *Oh yeah, here we go again, all spit and polish, yes sir, no sir, three bags full, sir.*

To my astonishment, this guy was okay and had a sense of humour, which was desperately needed here. Apparently, as I learned later, after seven months or so, the whole squadron was to depart the Persian Gulf forever, meet up with the Sixth Squadron that would be leaving Hong Kong, and then together return to the UK. It would be quite an event, as the Navy had been there for many years policing the Gulf. I now realized this was the real reason for the three-ringer.

Our main job here was to try and stop the gunrunners coming up the Indian Ocean into the Suez Canal, blow up the occasional underwater mine, and generally try and sort out the many little hot spots of unrest that seemed to be everywhere in the Persian Gulf.

We were actually classed as a mine hunter. Our wooden hull had to be magnetically degaussed from time to time. The ship would find the mine by sonar, but stay a safe distance away. The CDs would be in a small, inflatable Gemini boat, taking visual signals from the boat via a tiger tail on the main mast. Once they were above the mine, the CD would dive and carefully attach an explosive charge to it. The Gemini and divers would then be hoisted back on board and the mine detonated.

I was told our maximum time at sea, with strict water rationing, was ten days straight. *Okay, I'm liking it a wee bit better!* Our maximum speed was fifteen knots with a tail wind, so we weren't catching too many gunrunners. We always knew the telltale signs of the real gunrunners: a puff of smoke would appear above the clumsy looking, ratty dhow as their gas turbine was started, and over the horizon he would disappear, never to be seen again.

Chief Petty Officer, Clearance Diver, Allan Broadhurst

As usual, being tall and fit, I had been volunteered by the coxswain for boarding patrol. Clearance Diver, Chief Petty Officer Allan Broadhurst was the coxswain and ad hoc medic, among many other titles on board. All though friendship among lower ranks is frowned upon in the forces, the chief and I hit it off from the start. I had still not completely given up on changing branches, and the chief had my number! He constantly volunteered me for all sorts of things during my stay aboard. He knew I would never refuse.

'Okay men, I'm looking for volunteers to play rugby against a South African team of rather large, gnarly players. Firth, you've just volunteered. Thank you, dismissed.'

Boarding patrol

Stationed in the shore base was a team of Special Boat Section (SBS) Marines, a branch of the SAS, of which I'm sure everyone is familiar. SBS Marines were similar to the American Navy Seals, in that they were all fuckin' mental! They trained us in unarmed combat and what to look for if we had the misfortune of boarding a gunrunner. My pacifistic nature was being severely challenged and I was starting to wonder what the hell I was doing there.

One afternoon out on patrol, the ship's klaxon went off and I was awoken from a deep slumber. I had just completed an afternoon, last dog, and middle watch in a very hot engine room. 'Boarding party alert. Muster at the aft davit boat launch.'

We had practiced this many times, to the point that it was routine. I quickly got dressed and ran down to the muster area beside the davit that launched the Gemini. I checked out my sub machine gun, safety on, and attached a magazine with one spare taped to the side. I was the last on the Gemini, but first off!

My job when we reached the boat was to scramble on board the gunrunner's boat and tie up the painter (bow rope). The next man off assisted me in corralling everyone to the forward part of the upper deck. We both then had the safety off on our machine guns and one up the spout. One minor mistake, a trip or bump, and several rounds were going into the men crowded together ahead of us. The interpreter was next off, then the other four men, who searched the boat's compartments for other personnel or weapons. When they had completed their search, one of the men took my position. I then went down below into the engine room to do a search and take the serial number or whatever information I could get from the main engine. I was very careful and watched for trip wires, booby traps, and weapons.

It all seemed to be going relatively well. However, I did find a piece of a revolver hanging from a string into the bilges. I heard a bit of a ruckus on deck and immediately got an awful sickness in my stomach, like a premonition of impending doom. I returned to the upper deck to find one of our crew had found a woman dressed as usual in black from head to toe with the standard Islamic burqa covering her face. She was being very obstinate as she was pushed forward, and we couldn't see her hands. When the interpreter asked her to show her hands and remove her burqa, she was not having anything to do with it. Everyone was getting very nervous, and things were really not looking good. There was a lot of very heated discussion going on between the Arab men, who were corralled together, and the interpreter. The leading seaman guarding them was nervously clutching the trigger. We all knew at that point that in the next few seconds people were going to die.

Suddenly, the magic words were repeated over and again, 'Exercise, stand down,' to my astonishment and relief. The ridiculously stupid SBS had just risked their lives to prove a point.

The lady was not a lady, of course. He removed the black robe and we saw a thin strand of string attached to his/her waist going into the water. At the other end of the string was, of course, a weapon. He then proceeded to take the 'loaded' machine gun off the leading seaman and attempted to hit him in the head with the butt. He was furious, and was now showing us all the times that we had unwittingly let our guard down.

'Chief, I really don't want to do boarding party anymore.'

'Stuff it, Firth. Remember, you volunteered for this!' Oh yeah, sure I did – my ass!

Months later we had been following a very suspect vessel for a few days. Every time we got close he just motored off, being a bit faster than us. Most vessels there were embarrassingly faster than us. You could probably row a boat faster. We had been chasing him around a series of remote islands, and somehow we had managed to catch him anchored in a small cove. It was, as usual, late at night. I had been seriously hoping he'd got way!

The ominous feeling of imminent danger was again playing havoc with my bowels. The skipper had basically cornered him and he had no place to go. The ship's searchlights had the medium-sized dhow lit from stem to stern. Our forecastle Bofor 40mm gun was pointed directly at him, and the port-side Oerlikon machine gun was also manned. The interpreter was shouting orders in Arabic through a loud hailer from the bridge.

I just knew this one was for real. My stomach was just a-churnin'. Although I had just been woken from a deep sleep, again I was wide awake. Not wanting to show my trembling hands, I just got on with it and concentrated on not screwing up.

We boarded the large wooden boat and corralled about ten very scared men up to the forward upper deck. They all looked completely terrified. I knew I had a job to do, but I couldn't help thinking about their welfare. I was more scared that my finger might slip and I would mow down what might be innocent men. To them, we must have looked a formidable force. In minutes we had efficiently boarded and had the complete crew sitting or kneeling, huddled together on the forecastle, and half of the boat had already been thoroughly inspected.

The interpreter was vigilantly questioning the captain of the vessel, when unexpectedly we were all told to stand down. Another false alarm, much to our relief! We had inadvertently boarded a gold runner coming up from India. The interpreter asked to see the gold as proof. We were then showed into the captain's meager quarters, which apart from the small bed didn't really account for much. We were told the gold was under his bed.

Lo and behold, there it was, a basic brown paper-wrapped parcel about two to three inches thick by about ten inches square. It took two of us to drag it from under his bed. I could not believe how heavy it was. We undid the string, unwrapped the parcel, and there before our eyes was a solid, shiny block of gold. Seeing that the captain was still obviously very nervous – he had originally thought we were pirates – we left him be. The interpreter told us he was out of our jurisdiction. He was, however, reported to the Trucial Oman Scouts, who were the area military police.

Purple and orange

Life at sea was, for the most part, very mundane – eat, sleep, watch keep, fix engines, eat, sleep, etc. It seemed to me that my life was slipping by. I had brought some of my music LPs on board, and we had somehow purloined a record player. I had probably swapped it for beer from another sweeper crew. Being the flagship had its perks; the skipper turned a blind eye to us having more beer than we should have by regulations. The Royal Navy free daily tot of rum had only months prior ceased after hundreds of years of tradition. It had been replaced by an allowance of three cans of beer per day, and on most ships they would even force you to open all three cans at the same time so that you didn't hoard them. I was still pretty much teetotal, in that I didn't drink alcohol, but I still drew my beer since it was used as commerce below decks. The lads would hoard cases of beer that were hidden in every nook and cranny of the ship. The lads from the other sweepers were still under the strict regulations, so when we were in port they came on board and purchased cases of beer from us.

We decided one day that our living quarters needed cheering up! One of my albums, an LP by the band Deep Purple, which was also a favourite of the rest of the lads, had the colours orange and purple on the cover. Later that week, when the engineer officer came to do his weekly rounds, he was greeted with Deep Purple playing on the record player and a complete mess deck painted purple and orange! Brigham Young, one of the lads we had nicknamed 'The Dog' because of his knack of always getting into fights ashore, had painstakingly painted every rivet in the bulkheads alternately orange and purple! We had even purchased some purple and orange curtains from beer plunder money. The official white and naval grey was nowhere to be seen.

This was the late sixties; I think I was turning into a wannabe hippie! There was a revolution in music and a whole new way of thinking going on that I liked. The music I was listening to just enveloped me and took me somewhere else. Popular music that we heard on the radio all the time left me empty. But the music you sometimes had to search for – James Taylor, all the early blues players, Howling Wolf, Mississippi John Hurt, Crosby, Stills, and Nash, to mention only a few – really took me by storm. I couldn't get enough! There were times, though, I thought I was the only one that had been taken by this music. Laying strapped into my bunk with my bulky headphones over my ears, miles out to sea being tossed around like a cork, I found that I could mentally transport myself to a different place, away from all this emptiness.

America was still at war in Vietnam, and the Cold War with Russia seemingly hovered over everyone's head. The threat of nuclear war was the highest it had ever been. There wasn't a month that went by when another nuclear bomb had been tested to seemingly aggravate the other side into testing an even bigger one. Nixon the crook was in power in the US and it was a scary time. Men were returning from the senseless violence of war in Vietnam to be heckled in the streets by the peaceniks! It was like the whole world had gone crazy overnight. It wouldn't be proved until much later that many young men had been sent to be slaughtered in Vietnam because of one man's lies and greed for political power.

The world had experienced two massive wars this century, with violence and atrocities that a few people still alive today will regretfully take to their graves – sickening atrocities, with millions of ethnic people exterminated to appease a madman's wishes. Hadn't we had just about enough of this crap? And here I found myself serving in Her Majesty's armed forces, admittedly in only a very small way, but still adding or agreeing to make war. Any one of our 'trustworthy' politicians could decide tomorrow, probably more for political/financial reasons, that it would make sense for us fight on their behalf. I didn't profess to know all the political ramifications going on in the world at any given time, but I did know in my heart that war was wrong. I had heard the banter from men who should know better that when economies are struggling and people are jobless, it's time to have a war. Nothing improves a country's economy and well-being, especially if they are on the winning side, than a war! Anyone serving in the military, especially in the officer ranks, soared ahead in advancement during a war. This was the war machine in action, a self-serving monopoly, replicating many times over and seemingly out of control.

In my humble opinion at the time, I thought the whole world was at the very threshold of World War III. I also firmly believed that the new generation coming of age wanted change. Some of us believed there was another way. The peace movement might have started with a bunch of flower people prancing around in San Francisco, but it developed into a serious ban-the-bomb movement. Youth went to the streets in droves all around the world in protest.

If there is anything that can channel a message deeper into the average human being it has to be music. We were all profoundly afraid of what may be the end of mankind as we knew it. Now, unlike other eras of human destruction, we had made it possible to totally destroy the earth during war. I think we were all listening very acutely to any answers that might be out there, and we were very distrustful of the powers that be betraying us with the usual lies. I might not be able to remember every word to all the anti-war songs, but subliminally I think we all got the message. My guitar playing took on a whole new form. I wanted so much to be a part of the revolution I had seen, read about, and, seemingly from a distance, experienced.

I was also an avid reader of science fiction. Arthur C. Clarke was my all-time favourite, in that the fiction had to make sense and seem almost probable. America had just landed on the moon, and I had a picture of Neil Armstrong above my bunk. In another life I could see myself as an astronaut, as I'm sure millions of men my age did also. I would be the heroic adventurer furthering mankind's mission in space. I would have all the elaborate controls at my fingertips, flying my vessel into the unknown and returning to Earth to a hero's welcome. Okay, so I'm a dreamer.

People were landing on the moon, and I felt I was wasting my life doing something that I was beginning to see I was just not cut out to do.

I had made friends with some other like-minded guys who served in the base camp. I don't remember too many fond moments of Bahrain, excepting of course the desert. There really wasn't much for the lads in the base to do. There was a small bar and a swimming pool, but that was basically it. I had also started experimenting with mild drugs on my time off ashore. We would drive out to the desert, meet up with some of the Arab guys our age, and smoke a few joints.

Occasionally we went to the local open-air movies in town. It was there under the stars that I saw Stanley Kubrick's movie of Arthur C. Clarke's *2001: A Space Odyssey.* To this day it still remains one of my all-time favourite sci-fi movies. I had previously read the book, but wasn't prepared for such a magnificent rendition. A few weeks later we saw *Woodstock.* I was also probably experiencing my very first marijuana highs at both movies, which is probably another reason why they were so memorable.

My first big concert

A couple of people around the base had heard me play guitar, so I was asked to perform at their annual base 'Sod's Opera.' I had been practicing hard, as I would be performing for over 300 people, which were a mix of navy and army personnel and families stationed there in the base married quarters. Peeping out from the stage curtains, I was getting pretty nervous. There were so many people out there. The guy working the curtains was my friend, the infamous captain's driver. He was a short, burly guy with an infectious laugh. I was due to go on during a change of stage scenery that would happen quietly behind the curtains to my rear. Earlier, the captain's driver had given me a small chunk of hashish. We obviously couldn't smoke it, since we were in the base camp and would get caught for sure. He popped a small amount into his mouth and chewed it so I followed suit, thinking nothing of it. He told me it wouldn't do any harm and I might later feel a little high.

My time came and I played one of the favourites amongst the lads that I had written, 'ROMFT,' which was an acronym for 'Roll On My Fuckin' Time.' It was a blues tune with a beat to someone marching.

ROMFT (Marching Blues)

Left, left, left, right, left
Halt
Turn around, left, right, left
Marching along with the rest of the guys
Boots a shinin' and my gaitors so white
I've done some pretty stupid things in this life of mine
But none add up to how I got here

ROMFT
(Harmonica break)

Can you honestly agree that at fifteen years of age
A boy knows his mind enough to sign away his life?
And do you really understand that in this country dear to us
They think nothing of ruining a young boy's life?
Press gangs going around, maybe not the same
    but just as cruel
Trapping young boys in their web of misery
Would you like it to happen to one of yours?

ROMFT
(Harmonica)

Joined this here navy to see the world
All I saw night and day marching along

ROMFT

Roll...On...My...Fuckin'...Time
(Play 'Rule Britannia' on the harmonica and fade)
　　　　　　　　　　　　—Kevin Firth, circa 1970

    A lot of the big brass present were not too amused, and I had probably been marked as a possible troublemaker, but I did get huge applause. Encouraged by the audience, I was now flying. I could have got up from my stool and done a jig. The hashish had taken hold in a big way. To make matters worse, the captain's driver not ten feet from my left controlling the curtains was now on the floor in spasms of laughter. He couldn't believe I'd had the balls to play the song. Every time I tried in earnest to compose myself for the next song, he started laughing. I managed to start my next tune, 'Angela's Song,' which was supposed to be a touching love song. I got as far as the second verse and became a laughing blob. Luckily for me, pretty much half of the audience joined me in hysterical laughter that no one, excepting me of course, knew the reason for.

The desert

    The nearest town outside the camp, Manama, wasn't much. There was absolutely no booze for the drinkers and the women all dressed from head to toe in black; this was indeed a weird place to be. Just being in the town gave you the creeps. It seemed it was just a matter of time before someone would get in trouble.

Going out to the desert was quite different. I never knew how he finagled it, but one of the lads, the base captain's driver, often borrowed the gleaming black captain's car. Three of the base lads and I would very comfortably drive out along long, straight roads with nothing but desert and the odd oil pipeline on each side. We brought along some water, but rarely anything else, and we would generally stay overnight in the desert.

One of the lads, who had the nickname 'Brummie' because he was from Birmingham, had been there the longest, probably a wee bit too long if you ask me. If he happened to see a plane overhead, he immediately went to his knees in prayer fashion and pleaded, 'Big iron bird in the sky, take me home, take me from this godforsaken land. I beseech thee, take me home.' He knew all the places to go to buy huge slabs of cannabis resin for next to nothing, and where to pick up a local kid whose sole job was to roll large cone-shaped joints in the back of the car.

We once stopped at a tumble-down shack in the middle of nowhere beside an oasis, which was a small pond under some shade trees. It was quite a ways from the road; we had driven the last few miles over sand tracks. I asked why we were here, and Brummie replied in his fashion, 'Wait and ye shall see.' In the shade it must have been 120 degrees. We were dressed in our usual shorts and sandals, no shirts. Our skin was so dark and leathery from being in the sun, we were used to it!

Al Salaam a' alaykum

Eventually across the desert we saw a tiny figure coming toward us. As he got closer we saw he was herding goats. He eventually made it to the oasis and commenced watering his goats nearby. Once the goats were settled, he came over to us. He obviously knew Brummie, as he gave us the usual greeting,

'*Al Salaam a' alaykum.*' Brummie replied in the little bit of the lingo he knew. Brummie explained to us that this kid was not too much younger than we were and had never seen a TV or been into a town. He could not read or write; his only job in life was to bring his goats once a day to the watering hole, and then return to his father, who was very old and he helped to feed and basically keep alive. Such was his lot in life! After an hour or so he said his farewells and off he went with his goats, out into the midday scalding sun, and slowly disappeared into the distant haze.

My favourite place was a large hill that we could almost drive to the top of. The last half mile or so you had to climb, where you eventually came to an excellent lookout point. Facing west, you saw over roughly five miles of flat desert, some scattered palm trees, and then the blue ocean beyond. Sunset from there was ethereal. I generally climbed up there on my own, sometimes with my guitar. After a couple of weeks of noisy sweaty engine room and mind-numbing boredom out at sea, this place was so very welcome. It was usually easy to find my way back to the lads in the dark, even if the campfire hadn't been lit yet. There was always that gentle glow coming from the desert sand at night. The sheer quietness of the desert at night and the mass of stars in the heavens was also very gratifying.

We generally returned to Manama the following Sunday evening starving and bought barbecued food from the pavement vendors. Lord only knows what we ate, shish kebab dog most probably. Waking up on Mondays ready to go to sea were not my favourite times, with my stomach rumbling from the food and sometimes still a little bit high.

A Deltic engine is similar to a V engine, except at the top of the V there is another set of horizontally opposed pistons. Times this by eight rows, and it is one powerful engine. The main shaft had to be turned a complete 360 degrees by hand before starting to ensure lubrication had made it to all the moving parts. This was done with the use of a huge crow bar. There were two engines. After the laborious job of turning the engines, to start them you had to load a magazine cylinder with a large shotgun-type cartridge. For safety reasons, we returned to the small control room with protective acrylic windows, and with a hand carefully entrenched around the throttle, remotely fired the cartridge. After turning over an engine in an engine room that is so extremely hot, you are just about ready to drop.

Tragic and violent place

To me, the Persian Gulf seemed a tragic, violent place with antiquated laws. We were once refused entry in the Port of Oman because of a public hanging. Apparently, half a dozen people were hanging from poles above the mooring jetties.

We had been asked by the Trucial Oman Scouts to help sort out a skirmish that had turned violent. The interpreter directed us into an area of isolated islands, bays, and rocky outcroppings. It was hard to believe there were people actually living on these desolate islands. There didn't seem to be anything green or any signs of life, just hot, dry rock. We were even having some problems with our engines overheating because the seawater was so hot it wasn't doing too much in the way of cooling.

In those days all of our garbage went over the side, including oil from our bilges. I hate to think what pollution we must have caused. Within minutes we had a few small wooden boats coming up to our stern. The sad-looking beggars were rummaging through the garbage now floating on the water. Some of the lads were even throwing garbage directly into their boats; these locals seemed quite happy to oblige.

The interpreter and a few officers went ashore. Thankfully, the boarding party was not alerted to assist. When they returned, we were told what had happened. The interpreter explained that over a hundred years ago a family of people from one side of the island had raped the daughter of an elder from the other side. Every couple of years since then the violence escalated and repeated itself, with the odd murder thrown in. Sometimes the violence got out of hand, as too many dismembered corpses were seen floating around the bays. An official of sorts would come and the violence would cease for a while! Today we had just sorted it out – until the next time!

I was ashore in some small town in Oman when I saw this character walking toward me that looked like he was out of the movie *Lawrence of Arabia*. He was dressed in the usual white robe and headgear with the gold band, but he actually had the big fancy curly sword hanging from his hip. Well, this was a Kodak moment if ever I saw one. I pulled out my little Olympus camera, ready to take the shot. I was down on one knee about twenty feet away from him trying to focus in when I noticed through the viewfinder that he was not a happy chappie and was now in the process of taking his curly sword out and doing me a mischief. I realized very quickly that I was on my own (as usual) in a quiet back street. My brain told me *It's time to use the running skills, Kevin*. I heard a nasty gurgling voice in Arabic behind me, probably an insult on my parentage, as I took the corner at the end of the street, probably now doing about twenty miles an hour. Discretion is the better part of valor!

Sea snakes

During the day sailing around the various islands and bays we saw many sea snakes. You could easily count ten to fifteen in an hour in some areas.

The ship had anchored off in a bay and in the dead of the night when we got the 'Awkward' call. In minutes the total diving crew was all dressed in and heading out from the ship in the Gemini. It was pitch dark. The only lights we could see were the ones on the ship. The coxswain was driving the boat. None of us had any idea what the exercise would be. Sometimes we would be an attack group attaching limpet mines (magnetic tin lids) on the ship, while another group was the defending faction.

These exercises could get quite silly and sometimes dangerous. On the *Zulu*, I had seen men being stripped naked and tortured with freezing cold water from the fire hoses. They had even placed guys in the galley's walk-in freezer, all to get information about where the mines had been hidden underwater. I once saw a Marine hit someone over the head with the butt of his rifle. That same exercise, two men came back on board with broken arms. I was hoping this wasn't going to develop into something silly. Even this far in the navy, I had taken part in many exercises where lives were regularly put at risk. I understood that it made sense to run exercises to keep everyone on their toes in case we were asked to do it for real. Some men tended to lose reality, or maybe they had seen to many action movies, but in the thick of it you really needed to watch for these idiots.

When we were about a half mile away from the ship, the coxswain informed us that we were to find our way back to the ship *underwater*. If we were spotted we would have to go do it again. We had compasses on our wrists and were dropped off in pairs buddied together, which meant we had a six-foot length of rope attaching us together. The bright beams from the ship's searchlights were looking for us. If we were seen, they would inevitably throw thunder flashes at us. If one of those suckers landed close to your ears it could do damage. My partner and I were the only ones making bubbles, as the rest of the team had the rebreather sets. I think I was more worried about being surrounded by the damn poisonous sea snakes than being caught.

You couldn't see them in the pitch darkness.

Carbon monoxide poisoning

The coxswain ended up being someone I looked up to, and he also liked similar music to me. We could never be buddies, him being a chief and all, but sometimes we had conversations and he told me of concerts he had attended in London, including seeing Janis Joplin, whom he idolized. I could not understand why, with his years of experience, he still had to bow and scrape to much younger officers, who in my mind knew nothing.

I had been pulled over a few times by the diving officer, who was also second in charge under the skipper. For some reason he just had it in for me. The chief just told me to try and stay out of his way. One of the seemingly many minor offences was losing my ID card. It had been stolen from my pocket in the changing room of the base swimming pool. For that, I lost some pay, was given thirty days of number-nine punishment, and the loss of all shore leave until further notice. I had to muster outside his office in full number one uniform at 0600 and 2200 to be inspected, then work two extra hours, usually cleaning galley pots or peeling spuds. He seemed to relish in having this power over me, and never held back on his insults on why I thought I was different. It took so much willpower for me not to speak back, which it seemed is what he really wanted. I would come back to the mess spitting blood. Sometimes the chief would come in and try to settle me down, telling me, 'Now don't do anything silly. Just do your punishment and get over it.'

The whole team was involved in an exercise dive. I had been buddied up with the diving officer, much to my chagrin, because I was the only one again using the normal SABA set. The rest of the team were using their rebreather sets. Only a few minutes had passed when I started to feel sick and developed a pounding headache. When it had gotten pretty much unbearable, I gave the diving officer a tug on the rope, then four, to tell him I wanted to surface. I was signaling 'Problem with air, I want up' with my thumbs. He surprised me by flatly refusing and was now pulling me deeper. I hung on for another few minutes until I started to feel dizzy and was about ready to pass out. I then gave him an almighty tug and signalled 'I'm going up.' I literally had to drag him to the surface. I couldn't even pull myself up onto the boat after they had taken the set off my back. The men in the boat had to slide me on board.

The chief asked what the hell was wrong as the diving officer cursed at me. I could barely answer and just laid in the bottom of the boat, my head pounding. The chief looked at the pupils of my bloodshot eyes and the red colour of my skin. He knew there was something wrong and decided it was time to abort the dive and return me back on board the ship. He was pretty sure I had carbon monoxide poisoning, possibly from bad air in the breathing set. I laid in my bunk for a full twenty-four hours. The chief checked on me every couple of hours until the headache started to wane. He said he was going to have the set tested the next time we went into port at the base. I was shocked when the report came back that the air was clean. I felt like a bit of a twit, but was surprised that the diving officer wasn't gloating and jibing me with his insults.

Much later I told one of my friends ashore the story of the bad air, and he said it was a lie. They had indeed tested the set – and it was positive! Apparently, they had been doing some work nearby where the diesel air compressor was and had inadvertently put the exhaust too close to where the compressor air inlet was situated. Because of the test, they emptied all the diver breathing sets, moved the air inlet to a safer location, and recharged the sets.

Carbon monoxide poisoning is very serious, especially for divers, because at depth a tiny amount can make a huge difference. At only .32 percent, or 3200 ppm, death can occur within thirty minutes. I told the chief about my discovery; he replied that for my own good I should just drop it. However, I did notice that I was always included on pretty much every dive from then on. I helped out replacing one of the massive propellers on the ship, and even helped out on one of their bomb explosive jobs.

Chapter 27
G and T is Good for Me

There was a huge fanfare as the Ninth Minesweeper Squadron left Bahrain for the last time. Many people were on the jetty, even an army brass band witnessed the big move, so of course we got out the fire hoses and sprayed everyone.

We met up with the Sixth Squadron, which had similarly left Hong Kong for the last time. Somewhere in the middle of the Indian Ocean, the two squadrons linked together to form a convoy to return to the UK. It would take us over two months. We had a wonderful time stopping in ports in the Seychelles, South Africa, and beyond, all the way back to Rosyth, Scotland.

When you are part of the team you work hard and play hard, and that has remained my motto for most of my adult life. For instance, in the beautiful Seychelles, I had been ordered by the coxswain to a session ashore. I had come down with some weird chest infection and was taking this time off my engine room watch-keeping duties to get some sleep and try and recover before going back out to sea again.

One of the many duties the coxswain had was to be the ad hoc medic. His remedies were as follows: as my bunk bed had a slope up toward my feet, he had me sleeping the opposite way so the phlegm would drain the other way. It made sense to me.

He had also prescribed some nasty-tasting medicine, of which I'm sure he had no idea what it was. But he agreed it tasted really bad, so 'it must be good for you,' he added solicitously. *Okay, kind of makes sense too,* I thought. Then he ordered me to go ashore with him and the rest of the team for the 'ultimate cure' he promised would 'do the trick.' Oh, and the team would miss me if I didn't go, he added. I was trying, in my way, to get this man out of my face so I could quietly curl up and die in my bunk. He literally dragged me out of my bed, so I reluctantly gave in and headed to the shower to try and shake this awful bug out of my system.

I asked him what this amazing cure was all about as we walked to the nearest bar, stopping occasionally to cough up huge amounts of phlegm. There, in a very busy bar, he said with confidence in his voice, 'Okay, you ready for the cure?'

'Yeah, okay,' I said.

'Right, say after me,' he ordered, 'G and T is good for me.' He then proceeded to slide a huge glass of gin and tonic across the table toward me. My earlier vow to not drink alcohol had been somewhat weakened over the last few months and, feeling quite ill, I thought, *What more harm can it possibly do?* It seemed every few minutes he asked me to repeat the famous words, 'G and T is good for me,' and then along came another drink. After half a dozen of these glasses of elixir, I was miraculously cured! I was feeling wonderful and was up dancing with the ladies and thanking him for this wonderful cure. I don't remember coming back on board ship, but I do remember how I felt the following day!

Simon's Town, South Africa

Again, South Africa was a bit of an adventure. This time we went alongside in Simon's Town, about a one-hour train ride from Cape Town. As usual, the ship's company had been warned of all the places that were out of bounds and the punishment for being found there, which again was really silly, because that was, of course, where we were now all heading. We had caught an afternoon train heading into Cape Town, and we were all looking forward to our shore leave. Every one of the dozen or so shipmates was in high spirits and probably making a lot of noise. One of the lads tried to start up a lively conversation with the only other civilian sitting in the front of our carriage. To our complete shock, he immediately pulled out a revolver. The whole front of the carriage became very quiet, and as the rest of us started to realize what had just happened, we also were stunned into silence. He then started to laugh as he put away the pistol and told us he was just joking. He then commenced to give us all a lecture on protection while in Cape Town: if a black guy is following you, you take no chances; you turn around and shoot the kaffer. Most importantly, you make sure he is dead. If you accidentally run one over in your car, you reverse over him a few times, making doubly sure he is well and truly dead before you leave. Needless to say, by the time we reached Cape Town we were not in the same jovial mood. We did, however, make the best of it. Shore time anywhere was always such a relief.

I was in a popular disco with the boys and taking a breather from dancing, sitting at the bar talking to the black barman. This was a white-only bar, but the waiters and bar staff were all black. We were having a good conversation about music, but then, as always, no matter whom you were talking to, white or black, in South Africa, they usually, ever so conveniently, swayed the conversation toward the apartheid problem. We were obviously from another country by the uniforms we wore, and either side wanted to let the rest of the world know what was 'really going on.' To make a point, he picked up an empty can of beer from the bar, looked me square in the eyes, then said with a conviction that almost blew me of my seat, 'One day we will crush the whites!' as he crumpled the can. It sent shivers down my spine.

South Africa was a tinder box. The heavy burden of oppression was in the very air you breathed. Surprisingly to me, even talking to people of my generation, they still unfortunately believed that black people were somehow a different subspecies.

We had missed the last train out to Simon's Town, so decided, as with the many other sailors present, to just kip on a bench or whatever flat object we could find. It would only be a few hours before the first train out in the morning. It looked to be quite a modern train station. There were lads sleeping on the tops of lockers, on benches, and even on the shiny, tiled floor.

Two official-looking police officers came into the train station in the early hours of the night. Stretched out, I was luckily watching them as they came through the big glass doors. They were both identically dressed in khaki, with dark brown leather gun holsters attached to Sam Browne belts across their chests and midriffs. They had the riding breeches and matching brown leather knee-high riding boots. The peak visor fronts of their hats were down, almost touching their noses. It seemed to me that all they needed to finish off the image was a pair of SS insignias on their lapels and a swastika on their black arm bands. These two charmers almost looked like they were ready to break into the famous Nazi goose-step march as they zeroed in on an unsuspecting slumbering sailor. They dragged him to his feet by his lapels and proceeded to slap him around the head. The poor guy must have thought he'd awoken from a nightmare in a prisoner of war camp. They repeated the same procedure on a few other very surprised, snoozing sailors, until everyone had gotten the hint to sit correctly on the bench and at all costs do not sleep. By the time they had made their way over to my bench, my eyes were like saucers. *See these eyes? They are wide open!*

Throughout the now seemingly long night, they came into the station at hourly intervals. As they passed some of the lads, giving them their evil glare from under the visors, it almost looked like the lads where sitting to attention, staring off at some distant object, not wanting to make eye contact with the brutes.

Apartheid sadness

On the many visits I made to South Africa on various ships, I was always disappointed at what they had done to such a beautiful place, and I almost felt ashamed of my colour. I haven't returned to South Africa since apartheid was finally wiped out, but I'm sure it will take at least the rest of my lifetime before there is some semblance of peace. There is a lot of forgiving to be done by the black people for the atrocities made by some of the evil white race there.

The fated bosun's call

I was on duty watch during an officers' cock and ass (cocktail) party, and much to my dismay I also had to stand quartermaster's gangway duty. Usually this was a leading seaman's duty. My normal duty was to ensure the ship's generator was taken care of, taking hourly readings and sometimes catching up on service issues and oil changes during engine down times. The officer of the day informed me that, as I was the only leading hand on board, I had to go and change out of my overalls and into my number one whites. Thankfully it was the engineer officer; I don't think he liked it any more than I did. I had a lot of respect for the engineer officer. He had praised my work on a few occasions and tended to give me some slack when it was due. We would be expecting an admiral today, big brass for our little boat, but we were the flagship, so I guess we had it coming.

About an hour before the big brass arrived, I was duly informed that I had to pipe him on board. 'Get on yer bike,' I said under my breath. 'I'm a friggin stoker, not a deck swabber.'

'Sir, with all due respect,' I said, 'what are you talkin' about? I have never used a bosun's call.' This is a small tubular whistle apparatus. You blow into one end, and with your hand over an opening on the ball end, with much skill, it was possible to make shrill up and down notes. This had been handed down from before Admiral Nelson's time, when it was used to signal all sorts of events from the time of the watch change to all hands on deck. The seamen's branch had to master this contraption as part of their duty.

I had been ordered to 'pipe the side,' which was an honour given to a senior officer when embarking or disembarking ship, so I had to do it twice. Somebody in their infinite wisdom had screwed up the day's duty watch. It wasn't until everyone had disappeared ashore that they realized there wasn't another seaman on board. So it had fallen on me! And despite all my complaints, the officer of the day made me sit on the funnel deck and practice. *Toot tu tu too, toot tu tu too* (repeat three times), then a long reverberating *tooo u ooooo u oooooo*. The officer of the day was starting to get angry when I couldn't figure this thing out, but eventually I thought I might have gotten it down. He warned me in no uncertain terms that if I messed this up I was in big trouble.

My big moment approached as a shiny, black Rolls-Royce arrived and a Royal Marine in full colour uniform appeared from out of the car. He opened the car door for the admiral, then stood smartly to attention at the gangway on the shore side, sword in hand, pointed directly up in front of his nose. The officer of the day (a sub-lieutenant) and I were in spiffy gleaming whites and stood to attention beside the gangway on board the ship. All the gentry on the fo'c'sle, including the skipper, were under a large canvas awning. They were gazing down at this wondrous occasion. The admiral stepped onto the gangway, and I noticed that he had so many glittering gold rings and badges and medals that you would think he was the king of England.

As he reached the top of the gangway with, I thought, a rather pathetic excuse for a salute, I heard the officer of the day beside me officially shout the order, 'Bosun, pipe the side.'

What came out of the infernal instrument was not a 'pipe the side.' No, far from it; it was more of 'a cat just jumped up and bit my balls' kind of a pipe. The shrill bit at the end sounded like a gramophone record that had run out of torque. The admiral gave me a what-the-hell-was-that kind of look and disappeared up to the fo'c'sle. When he was completely out of earshot, I was taken by the scruff of the neck into a close-by compartment by the engineer officer and royally bollocked.

'Firth, you practice with that pipe until you have got it perfect! He will be leaving in two hours, and if you haven't got it right, then . . . well, forget ever going ashore again while you're on board this ship!' That was followed by 'I have never been so embarrassed.'

I practiced my little heart out until I thought that I had it down perfect. Funny though it seemed, I really didn't want to let the engineer officer down. I even called upon him before the admiral was due to leave to listen to my sweet call. He was now duly impressed.

My next big moment was almost upon me. The admiral was on his way down to the gangway. The officer and I were both stood rigid to attention and he whispered out the side of his mouth, 'Firth, do not let me down.' I was now sweating. He arrived and I heard, 'Bosun, pipe the side.' I made a big deal of smartly bringing the call up to my lips.

Just before the pipe touched my now-quivering lips, the admiral immediately turned around and looked at me with a pitiful look on his face. He held up his hand and said, 'Please, no thank you.'

CHAPTER 28

Returning to the UK on the *Brereton*
Ronnie and Richard, new ship's company!

We returned to the UK – Scotland to be exact. Our new temporary base was to be HMS Lochinvar, which was situated almost under the Forth Bridge at Port Edgar, the opposite side of the Forth River from Rosyth dockyard.

I had been away from the UK for just over nine months, and was surprised to receive a telephone call. The ship had tied up alongside and the shore-side power, water, and telephone lines had just been connected. My crazy brother Ronnie and his brother-in-law Richard had driven all the way up from Morecambe, Lancashire to meet me and take me home. They would never know how that one very thoughtful gesture had made me feel.

HMS Lochinvar was classed as a nuclear base; the subs regularly docked there. I thought it very doubtful that they would be allowed in, with the very strict security. Unbeknown to them, I would also not be allowed to leave until the following morning after completion of officer's rounds. It was early in the evening and I was trying to figure out the logistics of where they might stay for the night. I asked the duty officer, who happened to be the good engineer officer, if I could bring them aboard. However, all my pleading fell on very stony ground.

'Firth, are you in your right mind? Absolutely not. We would both be hung at the yardarm!'

I made some excuse to go onto the dock, probably to check on the water line connection, etc. I ran up to the main gate, which was heavily secured with police guards. I could see Ronnie's car parked just down the road from the main gate. I flashed my ID card to the guard and he allowed me through the gate. After a cheery greeting we got down to brass tacks. Neither one of them wanted, nor had the finances, to stay in a hotel for the night. Both of them had obviously had a few drinks at the local pub, so I asked Richard if he would wait for me in the pub. He was okay with that, as they were both heavy boozers. My idea was a long shot, but it was worth a try, given the circumstances.

Ronnie laid down in the back seat of his car with a cover over him, and I drove his car through the security gate waving my ID card at the now familiar guard. I parked close to the gangway, waited for a convenient moment, and waved at my buddy standing watch on the gangway to take him on board and down into our mess deck. I repeated the same procedure later and was successful in bringing Richard on board.

The cook added another two for supper and the lads brought out all of our remaining secret Asian Tiger beer. Ronnie and Richard had a wonderful evening on board a Royal Navy ship, as they were treated like royalty. They both got a taste of sleeping on a ship in the spare bunks we found them.

The following morning we had to clean up for officer's rounds, and my bags were packed for leaving. As we were having breakfast we were all trying to come up with ideas on how to hide Ron and Rich, when the officer of the day suddenly opened the curtain into our mess. He immediately saw Ron and Rich. *That's it*, I thought, *I have blown it and will probably be thrown into a navy prison as they throw away the keys. I am totally done for.* Much to my dumbfounding surprise, he stepped forward and, shaking their hands, cordially introduced himself to them.

I'm still not out of the soup yet! *I thought. He was probably up* with the skipper right now thinking of a suitable punishment, which would start with absence of leave. An hour later he arrived at our mess to finalize his rounds. As I smartly saluted him, he pulled me to one side and whispered in my ear, 'Firth, I know nothing about this, and if you get caught taking them through the gate, you are on your own.'

With a huge false confidence we waved at the guards as we drove through the gate. Smiling and waving, the guard shouted to us, 'Have a good leave, lads!'

Improved relations

Coming home to Marilyn was wonderful. She had waited for me, and our relationship became stronger knowing we could be separated for so long yet be together like this as though we had never parted. We were very happy and enjoyed each other's company. Although we both had heavy commitments in our young lives, we loved to go out on the town and have fun.

Leaves from the navy were sparse at best, but when I got home it was always like a honeymoon. We had many rough times with heated arguments, which were usually about money (more or less the lack of it). I was still sending an allotment from my meager navy pay home to my mum, which didn't sit well with Marilyn. To make things worse, my family wasn't too happy to see that I had started up a relationship with another lady with a child, the first one having done me so much emotional harm. I was beginning to see that I was being torn between the love I had for

Marilyn and the love of my family.

Contrary to how my family treated Marilyn, her mother and I got on real well right from the very start, and was more than I ever expected. She could be a tyrant with her Irish temper. I had once seen her throw one of her clogs at a neighbour, narrowly missing her head, for some small misdemeanor. However, it seemed I could do no wrong in her eyes. Her dad was a quiet, reserved, and proud man. He would sit by his fire smoking his pipe, sometimes telling me stories of his time in the war that I felt I could listen to for hours. They were both solid down-to-earth people that had worked very hard in their lives to end up with so little. I respected them tremendously in more ways than one.

Saturday mornings were a treat. I would come up with some lame excuse to go visit them a half dozen doors down the street from us. As this was her stew day, she would ask me to sit a while and have some stew and a coffee. I would weakly protest that I had to go, that I had so and so job to do, blah, blah. I'm sure she saw through me every time. Out from the tiny kitchen came this huge bowl of steaming and delicious rabbit stew. That was followed with a massive porcelain pot of granulated real coffee, not the instant type. Although there were many floaties in the coffee, it was the best I had ever had.

Leadership training course

After this leave I was sent on a leadership course in Portsmouth at *HMS Excellent* training base on Whale Island, which I thoroughly enjoyed. This was the build-up to becoming a petty officer, of which I was already technically qualified for. It was a six-week course, part of which was expedition training. Again, we were given more in-depth instruction on map reading and looking after oneself in the outdoors.

The maps were of a part of the New Forest in Southampton,

with many locations that we could choose at will. The more locations you made, the higher points you would receive, ending at a certain location on the map by a certain time. I loved this until they told us, 'But each one of you will take two junior sailors who have just joined the RN!'

Each competing team was dropped off separately from within a covered truck in the early hours of the morning. The first thing you had to do, pretty much in the dark, was to find out where you actually were on the map and then start to make as many points on the map as possible in the day. Each point had a question that could only be answered if you were actually there. For example: What number is on the gate beside the big oak tree?

I was twenty years old, leading two inquisitive but rather green fifteen-year-old lads. I had to keep my boys happy, so I took lots of chocolate. When they were moaning and wanted to rest I had to think up encouraging things to keep them going. I was in this race to be number one; orienteering or cross-country running, this was my game! But how was I going to drag around these two lads that didn't look particularly fit? I had to learn very quickly what leadership was all about if I was to get anywhere in this race.

I tried everything. 'Just think what your commanding officer is going to say to you lads if we come in first,' I said to try and spur them on. 'Two more mark points in the next hour and you get another chocolate bar,' which worked for a while until I ran out of chocolate. Then they got really tired.

I don't know how many miles we had covered in the day. The boys were knackered and about ready to give up. However, when we finally made it to camp, only minutes before the disqualification time, we came in jogging. My team came in with the highest mark by far. Not every team actually made it back, so we had to spend some of our evening searching for them.

The assault course back on base was again a wonderful experience – for me! Our leadership course entries were split up into four-man teams. The challenge was to take a large, heavy wooden barrel around the whole course, part of which was across open water. During part of the course we had to take the barrel across a small ravine; we were given two wooden planks, neither of which spanned the ravine, and some rope. One of the lads sprained his ankle on our final run, so I ended up carrying him on my back. That same chap later qualified for officer and ended up being a helicopter pilot. I later did the assault course on my own, which was suggested by the Chief PTO (physical training officer), whom I had made friends with during the course. I broke the course record.

We did some more interesting unarmed combat, of which I was usually the course guinea pig.

At the end of the course, I came out first overall in the class. I was also given a certificate of merit, but above all I made some great friends.

Mechanician training course, HMS *Sultan* engineering school

I reported to *HMS Sultan* engineering college for the petty officer technical engineering course. I had been previously informed that if I were to attain an eighty percent overall average on the final exams, I would be put forward for the two-year mechanician training course.

I had realized very quickly that marine engineering really didn't give you any qualifications in civvie street, no matter what they had told us in recruitment. It was a fictitious lie. I could make it to petty officer, even chief if I wanted to be a lifer, but in civilian life it would mean nothing. My original plan of getting some qualifications while doing my allotted time in the navy was crumbling. I felt like I had been conned. A mechanician, however, was a trade that was recognized in civilian life. I had worked so hard to pass any exam that I could to get advancement. This was the only way out of my predicament and I was more than confident that it would happen. After the two-year course I would have five more years in the navy and then be out with a trade, thank you very much! Everybody happy!

I studied so hard during the course. My science, math, and engineering were always up in the nineties. My English wasn't quite as good, and why that had any real bearing was beyond me. Toward the end of the course, my English had improved enough to tell me that out of the class of over twenty-two, three of us were going to go on to the mechanician training college.

I was failed! My average marks over the last couple of weeks of tests in English had been well over the eighty-percent mark. However, on the final English exam I received a miserable thirty percent. I was totally blown away. I could not believe what had just happened. I started to 'smell a fish' and was very angry. The mere thought of spending the next seven years going nowhere wasn't what I had in mind. I asked to see the training officer. He refused! I knew there was something going on, so I barged into his office demanding an explanation. At that point, they could have slapped me in irons. I didn't care. This was the ultimate insult.

The engineering training officer was obviously straight out of university and had never been on a ship. He would not show me my English results as to where I had failed so miserably. And I knew I hadn't. I stood up and said, 'Tell me right now what is going on, or I swear I'm going to wreck this place.'

He knew I meant business, so he sat me down and explained. 'Well, it's like this, Firth. Even though your record shows excellence in certain areas, the brass above me has decided because of your lack of respect and dress in some areas, we think it inappropriate.'

I then said, 'Okay, so what you are telling me is that because I don't go around saying "Yes sir, no sir, three bags full, sir," all the work I have done since joining up has been a complete waste of time?'

He never answered me. I stormed out of his office, slamming the door behind me, thinking I would probably have two military police waiting to escort me to the lock up.

After that the rot truly started to set in. I wasn't even allowed to buy myself out. You had to complete two-thirds of your man's time before you even had that choice. I would have to serve three more years minimum, which for me would be a prison sentence.

CHAPTER 29
New Skipper Aboard

I returned to the *Brereton* feeling very despondent. And to make matters worse, we had a new skipper on board who seemed to want to make a name for himself. The ship had been procured for fishery patrol. Our first patrol area was the northeast coast.

For the most part, the UK had a legally agreed fishing zone. Some neighbouring European countries totally ignored this fact and regularly poached within the UK zones. The UK fisheries, which were diminishing at an alarming rate, were fighting for their very livelihood. Countless generations of fishermen had fished these waters to make their living. For many it came to a financially abrupt end. Political push had caused the Royal Navy to get involved to police and regulate these waters.

Our new temporary base was at the South Shields fishing docks just east of Newcastle. We spent our maximum time at sea, ten days, and then returned to port to fill our fresh water tanks and store food. Most other boats would then get a couple of day's shore leave before the next haul. Not with this keen skipper! We'd turn her around in less than a full working day, and out we would go again, much to our disappointment. After the third or fourth tour, morale on board was getting pretty low.

At the end of one laborious trip we were forced into port because of a maintenance problem. We were informed that we would be in for only two days. I wanted to go home so much. It had been a few months since I had managed to get enough time off to make it home. Train timetables would not mesh to get me home and back in the limited time, so I contacted my brother-in-law Richard, who I knew worked close by. We met in a bar and I explained to him how desperately I wanted to go home. After many drinks, I had him whittled down. He said, 'I don't have insurance for any driver. So, see those car keys on the bar? If they were to go missing I wouldn't report them stolen until tomorrow night.'

I set off driving like a maniac, with no idea how to get home, driving over hills and dales and getting completely lost many times until I eventually made it home in the early hours of the morning. I managed to squeeze twelve glorious hours at home before having to return to leave the car and keys where I had found them. Thank you, Richard!

Put one across his bow

We had been trying to catch a Belgian fishing boat that we had seen regularly. He was way inside the zone. Again and again he fired up his engines and was gone, cheekily waving at us from his bridge. With our limited speed, we had no chance of catching him. Little did he know that our crazy skipper had contacted Whitehall and had been given permission from the admiralty to 'put one across his bow!'

On the third night we caught him again way inside the UK fishing grounds. The skipper called him on a loud hailer. 'Hold your position and prepare to be boarded.' He did his usual turn-about and the skipper called him again. 'Hold your position or we will fire on you.'

He must have thought, 'Yeah, sure, that ain't gonna happen.' Bang! A 40mm Bofor shell went careening across his bow. Needless to say, he stopped very quickly. The Gemini was launched, and the coxswain and I boarded him with instructions to have him follow the ship into port to have his nets confiscated and a heavy fine levied after the usual court hearing.

All of his crew were crowded in the bridge, probably around ten men, with the coxswain on one side of the bridge wings and me on the other. Every now and then we had to remind him to stay in view of the ship, which was easily seen at night, and to stop veering his course.

Neither one of us was armed. I'm not sure who made that decision, but at times it became a little nerve wracking. One of his crew reached up and above what looked to be a map cabinet and brought down a rifle. He then proceeded to point it directly at me. It wasn't the first time I had had a gun pointed at me, but it always had the same stomach churning effect. I tried to stay in composure and not show my fear. He then turned around and pointed it at the coxswain. I'm sure the coxswain felt the same as I did at that moment. *This could be it, mate. Your time's up!* I thought.

Just when things were getting really tense, everyone unbelievably started to laugh. He opened the magazine to show us that it was indeed empty. The skipper then offered us a drink, which under the situation we sensibly refused. We tied up alongside; he was tied up inboard of us so he could not escape for the next three days that he spent in and out of court.

He did have his nets confiscated, which apparently was worse than the fine. He and his crew seemed not to care too much about the outcome, as we all got pretty much acquainted drinking each other's booze every evening, the big joke being the looks on our faces when he pointed the rifle at us!

AWOL

On one of the granted weekend shore leaves, I made it home hitchhiking the distance, and as usual had a wonderful weekend. I returned back on time on the Monday morning to find the ship had already sailed on some emergency our skipper had volunteered for. Good sense told me to make my way back to the base in Scotland, as that is where I knew the ship was heading after this emergency. *Hmm!* I thought. *I wonder if I can sneak a few more days out of this?* So I headed back home, and a few days ended up being a week. I was now officially AWOL, a highly punishable offence. I just didn't care. I wanted out so bad it was affecting me in different ways. My hair was falling out in clumps.

After the week I knew the military police would be looking for me, and I didn't want the embarrassment of them showing up at Marilyn's house. I reluctantly headed back to the base in Scotland. Thankfully the ship was still at sea. No one was even looking for me. I thought that I might have conveniently slipped through the net. I stayed at the base until the ship returned two days later. I got away very lightly with two weeks number nine punishments and absence of leave at the skipper's discretion.

A bit of roughers

At one point the skipper decided to go to sea, even though we had warnings of severe gales off western Scotland. He just didn't seem to care. He was a two-ringer (lieutenant) wanting his half ring (lieutenant commander). We ended up being stuck in a heading of west for almost one week. It was so rough that it was too dangerous to turn about. When the weather was like that, and I had experienced it a few times, the brain went into remote. Sleep was in fits and starts, and you had to strap yourself into your bunk, unless of course you had a death wish.

Our living quarters was the most forward upper mess, so

when the ship hit a big wave, anything that was not totally screwed down became airborne and crashed into everything else. After a few days of this punishment nobody seemed to care. The deck of the mess was awash with all kinds of debris. The cook had basically given up. If you got hungry, which you generally didn't, you went into the galley at your own risk, as the deck was slippery as hell, and dug out last week's roast potatoes.

A shift in the engine room was a real treat. God forsake you if you fell onto a hot pipe. When the ship hit the crest of a big wave, sometimes both props would come completely out of the water. These Deltic engines were a wee bit temperamental; if you were not swift enough reducing the throttle, those engines had been known to explode, sending pistons up through the funnel.

Just getting to the engine room was risky business. A rope line was rigged from the aft door of the living quarters directly to the engine room hatch on deck. If a goffer (big wave) got you, over the side you went. Bye, bye! We can't come back and get you! The ship would keel over so far sometimes that you would wonder if it was ever going to come back. One of the lads in the mess slept with his life vest on. We ended up somewhere way out in the Atlantic Ocean before it was safe enough to turn around and return to Scotland.

We would be thinking how bad we were having it, but then occasionally we would see trawler boats not too much smaller than us taking the same punishment. It gave you a real appreciation for how tough those men must be to withstand that day in, day out.

In my many years at sea both in and out of the navy, I have witnessed severe hurricanes and even the tail end of a typhoon off Japan. When you see the sheer ferocity of what water and wind can do, it never fails to give you a tremendous respect and to always be on the ready; never, ever leave anything to chance.

This lunatic of a skipper was going to get us all killed to earn his lieutenant commander half ring.

CHAPTER 30
Secret Wedding

I eventually finished my time on the *Brereton* as it went in for a mini refit. I was owed four weeks' leave. This was going to be the most time I had ever had continuously with my sweetheart. We might have had a few hang ups, but overall we both knew we were happy to be with each other. Neither of us wanted marriage. We had both been through the wringer in our young lives. I was twenty years old with what seemed a whole lifetime behind me, and I'm sure she felt the same. We had talked about marriage on occasion and we agreed, why do we have to marry and possibly spoil what we have? I think just knowing we didn't *have* to helped us to make the final decision. Little Dominic needed a father. He was becoming a part of me and I had started to love him as my own.

One evening after Marilyn had just come home from a night out with her sister, I surprised her with the proposal. We decided that because of the flak that I knew I would get from my family (my sisters weren't keen and neither was my mum), that we would just go ahead and not tell anyone except Ronnie and Marilyn's sister, Stella.

I called Ronnie and told him to be at a certain place and be in a suit, and Marilyn did the same with Stella, with a note not to tell anyone. I'm sure they both knew what was about to happen. I donned a suit that had been made in Hong Kong, designed by yours truly. It was a dark blue, pinstriped affair, double breasted, with a matching a double-breasted waistcoat. It had tiny lapels and half-moon pockets. The jacket came almost down to my knees and flared with a big split at the back. My pants, of course, were wide bell-bottoms, also split up the sides, with buttons at the top. The material was so thin the hairs on my legs actually protruded through. I gave Marilyn the choice. It was either that suit or my silver one with the bright yellow lining.

The registry wedding went well even through my stammering, which made Ronnie and Stella giggle. We celebrated later in the Trades pub nearby. We were so very happy, and to have my big bro beside me only made it better. Beneath her tall, lightweight, and very beautiful frame, Marilyn was a strong woman. I trusted her and I felt she loved me. I knew whatever life threw at me in my crazy existence she would always be there for me, waiting for me to return. When I was with her I felt like I was in a sphere of sanity where I could feel honest, true love. Life was indeed good – until the draft chit came two days later! *Report to Brize Norton RAF Airbase to fly out to Cape Town, South Africa to join* HMS Lincoln.

I had been home only two weeks. This hit me like a train. I no more wanted to go than the man in the moon. We were both so sad. We were still celebrating our marriage and feeling wonderful, only to have been brought to this low, with no clue how long I might be away. It was heart breaking. I departed to many tears, and literally dragged myself away.

CHAPTER 31
HMS Lincoln
Redmond O'Connel

I joined *HMS Lincoln* and soon found out that it had a nickname throughout the fleet – the drinkin', stinkin' *Lincoln* – and it pretty much lived up to its name. She was 340 feet long with a displacement of 2,400 tons, a Salisbury class or type-61 aircraft detection frigate. With a complement of 235 men, the ship was almost as old as I was at the time and was just about ready to be mothballed.

After finding my bunk and stowing my gear, I was feeling pretty miserable. After the long flight it started to dawn on me just how much I was missing home and my new wife. For the first time in my adult life I was experiencing a duality – the Jekyll and Hyde life, as I used to call it – which would repeat itself pretty much for the rest of my life. Part of me was now addicted to travel and adventure. If danger was involved, that absurdly just put the icing on the cake. Situations and life events occurred on a regular basis that were almost impossible to explain to what I thought of as normal people back home. On the other hand, another part of me desperately needed love and companionship with a solid non-moving ground called home. Sanity, with an easy-going consistent daily lifestyle surrounded by a caring family, is what I imagined I desired. These two opposing desires sometimes tugged for my attention on a daily basis.

With all these thoughts whirring crazily around inside my head, I decided to go ashore and drown my sorrows. We, of course, had to wear uniform, which in the evening was our number one suit: black bell-bottoms, white front shirt, hat, and black shoes. Little did I know at the time that I was about to meet a very colourful character who would add much more fun and spice into my life. When you're just not looking, life's wibbly-wobbly way just lays out the red carpet in style.

Redmond O'Connel was the NAAFI (Navy, Army, and Air Force Institutes) manager and the only civilian on board the ship. He was from Clitheroe in Lancashire, not too far from where I grew up. Most large ships have a NAAFI shop. He ran this small shop in the main passageway and sold minimum items such as pop, snacks, chocolate bars, soap, etc. More importantly, he also dished out the beer every evening, a very essential task now that the centuries-old daily rum ration had been disbanded. Three cans per day with their tops off were handed out to all enlisted men over the age of eighteen not classed as teetotal.

As to our actual meeting, Redmond's version has always been a better story than what I recall. I was in no state to remember it anyhow, so I'll give you his.

Redmond came out of a nightclub and was heading back to the ship when he stepped off the curb to halt a cab and stepped on something soft and squishy in the gutter. This inanimate entity surprised him with a grunt as he stepped on it. He investigated further and looked down into the dark crevice. It indeed was a sailor in full uniform. Feeling benevolent and with a little sympathy, he reached down and dragged this wretched, now burbling, beast out of the gutter and sat me down in the cab that he had just hailed. He didn't recognize me, so he immediately concluded that I must be from the only other Royal Navy ship that was in harbour at the time.

Pulling up alongside the gangway of the other ship, he told me, 'Okay, mate, you're home,' to which I burbled something undecipherable. He assumed I was giving him a hard time, and said, 'Come on, mate. I did you a favour, now get the fuck out.' How I eventually made it back to my ship remains a mystery.

The next day I staggered up the metal steps and exited out of my hatchway from my shift down in the engine room, feeling like death warmed up. My tongue felt like it had grown a fungus on it, so I lined up for a pop only yards away at Red's shop. He was duly surprised, and we had a laugh when he told me of the previous evening's events. He apologized for not bringing me back to the ship, but had I been able to speak coherently he would have known better. I think 'drunken turd' did come into the conversation a few times.

In the coming weeks we quickly became the best of friends when we realized all the things we had in common. He played the guitar and we noticed that we had similar tastes in folk music. We were regulars down in the stokers' mess as we both sang and played for the lads. He introduced me to his banjo that he had been learning to play, and because I played the guitar finger picking style, it naturally became the instrument that I played most of the time.

Paddy Moriarty, also a stoker, joined us. He was a small Irish lad who played the button accordion. The three of us became a hit on board, and within weeks we were being invited into every mess at all hours of the night to play for as much free beer as we liked. Red named us 'Whistle Stop and Fart.' We performed at pretty much every port we went to in our time on the Lincoln and had a whole lot of laughs to boot.

I found out much later that, like me, Redmond came from a

broken home and his father was also an alcoholic.

The Mucky Duck

Redmond was a comedian and would do almost anything for a laugh. He had us in stitches many times with his jokes and antics. Wherever we played Moriarty would go into spasms of laughter with his funny guffaw of a laugh. I tried to keep some composure playing the banjo or guitar, with Redmond playing his twelve-string and doing most of the talking. Of course the many bars ashore loved us, as we would drag in most of the boys from the ship with us.

We had been playing in a bar in Gibraltar called the White Swan, which had the nickname the Mucky Duck, for a few nights and having a great time. On the third night, after performing one of our songs, an Australian band across the bar from us bravely gave us a contest. We heard in an irreverent strong Aussie accent:

> *Rule Britannia*
> *Marmalade and jam*
> *Stick three firecrackers up 'er bum*
> *Oh bang, bang,*
> *bang, bang, bang*

This just about floored the place. We thought, *Okay, these guys want to play,* so we gave them a version of our favourite, 'Dueling Banjos,' which we knew everyone loved. There was steam coming off my fingers when we finished. *Top that, mate,* we thought. Minutes later, from out of a dark corner of the pub, we heard our first rendering of 'The Shithouse Rock.' They started out snapping their fingers to a blues beat, and soon everyone joined in with a loud tapping of feet on the creaky wooden floorboards. This cute and innocent little ditty followed:

> *Sam, Sam the shithouse man*
> *He's the leader of the shithouse band*
> *Spends his time sniffing sanitary towels*
> *Listens to the heaving of the straining bowels*
> *It goes plip plop into the cot*
> *It goes plip plop into the pot*
> *Hoochy cookie cookie*
> *It's the shithouse rock.*

We were well and truly beaten!

We wandered over to find them, and for the next two mostly inebriated weeks had a lot of fun. There were three of them living on board a small twenty-six foot sailboat. They had been carpenter pals working in a city in Australia and had decided to tour the world. They sold everything they owned, bought this wreck of a boat, and between the three of them made it seaworthy and set off on their adventure. This was their second year on board. They would find work ashore, bartending or doing odd carpenter jobs until the boat was seaworthy, and then off they would go again. I think Red and I would have given our eyeteeth to join them.

During the same period, we also met two guys and a girl from France living in a ménage à trois relationship. One of them played a French version of the Northumbrian small pipes, which are similar to the famous bagpipes but have a bellows that can be pumped under your arm or by foot, as this chap was doing. The other chap played a comb with tracing paper over it, and the girl sang beautifully. They invited us on to their boat one evening after a brilliant night at the Mucky Duck.

Coming aboard this junky old boat, it reminded me of the

garbage boats you sometimes see in harbours that go around cleaning up rubbish. Going down below, however, it was miraculously transformed into a very comfortable, well-furnished and plush accommodation. Red velvet covered the walls and seats, and the rich mahogany tables and chairs were suitably placed. It was beautiful and such a surprise from what the upper deck looked like. They told us in their very good English that they had all been working in mundane office jobs in France and decided it was 'Time to go see what's out there.' We both admired their spirit of adventure and freedom, and once again wished we were free enough to follow suit.

Sod's Opera

Later that week we had volunteered to perform in the ships Sod's Opera. Having been out most of the afternoon with the Aussies and having been introduced to tequila, I was in no shape to perform.

A Sod's Opera is where the ship's company invents a play, or individuals perform whatever might be funny. Redmond came as a mailbag. He had a large blue mailbag that he had cut holes in for his head and arms, and he had a Groucho Marx bald head, nose, and moustache. I wanted to be the Monty Python 'my head hurts' character. I wore large hiking boots with my jeans turned up to my knees and a white collarless shirt with the arms turned up to my elbows. I held a large wooden carpenter's mallet, finished off with an army helmet that I had affixed a battery-operated propeller to the front of. I then attached tassels to the propellers that whizzed around in front of my eyes. The supply officer was the 'olde music hall' master of ceremonies with a little judge's wooden hand-carved gavel that had been handed down to him by his father. The skipper had just come out of hospital from having his appendix removed and was sitting front and center in a laid-back fashion because of the recent stitches. Our new a capella song that we had recently learned was called 'The Lunatic Song,' an old music hall favourite.

Lunatic Asylum

Outside a lunatic asylum
I was out breaking up stones
When along came a lunatic and said
Good morning, Mister Jones
How much a week duz tha get fer doing that?
Thirteen bob, I cried
He looked at me in a funny sort o' way
And this is what he cried.

Come inside, ya silly bugger, come inside

I thawt yer 'ad a bit more sense
Workin' fer a livin' so take my tip
Act a little strange and become a loon-a-tic
You gets three meals a regular
And two new suits a year
Thirteen bob a week
No wife and kids to keep

Come inside, ya silly bugger, come inside

In between verses I would say, 'My 'ead 'urts' and 'I ain't vewy clever but I can lift evy fings.'

We finished to uproarious laughter. The supply officer was doing the music hall come-to-order thing, tapping his little wooden gavel. I reached over and gave one all mighty smash with my big mallet, sending splinters of the hand-carved pieces into the crowd. The skipper was laughing so hard he had to be taken back to hospital to have his stitches fixed.

Oddball

This was the happiest ship that I had served on so far, with a little less focus on spit and polish and more on getting the job done. The skipper was down to earth and well respected by all.

The engineer officer was another person I respected tremendously. He had recognized early on that I was just here for the duration. My will had been broken to move ahead. My 'rap sheet' had been added to by every officer I had ever worked under. It must have been very colourful reading by now, but he left me alone. In fact, everyone knew to leave me alone. My nickname was Oddball, after the character in the movie *Kelley's Heroes* played by Donald Sutherland. I did my work and they basically let me be.

This was an old tub; there were only two ship's divers on board. The ship had a lot of leaks in the seawater cooling lines supplying the engines. The only way to fix this was to have someone bolt on a temporary cover plate outside on the ship's outer hull. That someone was always me. At all hours of the night in harbour, I was asked to don diving gear and listen for someone knocking on the hull from the inside to find the leaking seawater inlet.

I also volunteered to be ship's barber, so I was privy to all the scuttlebutt from the officers as to 'wots 'appening next' and 'where the hell were we going next.' This information was worth beer or favours! I also got to grow my hair a wee bit longer than most. The master at arms, the onboard military police, hated me and would have liked nothing more than to have me keel hauled.

We would be days out to sea, and on my time off I would

sneak into the NAAFI shop with a special knock. Red and I would practice new tunes while drinking what he called *breakages*. He was in charge of all the alcohol that came on board, including the wardroom liquors, which were banned from anyone below officer. As long as the top cap of the bottle was intact it was indeed breakage. Redmond had a knack of removing the cap and resealing it once we had finished the bottle, and then of course break the bottle. During our stay aboard, there were many such breakages of bottles. Returning to my bunk in the evening, the lads down in the mess always wondered how I could get half-corked when we were hundreds of miles out at sea.

This was a diesel ship. We had eight huge diesel engines in three separate engine rooms and four additional smaller diesel generators. We also made drinking water from seawater with steam evaporators down in one of the engine rooms. Some of the crew had learned that I could heat up cans of soup from one of the steam drains for a favour or two or a beer ashore. Red would also make a few shillings on the side selling them the soup. I got a bit fed up warming up soup on my watch after a while, so I showed a few of the lads how to do it themselves.

One lad came up to me in the very noisy engine room and said, 'It ate my soup, mate.' I went over to check and, sure enough, he had opened the wrong valves. Instead of heating up his tomato soup, his soup was now showing in my water level sight glass, which took a bit of explaining to the petty officer mechanic on his duty rounds.

UK Folkies

On our way back to the UK, we stopped off in the southwest of England in Cornwall. I was under punishment for something or other – by now that was situation normal, and part of my punishment was not being allowed civilian clothing ashore. I had

had another civvy suit made a few months back; this was my masterpiece. It was lime-green velvet in colour with bell-bottom trousers. The jacket had the wide lapels, as was the fashion at the time, but I had a gold trim around the edge of the lapel, which I thought was pretty groovy. I had Cuban heel cowboy boots and a bright yellow shirt with the collar turned over the lapels. And of course the sleeves of my shirt were also turned up over my jacket sleeves. I was the man!

No small wonder I was banned from wearing civvies. I had tried to go ashore with a hold-all bag with my colourful attire inside, but was caught by the officer of the day and sent below. Redmond had set up a gig at the local folk club; there was no way I was going to do it in uniform. It was summer and pretty warm. Later in the day I went up to catch the next liberty boat ashore. I had put on my suit underneath my uniform and topped it off with a large navy issue raincoat. I was a bit nervous when I was being inspected. The officer of the day asked me why was I wearing an overcoat. I nervously explained that I had heard on the weather forecast that there was going to be rain, mounds of sweat now dripping off my nose. I wasn't sure I had completely fooled him, but he eventually said, 'Okay, just go.' We had a brilliant time and met up with many like-minded folkies that just spurred us on.

The Lincoln was a Chatham-based ship in Kent, just southeast of London. We pulled up for a well-needed refit. This was in the very early seventies, and folk music in the UK was in its prime. You only had to pick up a local paper to see popular clubs advertised in various pubs. A large pub usually had a back room or second-floor room. Some larger, well-formed clubs even had a small hall.

Many much travelled folk stars toured the length and breadth of the UK, even going as far as Europe to perform. The setup was pretty much the same wherever you went. The main star would be advertised, and his fame determined the cost at the door, usually in the region of a pound or so. The evening would start with the resident band or singer, who would first explain who was going to play, and then they would start off the evening playing for fifteen or twenty minutes. They would then introduce the next three floor singers. These were generally people like me who had come early to get a set and were given free admittance for performing. The floor singers would get two to three songs. If you bombed you might get the hook, but if you did well you might get another song, or even a free drink. You never got heckled, and there was always silence while anyone was playing – that was the golden rule. After the floor singers, the main act would be introduced, who would play for forty-five minutes or so. Then there would be a break, or sometimes a raffle for music LPs. Then the whole evening would be repeated, this time of course with a different set of floor singers.

I introduced many shipmates to the folk clubs, who after the first time were as completely hooked as I was. It's difficult to explain the wondrous feeling of warmth and connection while listening to artists perform who usually exuded originality and character. All this while sitting in a room together with forty or fifty people in complete silence, and usually not more than a few rows away from the artist, seeing his or her every move and nuance, and hanging on every note that was masterfully played on their instrument. Allowing the story of the song to fill your every sense, this was an art in every meaning of the word. It sometimes completely overwhelmed me.

Some of the comedic acts also touring would literally have you rolling in your seat. When Red and I played together, comedy was our main theme. When I played on my own it was usually the complete opposite, very serious. There were a couple of excellent clubs in the area that Red and I frequented.

Red had purchased a button accordion and was taking some lessons from Gladys, an elderly retired teacher. Gladys was one of the many colourful characters we met and made friends with at the popular Gillingham Folk Club. She was quite matronly looking, slightly overweight, with short grey hair and rimmed glasses. Her easygoing way and warm smile caught your attention as soon as she spoke, allowing you to, quickly and with some guilt, swiftly change your opinion of her from her looks. I don't think she had ever married, and quite preferred to live the life of a spinster in her career as a lifelong academic. It was hard to guess her age, as she really didn't care too much about her looks or dress, but I would put her in her mid-to-late sixties at the time.

Gladys told us one day that the harmonies I sang with Red were, in fact, of a modal key and explained that some people think only in modal keys. She went on to explain that she had been doing some part-time research with mentally handicapped pupils at a local school. She had noticed some pupils just could not sing in tune with the rest of the choir. After testing them individually, she was astonished to realize that some of them were, in fact, hearing a kind of modal key.

I had not taken any formal training in music. Everything I had learned was from a few teach-yourself chord books. Like a lot of my contemporaries, I had learned through listening and finding chords or notes that complemented the songs. I also found very early on that tuning the guitar to various chords instead of the standard tuning, *E-A-D-G-B-E*, made things more interesting and would inevitably inspire me to write. I often wondered if this modal key thing Gladys talked about was my problem or, as I like to see it, my gift.

After Red had been transferred to *HMS Nubian* I spent many

evenings with Gladys talking mainly about music. Her untidy flat always seemed to be knee deep in music sheets, books, and musical instruments. Every conceivable shelf, table, or flat surface was spilling over with paper and open books. Even through all that confusion and mess, it felt very comfortable. She was such a dear old soul that I was comfortable enough at times to stray into more personal problems I needed answers to. How would I bridge this gap in my life between the yearning for adventure and this newfound music that touched my very being on the one hand, and my new wife and child waiting for me at a home that I longed for on the other? I yakked on so much about it that I once noticed she actually fell asleep.

Gladys enjoyed my music and songs that I had written so far, and made me promise never to go electric. By this she meant she wanted me to keep playing the acoustic guitar.

In a way, Gladys was my mentor in a time when I was very confused. Just talking with her helped me to face my demons. Through her I learned to sometimes use music as a cathartic practice. During many unhappy periods of my life I found playing music would take away the confusing and despairing thoughts, at least for a while, allowing me brief periods of rationality and therapeutic healing.

There is nothing more rewarding for a musician/writer/singer than, after much profound thought and usually some tears, putting together a jumble of words to a melody in some dark cellar or bedroom, then performing the song in front of similar minded people, and if all the planets are aligned and you indeed have five petals on your shamrock, your audience erupts into ecstatic pleasure. It has to be the closest thing to heaven!

Many musicians I have talked to or read about believed that the songs were always inside; you just need to be in the right place to bring them out. It is sometimes an uncanny and quite provoking process. After many months of trying to write something, one day a whole song appears right out of the blue. The words just flow, choruses drop into place, and the melody just keeps on getting better. *Wammo!* Right before your very eyes, in just a few hours your song is born. To have an experience like I just described cannot be valued in monetary terms.

Like some ancient Eastern wise person, and with very few words, Gladys set me on the rails and allowed me come to my own conclusions. I kept in contact with her for many years via Redmond, until he sadly informed me she had passed. I think she was probably the first stepping stone in my confidence building as I pushed forward to reach the personal musical rewards I have gained over the years.

I have always thought that this whole musical period of my life was, in some ways, the most rewarding. I have many warm memories of appreciating brilliant musicians on intimate evenings who inevitably went on to greater things. In those moments of clarity, those brief moments of connection when it seemed I was taken to a whole new level of existence, I was propelled forward in hopes that one day I just might have that gift to share my music and thoughts in the very same way – if I could keep the music pure.

The dope sub-lieutenant

The ship had sustained some damage to her asdic dome; this was a large rudder-like protrusion that was lowered from inside the ship through the ship's hull. To fix this, it would either need to have the ship put into dry dock, a very expensive procedure, or we could try and weld a new cowling underwater. Underwater (wet) welds are generally not good substitutes for dry welds, but the order was made to give it a try. I was given the task of setting up an underwater scaffold around the dome to allow a chief artificer who had his ship's diver qualification to perform the weld.

The ship was alongside the dock, and in between the ship and the concrete dock were the cats, large floating logs bolted together to form a dock bumper or spacer between the ship and the dock. They were around ten feet wide and twenty feet long with rubber bumper protection pads to prevent damage to the ship's side. Many ships were beside the dock wall, and these floating cats made a continuous line of floats. Scaffolding was erected on some of the cats for painting the ship's side and other maintenance. To my left was a continuous line of cats going up maybe three ships in length. To my right we had an opening where I could dive to get under the ship's hull.

I had been warned and I had heard many a sad story of divers who had gotten disoriented returning back to the surface. They had inadvertently gone the wrong way under the cats and eventually ran out of air, later found dead after floating up to the bottom of the cats. I wondered why they couldn't just follow their lifeline back to the surface to the dive tender. The four pulls and three bells, easily remembered by the 'Two's Company, Three's a Crowd' poem, would have your tender pull the lifeline, thereby gently pulling you to the surface, and of course giving you a direction to swim. So many things can go wrong during a dive, and the navy way is to always have a backup to everything.

I had a rather dozy sub-lieutenant, the only other diver on board, tending me. I realized very quickly that this chap was not on the ball and he kept letting my lifeline go slack. I was giving him signals and he was not replying, probably because the line was too slack or he was just plain bored. It was quite dark under the ship's hull beneath the cats. We were in a busy dockyard and the water was filthy, as usual. This was in an era when ships' toilets and oily bilges where flushed directly into the harbour. Therefore, most of my work was primarily by feel.

I was almost done and had equalized my set twice. It was time to come up! I had just a couple of things left to do, and I wanted to get it done on this dive, so I risked another couple of minutes. *Okay, I'm done,* I thought to myself. *Time to get out of this cold, black soup.* I gave the tender one pull to get his attention. I did not receive the standard one-pull reply. I repeated the procedure, but still no reply! I then gave him four pulls to tell him 'I'm coming up.' I was starting to get a little perturbed. My reserve air was probably not going to last much longer.

In the darkness, I quickly realized my line was slack as I head toward the cats. I started to gather up the slack lifeline and commenced pulling myself to the surface. *Boink!* My head hit the cat. He had let the lifeline get caught between the side of the ship and the cat, and it was now jammed tight. Rule number one: never cut your lifeline. I was eagerly pulling, trying to free the line from the cat. The other end of the lifeline was attached to my Sam Browne harness. I quickly noticed that I now had a whole pile of loose line that was now busy wrapping itself around me and tangling me up. I was thinking that I was going to run out of air soon. *I gotta do something or it's going to be curtains.*

I removed my knife from my ankle sheath and cut my lifeline. I took a calculated guess which way to go, and I eventually found the opening as I breathed the very last breath of air from the set. I looked up to see the dope sub-lieutenant holding the loose line going into the water on the dock. I stripped off my set and let it float away into the harbour. I scrambled onto the cat, removed my fins, and made my way up the ladder to the idiot staring into the sky holding a loose piece of rope. I grabbed him by the scruff of the neck and was about to pound him one when one of the helpers came to his rescue. I was calling him all the sons of bitches known to man, and he, with his toffee-nose accent, was telling me, 'I am going to get you court-martialed for threatening an officer.'

The engineer officer, a three-ring commander, came across the gangway and said, 'Shut it, Firth, before you get into more serious trouble.'

I was told to report to the engineer officer's wardroom after I was all cleaned up and changed. By now, I had taken a grasp of the situation I now found myself in and was pondering just where the hell I was going to end up this time. He explained to me that, under the situation, the officer involved had been told to drop all charges on the condition that nothing more was said. He had been stripped of his diver officer privilege, and would never be allowed to dive or be involved in diving while he was in the navy. I was still waiting with bated breath for my punishment. I had a weekend leave coming up and felt for sure I'd just screwed it!

The engineer officer was a pretty good egg. He was the only officer I had ever met in the navy with an accent. He had very obviously come from the London area. On the contrary, he surprised the hell out of me by congratulating me on the good job I was doing. The diving job was completed without a hitch. A ship's diver and PO from another ship helped us finish the work. The artificer diver even taught me how to do a decent underwater weld.

Redmond was sadly drafted to another ship as the refit got underway, and most of the ship's company were sent to *HMS Drake* navy base. I was billeted in the brand new Lord Mountbatten Building that he came to open a few weeks later. He seemed a nice old chap, and I was saddened when I heard he was murdered in Ireland by the IRA a few years later.

CHAPTER 32

The Druggy

I was on board the ship doing some work down below when I was paged to come to the gangway. I met two strange, what looked to me like civilians, because they both had long hair and crabby-looking jeans. They asked me my name and then quietly asked the officer of the day if they could speak to me privately. He seemed to know more about these strange chaps than I did and took us to a small, unoccupied room. Once there, they asked me questions about some other navy rating that they thought I might know. It was so strange. I kept asking them who they were and why they were asking me questions. After what seemed like ages of this bantering back and forth, they explained that they were undercover military police and that I had been linked to a person whom I had apparently smoked marijuana with. This supposedly occurred over a year ago in Portsmouth. A chill ran down my spine, but I still couldn't think or even remember who they were talking about. Maybe I was the wrong person anyway, so I decided to keep my cool and deny everything. They departed and I gasped a sigh of relief.

The very next day they returned! This time they had a purpose: my locker was completely cleaned out, even to emptying the dust from the bottom of the drawers. All of my clothes were packed into plastic bags and taken away for investigation. I tried to keep calm and protested what they were doing. These chaps kept telling me, 'You're a cool dude, Firth, but not cool enough. We are on to you, and you are going down.'

A week later they returned, explaining that they had found tiny particles of cannabis, what only amounted to milligrams, but enough to prove I was lying. I remained steadfast and still stuck to my story. I couldn't even think what the outcome would be if they knew I had smoked cannabis. I would probably be hung, drawn, and quartered, knowing the punishment system in the RN. I was then ordered to appear at the military police office ashore the following morning.

I sat in the waiting room with a bunch of other chaps. We were all wearing our number eight working gear. Strangely, so it seemed, everyone had a beard like me and we were all about the same height. The penny hadn't completely dropped yet, but I was starting to feel very uneasy with the usual sense of impending doom!

We were all made to line up shoulder to shoulder. My heart was pumping like mad when through the door came a lad I recognized. He came straight up to me, put his hand on my shoulder, and with a pitying expression on his face, said, 'Sorry.' To which a screaming master at arms shouted, 'Shut it, you're in enough trouble!'

The two undercover officers were grinning from ear to ear as I was dragged out to another room. They then asked me to 'fess up.' It was relatively easy now that I knew who they were talking about. I had gone on board *HMS Bulldog*, a hydrographic survey ship that was tied up alongside the *Brereton,* and I had met up with some like-minded chaps who enjoyed music. I struck up a friendship with one of the lads, and ashore one evening he pulled out a joint and we had a smoke. That, in its complete entirety, was it. The *Brereton* had sailed the very next day. I never set eyes on the lad again.

They asked me a whole bunch more questions and if I knew of anyone else. I said no, and lied that it had been the first and last time I had smoked pot! Okay, so I fibbed, and I probably won't go to heaven now.

I was a bit mystified as to where the milligrams came from that they had supposedly found. This one lad had done more damage to just about every person he'd met and smoked with in the navy. In order to reduce his punishment, fifteen men went down with him. I got busted and lost my hook. I was now right back to where I had started six years prior. I really didn't need the loss of pay either! I was only just keeping my family back home on the poor navy wages as it was. The worst of this whole situation I now found myself in was that I was listed as a druggy. For the next year and a half I served on the *Lincoln*, I literally couldn't go for a shit without the master at arms peering over the door. In harbour, the officer of the day came by my bed almost every night to shine his flashlight in my eyes and take a little sniff for drugs.

I asked the skipper if I could buy myself out, and unbelievably he tried to convince me to stay. Both he and the engineer officer said it would all blow over; I would get my leading hand rate back again in two years. I had a lot to offer and the navy would be losing out if I left. He refused my request the first time, so I said as politely as I could, 'Sir, what would you like me to do before you allow me to leave, because I can be real bad!'

He bade me to try to behave myself and to spend a little time thinking about it. In one more year I would be twenty-three, so I would have served two-thirds of my 'man's time.' I would then qualify to buy myself out; I just had to save 150 pounds. My pay was less than twenty-five pounds a week, and most of it was going to my responsibilities, my wife and child at home. It was going to be hard work saving the money.

There was no reason for me to continue in the RN. I had enjoyed the travelling and the camaraderie, even some of the work, but I had vastly outgrown being treated like a naughty child. At sixteen I had seen and done more than most men had ever experienced. I was far from being a boy, and for the most part I had been denied any childhood. I asked again months later, and this time the skipper reluctantly accepted.

I was home on a weekend leave. It was a Saturday evening; Marilyn was out on the town with her sister. I had my headphones on listening to some wonderful music and I was probably a little high. I couldn't afford to buy marijuana, but every now and again someone would give me a little when I was home. A loud knock came on the door; it was Biscuit, my old friend. I knew he had joined up years ago, but we had never bumped into each other in the navy or rarely been home at the same time. It was the same with Birdie, who was in the fleet air arm.

What a surprise! He had grown in height and had acquired a much larger personality, in that he was seemingly full of spunk and vinegar. From the conversation, he was definitely a navy man. He couldn't stop talking about all the things he had done. Admittedly, I was a little envious. He had done a lot of the things I would have liked to, as he had joined up as a clearance diver. He'd taken apart bombs in the Suez, and you name it. He had even been a part of a demanding rescue operation when a ferry had sunk in UK that had gained much national publicity.

Although I was suitably impressed, after all the things I had gone through over the last few years, I was in no mood to listen to stories about the wonderful navy. I think at the time he must have certainly felt that he was looking at a broken person, the same as I felt years earlier when I saw him ashen faced and working in a cotton mill. The proverbial shoe was now on a different foot.

We said our cheerios, and as he departed I was sure we would probably never see each other again. We were in two totally different worlds.

Ah! But life's wibbly-wobbly ways would prove me wrong.

CHAPTER 33
Spud Fight at the OK Corral

After the mini refit, the ship went on fishery patrol off Iceland. Apparently the Icelanders had indiscriminately decided to increase their fishing zone. These were the popular fishing grounds of many nations, Britain being one that had been there for many years. It had turned nasty when the Icelandic gunboats *Aegir* and *Thor* started to cut trawlers' nets with many dangerous maneuvers. The British tabloids aptly named it 'The Cod Wars.'

Many navy frigates were dispatched to help thwart these gunboats, usually working in pairs. The navy frigates circled the fishing fleets, giving them protection, staying between the gunboats and the trawlers. The small gunboats with icebreaking hulls were much more maneuverable than the large frigates and had on a few occasions even opened fire on the trawlers. One trawler had been holed below the water line.

We had been circling the fleet with the *Aegir* close on our starboard beam. His normal maneuver was to go immediately astern, and before we could follow suit, he coasted in behind us into the fishing fleet to do his damage. Our skipper wasn't going to let him get away with this after his second successful attempt had made a laughingstock out of us. This time he ordered the ship to go *full astern*, a dangerous engine maneuver on any ship and usually used only in emergency. The *Aegir* seemingly didn't care, and rammed us amidships, taking out most of our radio room with it. The hole was above water so we weren't about to sink. With its tough bow, the *Aegir* carried on into the fleet to again wreak havoc. We had to limp back to Chatham dockyard for a very expensive refit to fix the damage.

The well-respected skipper, Commander David Howard, was a bit of a character and he wasn't going to take any of this lying down. He had two railway lines menacingly protruding out of the stern end of the ship fixed to the quarterdeck. Someone had cheekily put up a London Underground sign saying 'Lincoln Junction.'[2]

This time out, the *Thor* had been trying to out maneuver us for a few days, and every time he came close enough he was unceremoniously bombarded with spuds. At one point the skipper came out of his bridge, obviously pissed as many spuds came his way, but he was now brandishing a revolver. I was one of the many spud throwers, and at the sight of the gun I never saw so many men trying to get down a small hatchway all at once. In anger, the *Thor* then tried his astern maneuver. The skipper bided his time until he had his foe with his weakened underbelly, his amidships, directly astern. The *Lincoln* lurched as the ship went full astern, puncturing the *Thor*. There was a loud creaking and groaning noise as we almost lifted the *Thor* out of the water. The order was then made to go ahead, and the railway spears were pulled out, showing two gaping holes in her hull. The *Thor* limped back into harbour with her tail between her legs.

Diplomatic relations with Iceland were threatened to be broken and the admiralty was wise to remove the *Lincoln* and our illustrious skipper from the brawl. The British tabloids made a

---

2 A picture of the incident can be found at http://www.forcesreunited.org.uk/forum/forumimageresizer.aspx?src=/forum/ uploads/18460/Lincoln 1974 lincoln junction.

meal out of this intelligence, and our skipper and the *Lincoln* returned to shore to a hero's welcome.

On one of these excursions to Iceland we came close by *HMS Nubian* that I knew Redmond was now serving on. He was on the forward deck. The news of me losing my hook had obviously reached him, and with a sad face he mimed me having my hook badge removed from my shirtsleeve, to which I nodded.

Not more than a month later we were in port storing ship, as was his ship, somewhere in Northern Scotland. He informed me that he had made a swap with our NAAFI manager, and he would be coming back to our ship. It was wonderful news! Things had been a bit too quiet without the crazy Red around.

Whether it was because the ship had done good or the skipper's influence, the next few months were filled with interesting runs ashore in the islands off Northern Scotland, Kolding in Denmark, and Den Helder in the Netherlands.

I don't know how I had managed it, but I was chosen as the fourth person on a weekend skiing trip to Aviemore in Scotland. The skipper drove the car with a couple of officers. We pitched the tent and decided, because of inclement weather, to find somewhere to eat in town. It was the first evening after a great day skiing. It was the first time I had ever tried skiing, and I thought I had picked it up pretty good. I had met a bunch of people and stayed in the bar until late. The weather had turned into wet rain, and I didn't fancy getting soaked finding my way back to our campsite. The lads I had met told me they had a spare bunk in their room, so I spent a warm night listening to the horrendous rain outside. In the morning I made it out to the campsite. The tent had collapsed in the middle of the night. The officers were soaked from head to toe and were in no mood to hear what a great evening I had had.

CHAPTER 34
Marilyn's Introduction to Red

I was home on a two-week leave. On a Saturday morning we were awoken by a loud knocking on our door. 'Who the hell is that?' my wife asked.

The front door opened (it was rarely locked) and in came Red, singing his head off. 'Come on, ya lazy buggers, get out of bed!' he shouted up the stairs.

Marilyn looked at me with shocked eyes, and I said, 'Oh, it's ... ah ... it's okay, it's only Red.'

I had already told her many tales about my crazy shipmate so she knew who he was, but what was he doing here? I had always found it so difficult, and still do to some extent, to explain my Jekyll-and-Hyde life. At home she knew me as a husband and a father, and whatever came with that. I didn't mix very well with the locals. In fact, if I ever tried to join in a conversation with someone about something I had done or somewhere I had been, I was immediately an outcast, almost ostracized. Conversations between most men in my local town were based on who had won the football or cricket match. With gossip on who was screwing whom, sometimes it was worse than some women. None of these subjects was something I was even remotely interested in.

Even though sea time is mind-numbingly boring, and in

some ways lonely, you always knew the men around you and whom you could trust. We were all thrust into situations where you just had to find your way or suffer the consequences. When I think back to some of my shipmates, when things got bad we all somehow managed to make fun of the situation. When things were good, we could look back and feel proud that we had pulled ourselves through it together and now it was time to party. And party we did!

Marilyn nervously came down the stairs and I introduced her to Red, who was comfortably making himself a coffee. He then came bouncing over like he had known her for years. Two hours later we were having whisky toddies (hot water, honey, and whisky). Four hours later we were in the pub and didn't return home until the early hours of the following morning, having had a thoroughly good day out. Wherever we went, Redmond the extrovert made friends by singing songs and telling jokes, the ultimate party animal. She thought he was fun, but was glad when he left the following day. He came in like a tornado and left quietly.

CHAPTER 35
De-Mobbing

A few months later I was in *HMS Nelson* barracks in Portsmouth handing in all of my navy kit. We had to do a three-day mini course on how to leave the navy and what to expect in civvie street. For some older hands, they had to do a one-week course to unscramble their brains and prepare for their freedom. These men had been told when to get up, when to eat, when to sleep, even when to take a shit, for the last twenty-six or thirty years. They had only done what they had been told to do. They had been brainwashed into what is okay and what is not okay. On the down side, no one from now on was going to look after them when they were sick, unless they had family. They had to find a job that was useful and would pay them to make a living to feed themselves and their families – if they still had families. They would inevitably wake up in the same bed in the same house and town, probably for their rest of their lives. They would, as I am doing right now, wonder if anyone else feels like they do now. They will yearn for camaraderie and the good times that maybe won't be there in their new lives.

It was very strange and coincidental to find Brian Reid, the lad I had joined up with. He was there de-mobbing, as were two or three other friends I had known well during my time in the

RN. Out of the twenty or so men, I knew almost a third. We were all buying ourselves out. I had served almost eight years, and unbelievably I still had to buy myself out. I had looked forward to this moment for so long. To me, the last few years had felt like a prison sentence. What exactly had I done wrong?

I remember waking up in the morning feeling weak with a strange sensation, almost like an anti-climax. Time and time again I kept imagining myself walking out of the gates. I was looking back at myself in a strange dream world.

Brian and Rosemary were still happily married and had a baby girl. He was playing guitar and singing in a country and western band, and was apparently doing quite well. I shook his hand and wished him, Rose, and the baby the best. We promised to stay in touch. I never saw or heard from them again. I remembered my mother's letter about lifelong friends.

When the moment came to walk out of those gates, I reminded myself how I hated everything about the navy and how it had cheated me – eight long years and I was leaving with nothing. Even in the last few days I was made to feel like a complete and utter failure. What terrible thing had I done to deserve this?

In this strange dream world I was experiencing, there was also an awful niggling feeling that I could not understand that still wanted to hold me back. I was horrified to think I might even get to the gate and turn back. It was like an invisible barrier I had to cross.

When the moment came and I stepped through, I felt nothing, absolutely nothing. I didn't jump for glee like I thought I would. I didn't turn around and give them the finger or even moon the officer of the day. I just quietly walked away, caught my train north, and wondered what lay ahead. How would my life unfold from now on?

Civvie Street

I arrived home still bewildered, as I was for the next week or so. One moment I was ecstatically happy, the next I felt lost and disjointed. Fortunately, I had to put all that aside quickly and start in earnest to find a job. What could I possibly do? I had searched my soul; I was twenty-three and I had a family to keep. I applied at a couple of machine shop factories, and was asked the same question over and over – where are your qualifications? You don't have a trade? You have to join a union; sign here to agree. I felt like I just wanted to stay away from anything to do with a union. I didn't want anyone telling me when I could work and when I couldn't. I had just left a job that wanted to rule my life. I wanted to be a free agent and be judged on what and how I produced. Sure, I could join the merchant navy. I might be starting with something already under my belt, but did I really want to go to sea again? No sir, I never wanted to feel that loneliness again, constantly missing home and my loved ones. I contemplated working in a music shop or even a diving shop. No, I didn't see myself being happy with that for very long. So I just kept my eye on the jobs column in the local newspaper, hoping that something might catch my eye.

I had thought briefly about getting a job on the oil rigs off Scotland as a diver, but it seemed divers were being killed left, right, and center. It seemed every other week there was another death in the newspapers or on the news on TV. I had heard stories of American companies paying off navy divers in Plymouth and Portsmouth to leave the navy to work offshore.

Valley Refrigeration and Shopfitting

Within a couple of weeks of leaving the navy I took a job with a business in Rawtenstall called Valley Refrigeration and Shopfitting. It was in the business of delivering and installing large commercial refrigerators. They had qualified and unionized fridge mechanics doing the actual installations. The shopfitting side of the company did the grunt work, delivering and placing these heavy fridges. They had four laborers/joiners (carpenters), including me, and one foreman. When I started with the company we did some minor shopfitting, installing shelving systems and counters in small corner stores and minor supermarkets. My basic pay was not much more than my miserable navy pay, hardly twenty-five pounds a week after deductions. After a month, they bought me a set of woodworking tools. Eventually I managed to buy an old second-hand Austin minivan, which I used to take my tools back and forth to the main office instead of taking the bus.

They had two trucks and we were set up in two teams of two men, unless we had a really heavy fridge to deliver, then we would all go. After the first few months I found that I was enjoying working with my hands. They had a large garage out back, and I was shown by the foreman how to build cabinets, checkout bays, and laminate counters. I liked staying back in the garage on my own building stuff very much. My days went quickly and I went home feeling like I had done an honest day's work.

In the next few months, the owner, Geoff, expanded more into the shopfitting side. We became very busy with lots of overtime. When the stores closed in the evenings or weekends, that was when we went to work. I didn't mind the extra cash, so I put in every hour I could. I noticed that my wage packet was somewhat reduced compared to the other men doing the same hours. I was told my tax bracket seemed to be the culprit. The owner's wife explained this was not her doing. The tax office had me on an emergency tax bracket. I would have to go to the local tax office to sort it out.

The tax office explained that I had been on emergency tax

for almost the last four years, coinciding with the date I was married. When I ask them to explain emergency tax, I was told it was basically the highest tax bracket until someone told them different. When I got married and took on two dependents right away, someone in the naval pay department had decided that until they knew more information I was put on emergency tax and then conveniently forgotten about. I said, 'Oh, well. Okay, how can I claim that money back?'

'Sorry, sir' they replied, 'it cannot be claimed back, and before we change your tax bracket, you will have to fill out these (many) forms.'

Wonderful. I learned an important lesson that day, which basically goes, 'A bird in the hand is worth two in the bush.' In future years I was almost always self-employed. The taxman can come to me at the end of the year and ask for his taxes, and I shall employ the best accountant I can afford – fuck you!

Although I spent a lot of time at work, I was home most evenings. Marilyn and I were happy for the most part. We did have many arguments, but they were all basically about money – usually the lack of it.

Dominic was a little toddler now and he just seemed to be part of me. We decided it was time that I adopted him and gave him my name. I couldn't even think of another person being his father. I just wanted to blank all those thoughts out of my head. She was my wife and he was my kid, and that was that! We put in for the adoption, and a social welfare officer came to see us and asked if we had told Dominic yet that I wasn't his biological father. I said, 'No, I don't want to tell him. I am his dad!' She agreed that under the circumstances, because of his age, that it was okay for now, but sooner or later we would have to tell him. The official adoption went through and we changed his name.

The social worker came to see us pretty much every year.

We were also trying for a child, but so far it wasn't to be, and I was getting a little anxious. I was starting to wonder if some of the weird and wonderful stuff I'd done in the navy with chemicals, radiation, or even diving had had a detrimental effect and I was now shooting blanks. Somebody said, 'Hey, start drinking Mackeson cream ale. That'll put lead in yer pencil, lad.'

CHAPTER 36
We're Having A Baby

I had been home just over a year and was regularly drinking Mackeson. I didn't honestly believe it would make any difference, but hey, no harm done. Marilyn gave me the wonderful news one evening that she was pregnant. I could have danced in the trees I was so happy.

We still lived in the rental council house close to Marilyn's mum and her sister right across the street. I'm sure she felt at ease knowing her family was so close, but I thought that renting was money going down the drain. I wanted to try and buy a house, a fixer upper, anything, but it would be ours and our investment would increase over time. We had to do something to try and get ahead. Again, many arguments were had over that to add to our financial woes.

Friday nights were our nights out together, if I wasn't working. It seemed we had to watch every penny. I could never figure out how all our so-called out of work friends managed to go out every night, and sometimes in the afternoons, getting well and truly plastered. We knew very few friends who actually officially worked. Most were on the dole (social security), or call it what you like. To me, the answer came in the form of all the damn deductions for this and that in my pay packet, and it was getting worse. I was starting to get very annoyed that this country was helping to keep people out of work. What was the point? If you were smart enough you could draw more money from the government than most of these people could ever possibly earn. To top that, we knew most of them had jobs on the side, getting paid under the table, so they were getting a double whammy. We would all sit down in the pub on a Friday night having a good old laugh.

I remember one chap said to me, 'You're working too hard, you know. Top Cemetery is full o' people like you.' Then he added, 'You know, yer a long time dead, mate.'

We seemed to be struggling but slowly getting ahead when heartless thieves stole my van from right in front of our house as we slept. All the tools I had managed to collect over the months to do my job were in the back of the van. I could have wept. Marilyn was getting close to having our child. We were putting every penny away for a deposit on a house. I thought, *Damn it, I'm cleaned out again.*

I managed to buy an old clunker of a van to get me to work, and I borrowed some tools to allow me to do my job until I could afford to buy new ones. I thought the insurance for the stolen car would come soon, but six weeks later, to my dismay, they found my minivan. It was beaten to death and barely ran. The insurance bailed out on me, the bastards! Lesson two: Insurance is definitely not to be trusted – beware!

On a cool morning on February 11, 1975, Marilyn's water broke. I went into panic mode; she was as cool as a cucumber. We had practiced what was going to happen and Marilyn had set aside all her needs in a bag. She was organized. I eventually got her out to the car after much prodding, and with her saying, 'Relax, it's okay.' I helped her into the van. The old clunker decided that of all days it didn't want to work today. I tried to start it, but the battery was dead.

'Can you get out and push, dear,' I stupidly asked without thinking. She gave me a nasty look. 'Oh, sorry, silly me. Okay, I'll get out,' I said, flustered.

I was trying to push start it down the street. Thank God it was a mini! I had this horrible thought that I might not be able to jump back into the car and my pregnant wife would sail on down the hill on her own with nobody in the driver's seat! Nope, she was still calmly sitting there. She was confident I would somehow manage. I skipped and dived into the van, one leg still dangerously hanging out of the car, and it started. 'Okay, love, we're on our way.'

I arrived at the hospital, and parking was sparse. I found a spot close to a wall, got out of the car, and ran round to help her. *Ah, shit!* I'd parked so close to the wall that she couldn't open her door. I received a strange look and then a stern, 'What are you doing?'

I jumped back in the car. 'Oh, sorry, love,' I said, trying to keep the utmost of self-control. I tried to start the engine but the battery was still flat! All kinds of profanities came from my mouth that I didn't know I had in me. I didn't dare to look at her. I knew I would get the you-really-are-a-stupid-idiot look. But no, she was still amazingly composed. I exited the car again and noticed some spectators had cruelly gathered on the curb to watch the show. I pushed the car out into the middle of the road, and just left it there. I quickly helped her out and we hastily made our way into the hospital.

She gently explained to me that she didn't want me to be with her during the birth and would like me to go home until I received a call. For a moment I wondered if it was my actions so far today. Did she not want me around where there were sharp instruments? She was being incredibly brave and wanted to stay in that frame of mind. She went on to explain that if I were there she thought she might weaken and lose some control. As much as I wanted to be there, I accepted her wishes. I respected her tenacity and felt a deep love for her. She was going through all of this for us, and I just wanted everything to go okay.

After a difficult birth, later that day I became the father of a beautiful little girl. An extremely tired Marilyn, looking like she had just experienced ten rounds in a boxing ring, told me to go look for a very long red baby with a loud cry. 'You can't mistake her,' she said.

With my nose pressed up against the glass window to the nursery, I knew exactly who she was talking about. All the other tiny quiet babies were laying there looking cozy. My little girl looked like she barely fit the length of her cot, and indeed she was quite red and screaming the place down. A great big chunk of my heart invisibly passed through the glass toward her. I knew from this day forth I would never be the same again. I also knew seeing my child for the first time would be a wonderful experience, but nobody could have possibly warned me of the surge of emotions now washing through my very core. My whole meaningless life had just started to take shape. It seemed I had been climbing an impossible, steep cliff for eternity, and my fingernails had only just this one magnificent moment found a purchase. I stood there having my epiphany when the nurse came to take her to her mum.

At the bedside, Marilyn asked me if I wanted to hold her. She was surprised, and probably a little confused, when I declined. She was not a small baby at nine pounds, thirteen ounces, but to me she still looked so fragile, and beside her mum she was very content. In comparison, I felt clumsy and a little unworthy. She was so precious that I didn't want to risk contaminating her with the bad karma I had been experiencing lately. I later reluctantly had to leave to pick Dominic up from his gran's house. I felt like I was walking on a soft fluffy cloud of contentment for the rest of the day, hardly believing what had just occurred.

Probably for the first time in my life, my heart wasn't pessimistic, wondering what could possibly go wrong next. On the contrary, I felt like I could move mountains; good things, no, great things, could just as easily happen. I now had another big reason to try and make something out of my life.

Marilyn did not want to name our baby until it was born, for fear of bad luck. I guess we were both feeling the same bad karma thing. We had played around with some names, but had never really decided on one. The little bracelet on her arm showed her as baby Marilyn. At the hospital we came up with the name Michaella. I had decided on the actual spelling when I went to register the name. I knew I would be happy when the time came, but I never knew I could feel as happy as I was right then. Every time I saw my baby girl, I had to prick myself to believe that this was actually happening in my life.

Marilyn had had a difficult birth and was quite ill for many months. She was having a hard time coping on her own and asked if I could take some time off work. My boss was particularly helpful and gave me a week off with pay. After the first week, and Marilyn still not ready to be on her own, I told him I needed more. He never hesitated, but suggested I go and ask for social assistance for as long as I liked. I had never been on any kind of assistance except while we were growing up. Remembering the embarrassment in my youth, I never wanted to be in that situation again. Being too proud wasn't going to help the desperate situation we found ourselves in, so I relented. My boss said that he would keep paying my wages, and when I returned the assistance would pay him back for his losses.

I had three weeks off, hardly enough for my sick wife. The

assistance reimbursed him for his losses. Being a little green in asking for assistance, I had mistakenly told the truth. Little did I know the assistance money had to be paid back! It was deducted out of my pay over the next three months. So much for assistance! Lesson 3: Look after yourself and yours, because no other fucker will.

CHAPTER 37
Our Very Own House

After much hard work between the two of us, Marilyn had taken a job at a local school in the kitchen making dinners. We eventually came up with enough money for a deposit on a small two-up and two-down street house at the other end of town. Forty-nine South Shore Street was a long street facing some lovely hills. The stone houses were built over a hundred years ago as homes for the people working at the local factories below at the bottom of Grane Road. It was going to need considerable work to modernize, but I was willing and ready to do whatever. This was our home as long as we could pay the mortgage.

Nobody had showed me how to renovate. I had learned a bit from the lads at work (some of them were qualified joiners), but most jobs I just figured out how to do myself. I knocked out walls, not sure if the house was going to collapse and take the rest of the street with it! The old kitchen was stripped out, and I built cabinets and counter tops; we now had a perfectly modern kitchen. I purloined some flat stone from an old farmhouse roof to clad the chimneybreast fieldstone style, and installed a gas fire with back boiler. We now had hot water.

Even though the walls of this house were eighteen inches

thick with stone, it still allowed the damp to seep through the walls, which I never did get a good handle on, as much as I tried. All in all, after a lot of toil and trouble and living in rubble and plaster dust, we eventually had a comfortable home.

I had mistakenly left some finishing plaster powder on my workbench on a piece of plastic paper in the small backyard. Marilyn was out and I was also trying to look after the mischievous Michaella, who was now a toddler. I was trying to get some work done on our house. I came out to the back yard to find Michaella covered from head to foot with the white powder, her little eyes peering out at me. 'Da Da' was all she had to say. She has always known how to twist me around her little finger – and usually get me in trouble from time to time.

Marilyn's night out with her sister was usually Saturday night. Dominic was playing out and I had fallen asleep on the couch. I awoke to Michaella tugging at me with a pair of scissors in her hand. Lord knows where she had got the scissors from, but as soon as my eyes cleared I was shocked to see she had managed to cut her long beautiful brown hair from her fringe all the way back on one side of her head. I was in deep shit. When her mum got home, I never heard the last of it.

CHAPTER 38
Feeling Restless

When I did have time to think in the very busy life that seemed to consume my every waking moment, I was starting to realize there were things I sorely missed. At twenty-six years old, I had achieved more than most men almost twice my age in my local town. Not one to blow my own trumpet, but by the time I was seventeen I had been halfway around the world! I'd had so many adventures and witnessed so much camaraderie, my new life paled by comparison. Is this what it was going to be like from now on? Working my fingers to the bone and listening to endless talk about football? My big world had now shrunk to this little village of Haslingden.

Socially, I always felt like an outcast with most of the locals. Gathered in the local pub on a Friday night, it was rare for me to get into much conversation. Most of the conversation was based on gossip. On rare occasions, the conversation sometimes developed into subjects I felt I could join, based on my experiences. I would immediately notice the strange looks coming my way, almost like I had grown two heads. I eventually figured it to be for one of two reasons: either they felt I was full of bullshit and lying to my back teeth, or they felt intimidated. *Who the hell does this guy think he is with his smart arse talk?* Feeling ostracized, most of the time I ended up drinking my fill and then staggering home to a Saturday morning hangover.

On the other hand, I dearly loved my home life. We still had our woes, but I'm sure no more than other couples trying to get ahead. I loved to be with my loving wife and children, even for a few hours in the evenings or on weekends. Taking long walks over the hills with my kids and dog made me feel whole and complete.

John Merchant, the landlord of the Commercial Hotel, had travelled and done a bit in his time and he kind of took a shine to me. He fictitiously thought of himself as the country gentleman, a retired army officer type. I never questioned him on it, because he always came across to me as being a genuine friend with a heart of gold.

During my time in the navy when I was on the *Brereton*, we ferried young officers back and forth from Dover to Le Havre in France for a month or so. I had volunteered to be tour guide, and I had developed quite a taste for red wine – the cheap stuff! At a few shillings a bottle, it certainly looked like a good deal to me. I had smuggled a hold-all full of this cheap stuff on Her Majesty's ship and brought it home. Marilyn noticed I was disappearing in the afternoons into the long grass behind our house with cheese and crackers. Then I would blatantly lie about the missing bottles in the cupboard. It was at this point that I realized this stuff was taking a hold of me.

Not long after, I found that the English pints of beer just weren't doing it for me, so I would ask John if he had some red wine he could sell me by the bottle, as by the glass it could get expensive. It was a very unusual request at the time for the local beer-scuppering English lads. Having given up trying to get on with the local lads, and having never been one to care about being popular, I felt even more ostracized and out of place sitting alone at my own small table with a bottle of red wine and a single glass, as if I was sitting in an outdoors café on the Avenue des Champs-Elysees. I tried my best to ignore the stares and snide whispering from the bar.

Sweet old John, a wine connoisseur in his time, mistakenly thought I was becoming an aficionado of the *Riojo* vino. He might have just handed over a cheap bottle of plonk, as at the time I would have been quite happy to slurp it back. Instead, he took me down to his dusty, well-stocked wine cellar to choose a few choice bottles of God knows what. After everyone had left the bar, we would graciously sit back and drink copiously on expensive wines from the vineyards of blah blah blah in France and talk about worldly things. He would bring out tasty cheeses and his delicious homemade pickles.

Over the years, he taught me how to taste and enjoy a good bottle of red to the fullest. At least once a month, if I was home, I ventured into his very busy pub, and over the crowds at the bar I would hear, 'Kevin, wine later this evening?' I was privileged he had taken the time to get to know me.

In that period of my life, John was like a small oasis in an isolated desert. I was trying so hard to be a good provider, a dutiful husband and father. Sometimes I thought I was getting into the routine and starting to see what I had to do to keep everyone happy. But this burning ambition I seemed to have been born with just kept getting in the way, making me feel unfulfilled. I had had my fun. Now it was time to settle down to business, I tried to convince myself. Sometimes, though, I felt that I was slowly falling into a rut. The Saturday morning hangovers were becoming a little too frequent – that is, if I wasn't working.

Life's wibbly-wobbly way came to the rescue once again.

My ol' shipmate comes to the rescue

One rare sunny summer's day, I was alerted to a loud knocking on our front door. I was totally gobsmacked to see my old shipmate, Mr. Redmond O'Connel, standing there in person as if he had appeared out of a magician's hat. I had been out of the navy a couple of years and he was a sight for sore eyes.

Thinking back, in some ways, the last years in the navy had felt almost like a prison sentence. My only crime had been trying to deny a contract I had signed at the tender age of fifteen. I had experienced years of silly punishments for petty military crimes. I was obviously not suited to be an underdog, and my intelligence was constantly being insulted. Through all of those lows there were spikes of many wonderful memories. During obscure thoughts, I wondered if those things really happened to me. Was I the main actor in this play, or just some figment of my overactive imagination?

Redmond had also left the navy and had come home to Lancashire. His mother and sister still lived in Clitheroe. He had come out with a bit of a nest egg from savings and from wherever he could make a few shillings. He had managed to buy a house with many rooms that he then rented out. He was also selling kitchen cabinets and whatever else he could get his hands on. He lived about fifteen miles from me in Nelson. Marilyn was not too enthralled at the idea of him showing up out of the blue, as she knew we could get into a whole lot of mischief together.

We started to play music together again and called ourselves Clog Butty. Moriarty was sorely missed, but we were now trying our hand at Lancashire folk music. We got a few gigs here and there. The money wasn't anything to write home about, but we had a lot of fun. Comedy was our main theme again.

Since leaving the navy, I had gone to the occasional local folk club here and there over the last couple years. That had given me my out, as it were. There I could meet like-minded people and speak the language of music. Most of the clubs were staunchly traditional, where my type of contemporary singer/songwriter material wasn't as well received. But I did well on occasion and opened for a couple of big bands, and I did a little radio. I was still experimenting with writing songs, but since I had left the navy, they were few and far between. For the most part, my music was also becoming a distant memory. With Red around, I felt a new surge. We did a little traditional Lancashire folk music, but I always managed to throw in a couple of my songs. I used to wear clogs that had steel toecaps. This was Lancashire when all was said and done. It rains all the friggin' time and my toenails would go rusty. He would, of course, try to embarrass me during our act, showing the crowds that not only did I have holes in my socks, I also had rusty toes!

For a time I wondered what it would be like to tour, to live the life of a musician. Maybe that is what I needed, to be appreciated by being on a stage. I knew there was something missing and that I would not be happy until I found it. I envied some of the professionals we had met, but I knew most of them didn't have the commitments I had taken on. Marilyn would always ground me. 'This is your life you have chosen, and that's all there is to it.'

I knew even without Marilyn's persuasive influence that I had made an important choice. As much as music filled my soul and gave me so much, I didn't want to be a starving musician. My family always came first. I had been poor once and I knew what that felt like. I wasn't going to go back to that. I always admired the stamina of the many successful musicians that made that tough decision and stuck it out. There have been times when I regretted that decision, but overall when I think of the other things I have accomplished, I know it was the right decision.

After I disappeared for two days, things got a bit tense with Red and Marilyn, to the point he was banned from our house.

She temporarily left me and went to her mother's. I knew I was in big trouble, and deservedly so. She eventually forgave me and told me what her mother had said. 'You know, Kevin works so hard. He's just a bit of a binge drinker. If he goes off the rails every now and again, well, that's okay, as long as he doesn't do it all the time.' God bless her socks. I was saved again, but I had promised to cool my heels and get back on track to becoming a dutiful husband once again.

Shortly after that, Red informed me he was leaving the UK. He had previously formed a relationship with an Australian girl, who had just divorced one of our navy friends in Portsmouth that I had originally introduced him to. Redmond was a confirmed bachelor, but I think he had fallen for her lock, stock, and barrel. She was indeed a beautiful girl, but she eventually left him and went back to Australia. He was not a happy camper after that. I went to his house to see him off. He was leaving for California. All he had was his guitar, his button accordion, a hold-all with a few clothes, and a couple hundred quid in his pocket. I knew Red would not return. He was looking for his dream, and like myself, he had seen enough of the world to know there were more adventures and opportunities to be had elsewhere.

I had made my bed, as it were, and had to put all that behind me. It was time to buckle down. The brief couple of years while Red was around, it was a tonic to my being whenever we got together. This close friend, who kept popping into my life, gave me reminders of something to reach for, and now he was leaving again. Each time he appeared, he allowed me to escape into a world of song and mirth, camaraderie and deep friendship. It dawned on me at that very moment of his leaving that I thought I could never love another man the way I loved my brother. We said our farewells and I drove away with a heavy heart and tears in my eyes. I stopped at a pub on the way home, had a beer, and quietly wished him well.

Restless Hearts

That dark cold night so many years ago
When you moved on
Plane took you away
America you were bound
Leaving behind all these gray faces
Took your guitar and your squeeze box too
Alone I had another beer and wished you well

You and I, we met far from Lancashire
On a different shore
In a different time
Two kids with a laugh and a song
We raised hell, Oh God what a time we had
No worries what tomorrow will bring
For the day is where we were

(Chorus)
Boats and trains and planes
We're always movin' on
Restless hearts
A curse to all we love
We're always movin' on
Restless hearts

Leaving home to sad farewells
So many times
It don't change
Still breaks your heart

You're the only one to take your path
It's a scary road but you take it anyway
Somewhere along the way I caught this train
And somehow through this fog I can't get off

(Repeat Chorus)

—Kevin Firth, 5th February 2009

Six weeks later he called me on the phone. He was at a party in someone's big house in LA. He had their phone in a washroom calling long distance. He needed money! I wired him some money, which he duly returned a few months later. We stayed in touch over the years, but it was over twenty years before I saw him in person again. Each time we have met since, we always seem to pick up where we left off and sing songs like it was only yesterday.

CHAPTER 39
Biscuit Reappears

Over the next two years Valley Refrigeration and Shopfitting expanded again, purchasing an old cotton factory. The glory of the cotton factories in the valley with their Victorian-style slave labor was coming to an abrupt end. When I wasn't taking as much overtime as I could handle at work, I was working on the house, to the point I started suffering from exhaustion. I had problems breathing and started with a strange rash on my arms. The doctor suggested I take some time off and put my feet up. At this point that was totally impossible, so I soldiered on, taking time off when I could. I was starting to realize there weren't enough hours in a day to come up with a fair pay packet to get ahead.

Biscuit, my old friend, appeared one day out of the blue. I hadn't seen him since his visit a few years back. He was visiting his mum, who lived not too far from where we lived. I had visited her a few times, and she kept me up to date on what her kids were doing. I was, however, surprised that he had bought himself out of the navy not too much longer after I had. He had married a WREN who was from Bristol. The pull of the North Sea and the oil rigs with their promise of big money had taken him out of the navy.

He had an incredible story of heading up to Aberdeen with only a few pounds in his pocket and being hired by a fledgling diving company, Sub Sea International. Most of his accomplices from the navy were working for the same American company and doing very well for themselves. There was always a shortage of trained divers, and military divers, mainly from the navy, seemed to do well. He told me that most accidents had usually been proven to be human error. Military divers tended to respect training and discipline. Safety had improved vastly and new regulations appeared almost weekly.

He asked me if I would like to give it a go. He was now a well-revered diving supervisor, having gained much experience in his two years. He told me with my experience he could get me a job with no problem at all. I was so tempted by the offer, but Marilyn was having none of it. She had seen the news on TV and read the same papers. 'You have two kids, Kevin. Just what are you thinking about?' She was always the sensible one and that would generally ground me right there.

'Would love to, mate,' I told Biscuit, 'but I have made my bed and I have to sleep in it. Thanks for the offer, though,' I quickly added.

I was doing relatively okay. Work was still keeping me very busy. A few people had come and gone, but I had stuck it out. I was starting to think I might be next in line for the foreman job and a raise. Two qualified joiners, one with shopfitting experience from the competition, had settled in. They tended to work together, and I had noticed that even though I could do any of the shopfitting jobs just as well if not better, now I was getting all the monkey jobs. Roland, my partner over the last two years, had just quit. I then got pushed aside, and one of the new hands got the foreman job. The company also hired a new manager from our big competition. He was also a qualified carpenter and knew the other two guys quite well. I was starting to be treated like a laborer. I stuck it out. It was just work when all was said and done, but I was also starting to get very bored. Those guys all seemed to stick together like thieves. And worse, they thought they knew it all.

When I went out for a drink on Friday nights, I generally drank on my own. I just couldn't seem to get into the conversations the other men were having, and the more I tried the more I felt ostracized. I returned home inebriated a lot, and I hadn't picked up my guitar in months. Arguing was all Marilyn and I seemed to do. She was starting to realize I was not a happy camper.

Biscuit comes to the rescue

Biscuit came to the rescue, bless his little cotton socks! This time he brought his wife, Lynne, along. We all went out for dinner and then a drink at the commercial pub. Lynne and Marilyn seemed to get on like a house on fire. She was telling Marilyn about the big house they had just bought; she was not showing off, just very proud at where they both were in life. They had a nice car and really didn't worry about money.

'Yeah, sure, Biscuit seems to always be away at work, but I have the dogs and the kennels to look after,' she comfortably added.

I could see Marilyn was starting to come around to the idea. Biscuit was telling me, 'Yeah, sure, there are accidents,' but from his point of view it was mainly because of lack of experience.[3] He had a strict code offshore. Anyone who didn't toe the line was on the next chopper ashore. In the last two years he had only witnessed one fatal accident, and that, he confidentially said, was mostly due to human error. He had already talked me into it two hours ago, but Marilyn was still on the fence.

I knew if I didn't do something different very soon, espe-

---
3   http://www.docstoc.com/docs/158863728/Expensive-Knowledge-Fin

cially with my work life, something drastic would happen. I was twenty-six years old and still going nowhere. I had always felt deep inside that if I followed my instincts something good would come and I would be successful one day.

I loved my wife and kids so much, and I wanted them to have better than I ever did. Sometimes I honestly felt I was becoming my father with the booze, but I knew I wasn't addicted. One nasty hangover would put me off drinking for a while, plus I really only drank on weekends. There was no way I could drink *and* work. Some of our arguments did tend to go ballistic, but we never got violent.

The very next day we talked about me going offshore. I promised that if I thought things were too dangerous, I would quit and come home. 'Let's give it a probationary period,' I said. I would be away for two weeks and then home for two weeks. A holiday every two weeks, how hard could that be? She gave me the green light. I immediately called Biscuit and told him the good news. Within the next few weeks I had quit my job and was heading north to Aberdeen on the overnight train.

CHAPTER 40
SEDCO 707

Biscuit had told me what to expect, and I kind of knew a little bit about the physiology behind deep sea diving. I had read up on it, and Biscuit loaned me some manuals to freshen up. We stopped in to the Sub Sea office and I was introduced to some of the important people there. I was thinking how lucky I was to be introduced by Biscuit, who was obviously thought very highly of by the way the office personnel treated him. They took all my information and I was told I would be making $1,100 US per month. I had no idea what that meant, but it sounded like a lot. When Biscuit showed me how to figure it out with the newspaper exchange rates, I was flabbergasted.

'For only two weeks' work?' I said. 'I'm liking this already!'

He told me, 'We are going to be pretty busy finishing off installing the diving system on the SEDCO 707. No such thing as overtime. We work until it's finished.'

'Hey, I'm not shy of a day's work. Let me at her,' I said.

The following day we each donned survival suits and caught the chopper offshore. Everything was exciting and I was loving every moment.

We landed on what seemed in the air to be a tiny speck on the water. Many years ago I had landed on the *Zulu* on a chopper after a shore exercise in the Persian Gulf that had gone wrong. A few people had got hurt, and we were being flown back to the ship. I had picked up a few poisonous sea urchin spines in my foot. I remembered what it felt like to land on a moving deck at sea.

When we disembarked, the oil rig was massive. I couldn't get over how big it was, and the whole thing floated. It felt like the deck was almost the size of a soccer pitch, with the huge derrick ever so slowly swaying with the movement of the sea. Even though the weather wasn't the greatest, I could hardly feel any movement. We took off our survival gear for the people who were now returning to shore, and went down below into the living quarters. I was to learn very quickly how these floating exploratory drilling platforms worked and the layout underwater, just in case I had to do a dive.

The main deck of a floating oil rig is attached to between four and six legs. These legs are hollow and in the region of twenty feet in diameter. The upper part of the inside of these legs, above the water line for all intents and purposes, is usually dry and used for storage or control rooms. Below water, roughly thirty to forty feet, depending how the rig is ballasted, they are attached to the two massive ballast tanks that are in the region of sixty feet in diameter and the length of the whole rig. The moon pool is usually at the main deck level, or one below, in the dead center of the rig. That is where the drilling collars go down inside a large steel pipe. Just above the moon pool, the large steel pipe is attached to a sliding, telescoping compensator that, with a series of rams and heavy cables, takes into account not only the rise and fall of the rig, but also the sway. Looking down through the moon pool opening, we were around eighty feet from the sea, or the interface, as we liked to call it. Two to three deck levels up is the drill deck where all the action was, similar to a land drilling platform. Way down on the seabed, usually around three to five hundred feet, there is the blowout preventer (BOP), again very similar to a land drilling rig set up.

The BOP was the main reason why we divers were out there – for insurance purposes. The BOP is what hopefully stops any gas, oil, or mud from blowing out. It has three huge hydraulic rams, so that one can cut the drill collar under emergency situations while the other two seal the hole. It is a big piece of equipment, roughly thirty feet high by about fifteen feet square, that can be activated remotely from the many hydraulic lines coming down from the drill floor. There were four guide wires going down from the moon pool attached to the four legs that held the BOP in place on the guide base. They usually sent down various tools on these wires, and there was also a frame carrying a low-light, remotely operated video camera. From time to time, all of that stuff refused to function or, worse, broke and refused to come to the surface to be fixed despite all their sustained efforts. They would try almost anything before committing the divers, because to do so would admit failure. From their point of view, the lazy, no good divers, who did nothing all day, shouldn't be out there in the first place. Add to that the cost of having a team of deep-sea divers out there with all the space that they took up and their damn equipment and reams of helium gas bottles. Yep, insurance is why we were out there!

The cost of operating a drilling rig for just one day was over a $100,000, give or take a few thousand. So if that drill wasn't busy drilling away, it undoubtedly caught the eye of some bean counter sitting on his luxury leather couch twenty-six floors up somewhere in Houston. He might even spill his scotch as the Dolly Parton lookalikes did naughty things to his body.

I was introduced to the other four divers, two of whom were ex-navy, one ex-army, and the other an ex-dockyard hard hat diver. The former army diver was the assistant supervisor. We were berthed in two quite comfortable rooms, each with two sets of double bunks. We quickly got changed into overalls and set to work. Biscuit had only one thing on his mind, and that was to have this dive system up and running ASAP, as that is when the diving company started to get paid. We started at seven and stopped for meals and occasional breaks. We worked until midnight some nights. I was working directly with Biscuit. He had impressed the hell out me by moving huge pieces of equipment from one place to another. His seamanship was impeccable and I was learning a lot. With the aid of several winches and perfectly placed blocks stropped from wherever, he could find a purchase. He was making it look too easy.

I had no problem with the mechanics and installing the tubing and hoses from the complicated dive control room (dive shack). I was starting to feel like I had landed on my feet. The lads were brilliant and we all seemed to be on the same wavelength. Everything seemed so familiar. I was part of a team, and the camaraderie I had been missing these past years was all around me. Humour was typical for ex-military, plus Biscuit and I had all of our history as kids to laugh about. The harder and dirtier the work, and the added element of danger, just made it more interesting. When the system was up and running two weeks later, I felt a sense of achievement. It was a good start for me, to see how it was all put together. Meals on board were like dining in a four-star restaurant. The rig worked on twelve-hour shifts, so you could have steak for breakfast if you wanted, or even dinner at midnight if you were so inclined.

A bit of techy information

Saturation diving systems had only been around since the early 1960s. A Swiss guy named Hannes Keller was probably the first to come up with the technical savvy how to get men safely back and forth from the deeper water depths that were now required..[4] Dr. George Bond of the US Navy came up with the first theories for saturation diving..[5] Basically, at any given depth a diver will eventually become saturated with inert gas after a certain period of time. It doesn't matter if he stays for four hours or a month. The amount of time to decompress to allow the inert gas that has been absorbed (usually helium) to dissolve remains the same.

Jacques Cousteau's Conshelf underwater habitat and Dr. Bond's experimental diving unit paved the way for safe practical use of diving work at depth. But leaving the entire system underwater was quickly recognized as being very expensive and prone to problems. It made better sense to have the saturation diving deck decompression chambers (DDC) on the surface on a diving ship or platform. To transport the divers to depth, they used a submersible diving chamber (SDC), better known as a diving bell.

The US and British Royal navies performed many manned experimental dives to come up with the safe diving tables still being used commercially today. With this new technology, if a diving task was going to need more than one short-duration bounce dive, it was decided it was better to leave the diver under pressure, because in a few hours his body would be saturated with the inert gas, so it wouldn't matter if he stayed there for weeks! His decompression time would always remain the same. Helium is quite an expensive gas, so there would be a considerable financial saving. The time involved in keeping bouncing divers at depth and decompressing them would be considerable. Bounce diving is also much more dangerous, with the likelihood of decompression sickness (the bends) being more likely to oc-

---

4. http://www.divinghistory.com/id25.html
5. http://en.wikipedia.org/wiki/George F. Bond

cur than a slow saturation dive decompression.

With the massive search for offshore oil and gas booming throughout the world, none more so than in the North Sea off Scotland and Norway, the need to put human hands on the seabed was imperative. A faulty twenty-dollar hydraulic hose could bring a complete halt to a very costly drilling operation for days, to the point that a drilling operation would not even be allowed to work by the insurance companies unless they had an approved diving service company on board.

Deep sea diving had become big business, and the technology had advanced at an alarming rate since the days of Jacques Cousteau. Sadly for some, though, it seemed the need, and a little greed, had come before the technology. In this rush to get divers on the bottom, adequate training to use the dangerous, evolving technology was not required. Safety procedures were, for the most part, nonexistent. And similar to the Klondike gold rush, many men over the previous few years had lost their lives.

Pipelines had to be connected. Huge permanently placed oil platforms, some as large as small towns, were now pumping oil directly to the Scottish mainland. Some other platforms had complicated underwater plumbing arrangements, where massive oil tankers could connect directly to the source. It was rare to see less than one or two of these tankers lined up waiting to connect. The underwater machinery and pipelines for these connections also needed underwater maintenance from time to time.

At any one time in the North Sea, there was a huge amount of diving work being achieved. There were air diving jobs around, but that only took you down to a regulation depth of 150 feet. You generally got paid by the foot, and sometimes time under pressure. They generally worked on the platforms, structures that were permanently fixed to the seabed. There was a small decompression chamber on the platform for emergencies or surface oxygen decompression diving. To work on the seabed in the North Sea, you had to be prepared to dive anywhere from 300.[6] to 600 feet..[7]

The standard Sub Sea offshore dive system we had just installed on the SEDCO 707 consisted of the diving bell, which was basically a heavy steel sphere about five feet in circumference. I'm guessing the steel was about an inch thick, if not more. It had several portholes with a thick, clear acrylic material for viewing. It had a heavy inner door that closed and sealed from inside with the use of an O-ring to the hatchway seal. It also had an outer door that hinged outward. From the inside of the bell, you would pull upward with a rope attached to a handle. The water pressure would then hold the door closed on its O-ring seal. The whole bell sat on a bell stage, which was a circular frame with many large emergency helium/O2 gas bottles attached to the frame (the percentage of the mix would be set by the working depth of water).

Inside the bell were two regulation 120-foot diver umbilicals. The hoses consisted of a mixed He/O2 breathing gas line, a small quarter-inch open-ended hose that accurately gave the supervisor the actual depth of the diver, a hot water supply line, a communication line, and sometimes a line for video and a larger hose for reclaiming the helium back to the surface. At the end of these umbilicals were connected Kirby Morgan band masks (KMBM)[8] with special neoprene hoods that had speakers over your ears, or on better jobs, a full KM superlight helmet..[9] There was a device called a scrubber that basically, with the use of a powder called Sodasorb and an electrical fan, caused a chemical

---

6. Typical dive system: http://www.youtube.com/watch?v=YcSduoKj6KU
7. Big dive system: http://www.youtube.com/watch?v=B3BWSMrgi3I
8. http://kmdsi.com/products/bandmasks/kmb-bandmask-18
9. http://www.kirbymorgan.com/products/helmets/superlite-17b

reaction that scrubbed the environment in the bell of poisonous CO_2 that the divers exhaled. There were many valves and switches, and with the very feeble twelve-volt light that tended not to work from time to time, you had to know exactly where everything was blindfolded!

The bell and stage normally sat on the diving moon pool's sliding door. The main winch lifted the heavy bell and stage. The moon pool door was slid open on its rails by a small winch and the bell and stage was lowered down through the opening. Eighty or so feet below it reached the sea. The main bell umbilical also had to be let out and attached every fifty feet to the main winch cable holding the bell (much newer systems had a separate umbilical winch).

When the bell returned to surface after the dive, it was raised above the moon pool, the door was closed, and the bell and stage were lowered onto the moon pool door. The bell stage was then removed. The bell was lifted off the stage and, through a series of rails or hydraulics, was moved directly over the transfer chamber. The bottom door to the bell was then opened and the same sealing face sealed onto the top hatchway of the transfer chamber.

The deck decompression chamber consisted of the main transfer chamber, a living chamber, and a decompression chamber. The main transfer chamber had an upper hatchway to allow the bell to be sealed. Once the hatchway was sealed (in our case, the two flanges were bolted together with stainless steel bolts), the supervisor in the dive shack pressurized the entryway from the bell into the transfer chamber. Once the pressure in the bell and the entryway was equalized, the divers in the bell could open their inside hatch. The top inside door from the transfer chamber to the bell could be undogged, thus allowing the divers to climb down from the bell into the transfer chamber.

Once inside, they pulled up the upper hatch and sealed the

transfer chamber from the bell. Inside the small transfer chamber, not too much bigger than the bell, there was a shower, a toilet, and a medical lock to allow wet clothes to be sent out and dry clothes brought inside. There were two more vertical hatchways inside the transfer chamber, one leading into the living chamber and the other into the decompression chamber. Both identical chambers had two bunks with an identical medical lock system to allow food and clothes to be passed into and out of the chambers.

CHAPTER 41
Me and My Big Mouth

I came off the rig after my two weeks totally enthralled by it all. We had worked hard, and the final pressure test of the complete system and showing that the bell could be raised and lowered gave us the final green light. We came off the chopper at Aberdeen Heliport and went directly to the Sub Sea office. Biscuit wanted to introduce me to Jack Highly, who was in charge of construction diving and installation of dive systems. This guy was a big wheel and had obviously taken a shine to Biscuit. He was quite impressed that the SEDCO 707 installation had gone so well.

I really wanted to go home. Even though the work was brilliant, I still missed my family. I couldn't wait to tell Marilyn everything. Biscuit suggested we stay the night and go out for dinner with Mr. Highly. I felt that I might be jumping the gun here, and I was probably acting a little above my station, but what harm could it do?

We set off in his car and picked up his girlfriend, who sat next to me in the back of the car. I was a bit nervous, wanting to make a good impression by trying to keep up with the various conversations. We arrived at the restaurant and his girlfriend hopped out and ran inside, as it was quite cold. He was making some derogatory remark about his car and I, wanting to make conversation, thought I'd make a funny remark and said, 'Oh, you shouldn't talk about her like that.'

I was mortified when I realized that he thought I was talking about his girlfriend. He then proceeded to make excuses for her, saying, 'Oh, she's not all that bad really. She can be a bit of a pain, but I'm not really serious.' He and Biscuit both gave me strange looks, like *Who the fuck are you?* I was thinking I had just completely screwed it and looked for a big hole to crawl into.

Always engage brain before opening mouth, Kevin.

Feeling like a millionaire

I went home the following day full of vim and vigor. Eleven hundred US dollars (or the equivalent of 350 pounds per week) was now deposited into my bank account and I had two weeks off! I couldn't believe my good fortune. A few times while I was away I had a pang for home. I missed Marilyn and the kids, but for the most part I was so busy it had come and gone pretty fast.

I walked into my house and little Michaella jumped up off her chair with a shocked look on her face and ran crying to her mum in the kitchen. My heart dropped. Had she forgotten me so soon? It took a few minutes before she would come to me, but eventually we seemed to get back to normal. Just the thought of her not loving me even for a minute played on my mind. Dominic was so happy to see me, but he had been bad for something or other and Marilyn had me scold him for it, which I hated to do so soon after returning home. We took the kids up to her mother's house to be babysat, and went out on the town to celebrate. I don't think we were ever as happy as we were then. For once in my life I felt successful!

Divers were classed as self-employed and could write off travel costs and all kinds of things. I eventually hired an accountant that dealt only with North Sea divers and professional footballers. I was legally paying less tax than I was when I was a shopfitter, which meant more cash in our kitty. The money arguments pretty much came to an end, and things became much easier for us.

First time in the bell

I had to have my first diver's medical in Aberdeen before I went out to the rig. The company thought of everything, and had booked me into a B&B that I would become very familiar with over the next few years. The medical was similar to the ones I had in the navy, but much more stringent. I was poked and prodded, X-rayed and thoroughly tested from head to toe and passed without a problem.

I met another diver in the B&B, who was also scheduled for a medical and, coincidentally, would be flying out with me to the rig the following day. His name was Don Weir, and he was from Dunfermaline, close to Edinburgh. It was my second trip out and I already felt like an old hand.

Another supervisor was now in charge, as the system was basically up and running. Mike Welham was ex-military SAS, and he liked us all to know that fact. Once we got to know him he settled down and became one of the lads. He seemed to know what he was doing and kept us all on our toes.

I was just as keen to know this system back to front as I was when I was first in the navy. While the lads where playing cards, I would be out on deck tracing every line and trying to figure out what it did. Biscuit had told me earlier that the definition of a rig diver was long periods of absolute boredom punctuated by short periods of sheer panic. He had recommended that I learn everything I could, especially the inside of the bell.

'Don't rest until you know where every valve is blindfolded,' he said. 'That way you won't join the ranks of the many dead divers that have passed on before you.' I knew that Biscuit had stuck his neck out for me, and I sure as hell didn't want to disappoint him. Remembering my navy engineering, I had drawn every single line in a book and colour coded them, explaining exactly what their function was. When Mike wanted me to check on something, I knew exactly where to look.

However, from time to time I did get the heebie-jeebies, as I'm sure most of the lads did. It was only a matter of time before the rig had a problem down below and we would be called upon to fulfil what we were actually being paid for. Ian Beeton, the assistant supervisor, was the only one out of the whole crew that had ever done a deep heliox bell dive. Even the two ex-navy guys had never done a deep one, and one of them was an ex-clearance diver. I had never used the Kirby Morgan Mk9 band mask, and as much as I played around with it, taking it apart and putting it back together, was I going to screw up on my first dive? *Whatever happens, please don't let me screw up!*

I should also explain here that extra money for diving or 'going in the pot' (decompression chamber) means you get paid an additional eleven dollars an hour for every hour you spend actually under pressure. This may not sound like a lot considering the risk you were taking, but even when you were sleeping during a three-day decompression, yes folks, you were still quietly making an extra eleven dollars an hour. Wonderful! There is also a rate per foot when you do a working surface air dive and it increases the deeper you go, up to a maximum of the regulation 150 feet.

The goal was to prove to the supervisor that you knew what you were doing and were not going to screw up and possibly cost him his job. It helped if you could prove that on deck you were savvy enough to complete virtually any task. He would remind us quite often, 'You can teach a monkey to dive. It's what you do while you're down there that counts.'

When the rig was on down time, waiting for you to finish whatever emergency task they had sent you down there to complete, all eyes were on you! Sometimes quite literally, as you were probably being videoed by the camera on the BOP guide wires. The company rep, tool pusher, and even the driller would be squeezed into the dive shack watching your progress. Oh, and that bean counter back in Houston? Well, he wouldn't be a happy camper either right now. So, you were really under pressure, in more ways than one!

My day had come to show what I was made of. Mike said, 'Okay, we're going to do a practice diver recovery,' which was probably about time. I'd been on the rig for about three months and I had never even seen a surface dive. I was beginning to think this was all just a sham and an accident just waiting to happen. I wanted to get the first dive over with so I could stop dreaming about all the things that could happen.

Everyone seemed to have their tales about how this and that guy had 'bitten the bullet.' Dave Asquith, the ex-navy ship's diver like myself, had a horrific story that he shared with us one evening. He was doing his first bell practice diver recovery and was out beneath the pontoons at a depth of a hundred feet or so, at the full length of his umbilical. The inexperienced bellman, instead of opening his own air valve, erroneously closed the diver's supply valve. This was before the regulation to always have an emergency bailout bottle on your back came into law. He went on to tell us that his air just stopped mid-breath, and he swam as hard as he could returning to the bell, but he realized he wasn't going to make it. He said, 'Everything went so peaceful and blue, and all I could think about was how they were going to find me stuck under the pontoon.'

He had physically died. What started out as a practice recovery ended up being for real. The diver bellman recovered him and brought him back to the bell. He managed to resuscitate him with mouth-to-mouth. They brought up the bell and put him and a medic into the decompression chamber. He was put on pure oxygen. He said that from the moment he passed out he knew nothing until he awoke in an intensive care ward in an Aberdeen hospital. He brought himself back to health over the next few months and miraculously returned to diving.

Dave probably wasn't what you would think a deep-sea diver should look like. He was small and skinny, and smoked strong rollup cigarettes like a factory chimney. It is so true that you should never judge a book by its cover. He was as tough as old nails. If there was anyone I would trust to be in the bell with me, it would be Dave. He was from North Yorkshire, and there was just no bullshit about him. He had two spells in the Navy DQs (detention quarters), and was virtually uncrackable! They just gave up and let him go. He quietly went about his work, and if there were any tough jobs around, Dave was our man.

I was relieved to know that Ian Beeton was going to be with me. This was only going to be an air dive at around fifty feet in the bell. One of my small worries was that this was the first time the bell had been tested in the water manned. I was thinking, *Ian has done this before. He knows what he's doing.*

We got dressed in and climbed into the bell. We had gone through the checklist procedure many times, but we went through it one more time. *Okay, let's just get on with it!* We closed the bottom door to the bell and dogged it (latched it closed). The bell with the stage attached was lifted and the moon pool door slid open. I was looking through one of the lower portholes and could see eighty or so feet to the sea below us.

Mike the supervisor was out on deck watching the bell being

lowered, so we were not in communication with him as the radio was in the dive shack. The bell started to lower, but it was doing it in a weird jerking-and-stopping kind of movement. Ian looked at me a little wild eyed and we each had a nervous titter. 'Don't worry,' he said, 'it's the star motor drive system kicking in. It'll soon stop.'

It didn't stop! We were now getting closer to the interface. Bounce, bounce, bounce we went. The sea was about ten feet away when the bouncing caused the bottom door to bounce off the latch and swing wide open. We were both now looking at the waves coming closer. I looked at Ian with an obvious questioning look. *Is this supposed to happen?*

He called topside, 'All stop on the bell!'

No reply!

'All stop on the bell!'

Nothing – still no reply.

The supervisor was on deck. He was also not too keen on all this bouncing, so he was still outside watching the bell going into the water. He obviously couldn't see that our door had opened from above. Ian then jumped out of the bell onto the bell stage below. For a split second he looked up at me and out toward the sea. I could instantly read his mind – he was going to jump and leave me to it. I was all connected up ready for the dive with the mask on my knee. I immediately grabbed his collar. *Not likely, mate,* I thought, and I half dragged him in. He had the rope to the door with him. As we hit the interface, the door slammed shut as a foot of water sloshed in before the door made a seal. The rest of the dive went without a hitch. I locked out no problem, and Ian then came out to exercise recover me. We then swapped over, and he went out and I recovered him.

Basically, the exercise went as follows: The diver goes out and swims approximately fifty feet away from the bell; he then pretends to be lifeless. The supervisor communicates to the bellman to recover the diver. He immediately puts his mask on, goes out, and drags him back to the bell. He attaches a pulley hook to his harness, climbs into the bell, removes his own mask, and then winches the diver into the bell. He takes off the diver's mask and pretends to give him mouth-to-mouth resuscitation (we made kissing noises on the speaker). The supervisor would be timing the exercise. If you hadn't brought the diver back within three minutes he would be pronounced dead, and depending on the supervisor, you could get sent ashore – i.e., lose your job!

I felt a lot more confident now that I had at least done a bell dive and used all this new technology. To be in the water and not be cold was definitely a bonus, and having full communication to the surface was also reassuring. The hot water suits we wore were like a baggy neoprene wet suit, excepting that it had many small hoses running through it like veins that had tiny pinprick holes. The hot water hose from the umbilical connected directly into the suit via a shutoff valve. You could control the pressure but not the temperature.[10]

Over the next months we did many air dives over the side of the rig from a metal stage hung from one of the rigs cranes to do inspections on the hull of the pontoons. We cleaned the rig's thrusters and worked on problems the rig had been having with the anchor mooring equipment. I was feeling a lot more confident with the suit and the band mask by now.

Late one night, out of the blue we were woken and told there was a problem with the BOP and we had to dive right away. It was three in the morning, the bewitching hour (everything always seems to happen at three in the morning). It was in the middle of winter, and the sea was only just acceptable to commit

---

10. http://www.history.navy.mil/museums/keyport/SkinThey'reIn/Photos/hotwatersuit.jpg

a dive. Hey, this was the first time they had asked for a deep dive in almost a year. We couldn't very well refuse! I felt that familiar queasiness in my stomach. *Could this be it, Kevin? Your time has come to do or die!'*

Dave Asquith shows his mettle

'First come, first served,' Mike said. So Dave and one of the other lads got the dive. I could see that even tough old Dave was showing a bit of nervousness, but he just got on with it in his own way. They completed the dive at 350 feet, and Dave was probably in the water for an hour and a half fixing a hydraulic hose, then videoing it to prove it wasn't leaking. I squeezed into the dive shack to see Dave on the TV monitor and felt a huge admiration for his toughness. Mike was relaying messages to him from the rig tool pusher. I had a heck of a time understanding Dave's replies, as it was like listening to a high-pitched Donald Duck voice, even though our special diver radios were supposed to unscramble that helium effect. All of this cool technology, and seeing Dave in amongst all the hoses and machinery hundreds of feet below, reminded me of the Neil Armstrong picture I used to have above my bunk bed. I wanted this so badly, but the question now running through my head was if I would have the right stuff to be where Dave was right now.

The dive was a success and the bell returned on deck. I peered through the port at my buddy Dave in the tiny dark bell and gave him the thumbs-up. He smiled and returned the gesture. Inside, the bell was now pressurized more or less to the same depth of the seabed below us at around 350 feet (175 pounds per square inch). They were breathing a mix of 90 percent helium and 10 percent oxygen. Dave would be feeling quite cold. As he had been the diver, he was wet; add to that the effect of the helium environment. Therefore, it was important to get the bell locked onto the system as quickly as possible to get the warmth of the decompression chamber.

They were in decompression for three and half days. We set up a watch system to feed and clothe them, and between Mike and Ian, they ran the complicated decompression schedule. Oxygen and CO2 levels had to be constantly monitored accurately from sensors inside the chamber. The chamber heating system, utilizing the same hot water machine used for diving, had to be carefully monitored. One of the side effects of breathing helium is that your body's thermostat completely shuts down. External heat has to be supplied to keep the body temperature within its normal range. We had been warned that if the hot water machine failed while the diver was locked out (in the water), he would have only minutes to return to the bell before hypothermia kicked in.

I was starting to get used to the fact that all of this wonderful technology tended to break down regularly! I was learning real fast that I had to be a jack-of-all-trades – a plumber, an electrician, a welder, a mechanic, and whatever else Mike instructed me to try and fix.

Dave mimed through the chamber port that he was ready for a ciggy, so I taped one on the view port for him. He gave me royal shit when he got out. For obvious reasons, nothing flammable was allowed inside the chamber at any time. With the high oxygen levels, it would be like a bomb!

The whole dive system had worked reasonably well with no horrible surprises, but we had come up with numerous faults that had to be sorted before any more diving was done. With their experience so far, Mike and Ian just shrugged their shoulders as though as to say, 'This is the norm. Get used to it!'

You didn't have to be a scientist to understand that the two guys in the pot were completely at the mercy of the supervisor and deck crew. The huge amount of equipment and manpower needed to get one diver on the bottom to replace a simple hose fitting was mindboggling. Then take into consideration that the diver was breathing over ten times the volume of the expensive helium gas at depth. Consider also that the bell, transfer chamber, and one decompression chamber also pressurized with the same helium/oxygen mix. I now saw why we had racks upon racks of the Heliox and pure oxygen bottles taking up huge portions of the rig's deck.

This job has many crazy characters

I met so many interesting characters in my first year on the 707. I guess it came with the job! We all knew how risky the work was, and even though we constantly tried to scare the living shit out of each other with scary stories, we didn't dwell on our individual fears. I don't know what it was that drew so many different and sometimes extremely funny characters to this dangerous job. They mostly tended to have a devil-may-care attitude. I often thought it might be, 'Oh, well, sooner or later my luck's going to run out, so I might as well have a fuckin' good time while I'm here!'

One of the craziest guys I had met so far was Creature Foot. His real name was Neville Bartholomew Foote, and he had apparently come from a wealthy upper class family who had been shocked when he had enlisted in the Royal Navy. He had joined as a clearance diver and served in a bomb disposal squad, much to his family's utter dismay. His nickname came from the fact that he jokingly (I think) thought of himself as a dog. Not any old kind of dog, no, he was a purebred hound. We all soon got used to his barks when he was working on deck. And before he went to sleep at night, he would love a belly tickle. When Biscuit went ashore (he served with Biscuit in the navy) he would whimper and howl, 'I miss my Biscuit.' Sometimes we would return to our room and find bones on his pillow that he told us he liked to nibble on from time to time. We made him a rope lead and took turns taking him out on deck for his evening stroll. He would sniff around, then cock his leg and pee over the side. The roustabout crew couldn't make head nor sense out of what was going on at meal times when he gnawed away at a big old shank bone, growling and snapping at anyone that came near his table.

All the silliness aside, this guy knew his stuff. He had apparently been sent out to a job Sub Sea had off Brazil, where he did a record 600-foot dive. During the dive, he surprised the tool pusher when, instead of saying 'We have a seal' (meaning the bottom door of the bell had sealed when going through the interface), Biscuit, the supervisor, knew exactly what was going on when Creature started barking like a seal!

On the way out to the heliport to fly to the rig off-shore in Brazil, Creature and Biscuit picked up some dried cow patties from a field. The next day on the rig the captain was dumbfounded as to how cow patties had appeared on the helideck overnight a hundred or so miles out at sea.

Two weeks with Creature went by so fast. I learned a lot from him technically, and the laughs we had I will always remember.

I had mentioned my fears to Biscuit and he said, 'Ah, just ignore it. Everyone has that same fear. It keeps you on your toes. As long as you are smart enough to know as much about the bell and systems and know exactly what the job is you've been asked to do, then you'll be okay. You have to just get on with it.'

A few weeks later, the head office called me at home and said they had enrolled me on a mixed gas, deep-sea bell diving course at Fort William, Scotland. I had a sneaky feeling that my friend in high places, Biscuit, had again pulled some strings for me. Regulations were getting stiffer by the month in the North

Sea regarding diving. There were still too many accidents occurring due to human error that could have been averted with correct training. The oil companies were now starting to ask for qualifications. Most of the ex-navy CD divers did not have mixed gas bell diving experience, not to mention the many cowboys that were trying to play the part. The Norwegian Directorate had the highest safety record around and basically policed the North Sea regulations. In the next couple of years, if you didn't have a certificate issued by them or you weren't suitably grandfathered, you just didn't get offshore, period.

Gone were the cowboy days when men were literally picked up off the street and the following day were sat in a diving bell with less than a fifty percent chance of making it back to the surface in one piece. Those jobs were also run by supervisors who didn't have a clue.

Like any oil company, when a job needed to be done, adequate safety was not an issue. Just get it done, and here's a bunch of cash. In my offshore career, I witnessed many times that the big decision makers who should have had more sense quite regularly and recklessly risked other people's lives.

CHAPTER 42
Fort William

I was feeling quite prosperous and contemplating how my life had changed in the last little while as I drove my new(ish) sports car. I passed the heathered glens and dales of Scotland, where beautiful snow-capped mountains beckoned me to an unknown but fascinating future. If only I could just cast all the doubts out of my head, the niggling feeling that sooner or later, as always, I was going to screw up and this whole thing would come toppling down on my head. I knew that I needed to stay positive if I was to appease this feeling that I had been born with. Like a monkey on my shoulder, it constantly reminded me that I had a destiny, and if I didn't take the correct path I might lose it forever. I would never be happy with mundane. But was I going to die trying?

I met up with the other fifteen lads taking the course in the hotel where we were staying. It seemed that I was the only one who was actually working offshore as a diver. These lads had paid for the course and were hoping to get the work.

I made friends with a South African chap right away. He seemed to have that same confident yet quiet attitude. I had already met enough divers in the last year to see through the bullshitters, and knew the ones I could trust. He had that little bit of craziness and whatever it was that gave me a feeling he would do well on the course and be someone to trust if I were in a fix. This guy would walk down the main street in Fort William eating a T-bone steak out of a brown paper bag raw!

I found the course extremely interesting, and the couple of weeks of classwork seemed to fly by. I was now able to put all the missing links together, figuring out the complicated gas mixes and partial pressures normally done by the supervisor. It became somewhat easy now that I knew the formulas and equations. A humourous ex-navy chief CD kept me on the edge of my seat. He taught us everything we needed to know about diving physiology, and more. I found out later that he had been one of the original navy hardhat divers that was experimented on to come up with the tables being used today. I felt privileged to know him when I learned that this modest pioneer was actually mentioned by name in the diving manual that had been our bible.

The rest of the course was pretty much practical. The diving system was on a barge called *Deep Diver One*, which was towed out to the middle of Loch Linnhe and anchored in position.

As with every diving system, there was always something to fix or update. We spent the first few days working on the system, getting it ready for our working dives in the coming weeks. I guess I had been a bit spoiled with our system out on the rig. Even though it probably didn't look very pretty and there were a few flaws, at least it worked. This being a school, I was a bit surprised that it really didn't look up to par. It didn't have a bell stage, for one. It had the emergency gas bottles strapped to the side off the actual bell. I had been told back on our Sub Sea system that if the bell was to lose the main lift wire or there was a fault with the hydraulic lift winch, causing the bell to be dropped to the seabed, it was at least possible for the divers to exit the bell. There had been accidents where this had actually happened.

If there wasn't a bell stage in place, there would be nothing between the bell and the seabed to allow the bottom door to open. You were basically trapped.

When I pointed this out to the supervisor, John McCabe, he said, 'Okay, but where are you going to go if you do get out of the bell on the bottom? You sure as hell can't come to the surface.' Not wanting to sound like a know-it-all, I still pointed out a few other scenarios. He just ignored me.

A few changes had been made to the bell weight and flotation system prior to the course, and we were having a problem getting it to sink. I could not believe we were messing about with this on an official course, and I was starting to lose confidence. When the problem was eventually sorted, their explanation was thermoclines. Loch Linnhe is tidal, but a lot of freshwater came from the surrounding snow-capped mountains. Ben Nevis, the tallest mountain in the British Isles, sat there majestically front and center, reminding us of the beautiful ruggedness of this countryside. The bell floatation acts differently, depending on the salt content in the water, we were told. I wasn't completely buying it. The whole idea behind the bell flotation was that if the bell lost its lift wire, it would be possible to jettison external weights from the inside of the bell, therefore allowing the bell to float to the surface to be recovered.

I had heard an alarming story from a couple of the lads working on the barge that a few months prior they had had a serious accident. The bell returned from a deep heliox dive and was lifted onto the transfer chamber. But during the equalization process, which allowed the divers to go from the bell into the hatchway to the transfer chamber, one of the flange seal O-rings gave way and almost surfaced the three divers. Fortunately, they had made it into the transfer chamber. They managed to quickly seal the top hatch to the transfer chamber, thereby not evacuating the complete system. Because of the rapid decompression, one of the three men developed a spinal bend and was paralyzed. He never walked again.

Things started to look up after we completed a couple of manned bell runs at thirty or so feet that went relatively well. I was the only one to have actually done one before. This was a three-man bell, with seemingly lots of space compared to the one out on the rig, and we could actually stand up inside. We even did a couple of emergency diver recoveries. I was starting to gain a bit more confidence in the equipment and trusting the topside control.

We were using the relatively new Kirby Morgan 17A superlight helmet. This was a full helmet, so your head and communications were always dry. I felt I was looking and feeling more like my hero astronaut every day.

Compared again to the system out on the rig, the transfer chamber was large and spacious, and the single, six-man decompression chamber seemed positively huge in comparison. All sixteen of us squished into the six-man decompression chamber for a 150-foot air chamber dive. I had done this before in the navy, so I was trying my best to be the professional diver and not get silly as we got close to the bottom. Even breathing air under pressure changes your voice somewhat. However, somebody then cracked a funny and we all fell about laughing. When the pot surfaced and the supervisor opened the hatch, he found sixteen divers in a big heap on the floor in uncontrollable laughter – so much for professional divers!

The following week, three of us climbed into the bell and were lowered 250 feet into the cold, pitch-black waters of Loch Linnhe. We blew the bell down with a mixture of heliox, and I locked out for an emergency diver recovery drill. We were returned to the decompression chamber and, using the Royal Navy Ciria bounce diving tables, we decompressed in fifty-seven minutes.

The next day, six of us, including my new South African buddy, were blown down to 300 feet, again using heliox in the chamber. Later, my South African friend and two other lads climbed up into the bell. The door was sealed and the bell was consequently lowered to 300 feet. He was the first diver to lock out. He luckily noticed that the bell was still descending. He told topside, and before they could fix the winch problem, the bell had almost hit the seabed. Only his quick thinking and putting a large wrench from the bell toolbox between the bottom door and the seal prevented his umbilical hose from getting pinched off. He was told not to tell us until we returned from our dive, which was not without problems. My earlier question to the supervisor about the validity of a bell stage unfortunately now made sense.

When the bell had been returned to the system, we replaced the three wet divers in the bell. We replaced the Sodasorb canister on the scrubber, and closed and sealed the top door. After undocking the bell/transfer chamber clamp, we were lifted into the water and sent to the bottom. I locked out first. We were at 300 feet and one of the other divers was supposed to 'emergency' recover me. It was so black I couldn't even see the seabed. Then, without warning, the bell outside lights suddenly went off and I was plunged into complete darkness. I waited for a few minutes, isolated in a void of complete darkness, and then decided, as my hot water pressure had also ceased, to head back. I climbed back along my umbilical and put my head into the bell. It too was in complete darkness and the scrubber had also stopped. We had no communications. There had been a complete power and comm loss.

I climbed into the bell and we closed both hatches. It was eerily quiet, and with no hot water circulation around my suit, I was starting to get cold. I was starting to shiver, because I was the only one that was wet. In the ominous silence, we tried to come up with reasons for our situation and what, if anything, we could do. In an attempt to keep up our morale, and remembering my navy days, I suggested that this might be a sick ploy to see how we would react under pressure. Fifteen minutes later everything came to life with a very exasperated voice on the comm. 'Is the diver back? Is everything okay?'

It was indeed for real. They had lost generator power. It was so nice to return to the warm chamber. I was still shivering. We were now in a saturation dive and the chamber was pressurized to the same as the bottom working depth.

We had all agreed prior to coming into the chamber to be part of an experiment. There was a study being done on hypothermia during helium dives. A lady technician had shown us a bunch of wires coming out of the hull of the chamber with little thermometer probes at the end that had to be put onto our bodies at certain locations. One of the probes had to be inserted . . . well, you know where! Once she was showing a reading on her terminal outside she would give us the okay. We would then try and ignore the wires and catch some sleep.

During the evening the barge was moved to a deeper location, where the following day another series of dives was to be accomplished. I was hoping all the problems with the system had been ironed out and we weren't going to get any more surprises.

We were lowered to 350 feet, where we blew down the bell the additional fifty feet to bottom depth. Each of us, one at time, locked out to find a frame with a pipe flange on the seabed and take off or add some nuts and bolts. Finding the frame was the biggest hurdle, because as you got further away from the bell lights it became much darker, with the black mud on the bottom not helping any. (In those days it was rare to have helmet-mounted lights and video – we sure didn't). We each did what was required, then the bell was brought back to the surface. We all climbed into the chamber and were asked right away to plug in with the wires.

It had become a joke with the young lady technician that as we inserted the last anal probe, which at times was quite difficult to show a reading, she would say, 'Come on, Kevin. Just put it in . . . just a little further . . . another inch. Ah, we're getting a lovely reading now, thank you!' She told us later that the readings showed that each one of us showed signs of hypothermia. The symptoms of hypothermia are confusion and loss of coordination, not something you want to be dealing with during dangerous operations.

After the other team finished their dives, we started to decompress. Again, we were using the Royal Navy Ciria sat tables, which was decompression in steps twenty-four hours a day. It was a little uncomfortable when you are trying to sleep, as your ears pop and wake you. The US Navy sat tables we had used on Dave and his partner seemed to make better sense and were much more comfortable. Those tables utilized a continuous slow, linear decompression during the day, with a rest at night to allow for sleeping. Our decompression would take us almost four days. I wasn't sleeping much, with my ears popping, and dreaming like crazy when I did nod off. It was March of 1979 and I had my twenty-eighth birthday during the decompression. Looking around, I realized I was the oldest. This was most definitely a young man's job.

The following day I awoke with an annoying pain in my jaw, and it steadily got worse. By day two I was getting worried that it might be decompression sickness. In the last day of decompression it started to ease a little, so I knew it probably wasn't the bends. After about a week the pain went away. Looking back, it was probably an ear infection, which was rampant in decompression chambers.

I loved Fort William. Everyone was so friendly. It was large enough to be a town but felt more like a village atmosphere. It serviced mountain climbers, skiers, and people from the campsites. The tourist season had started. The nightlife was brilliant, which occasionally played havoc with school or work the next day. It was almost a duty to play the reckless deep-sea diver and show that I could play harder and longer than you. I was still receiving my offshore pay, so money wasn't an issue either.

I met John Penny in a bar one evening. He was a diver that lived in Fort William and also worked for Sub Sea. Little did I know what more coincidences were heading my way.

I finished the course with flying colours and was confident that a good report was heading out to the powers that be at Sub Sea. Their money had been well spent. It was hard to believe that I had done so well, considering all the partying I had done! I was a lot more confident having completed the course and being shown the correct way. A lot of my questions had been answered and the practical dives had quelled any lingering fears. In this business, the more you know, the longer you live.

I said my cheerios to all the lads that had made it through the course. I never did see any of them again. I then returned home. The drive back was gorgeous and I was feeling good. I was confident and ready now to push myself forward to even better rewards. I was going to try and get on one of the big construction jobs, but mostly I wanted to be an important part of a team.

A few weeks later I received my license to deep-sea gas dive from the Norwegian Directorate and was informed that only 2,000 divers in the world had this certification!

Things at home were relatively okay. I had been away for a month. I was usually only away for two weeks. The kids had been hard work for Marilyn in my absence, and I was constantly asked to give them a scolding for one reason or another. I hated doing this. I missed them so much when I was away, the last thing I wanted to do was give them a hard time when I first arrived home. I knew Marilyn was not having a good time with this. It was hard for her to single-handedly look after the kids while I was away. If I didn't give the kids discipline, then I was accused of not caring. But our lives had improved overall, and through all the new problems we were still very happy.

Again, I felt the familiar Jekyll-and-Hyde life was returning. I was trying to be the supportive husband and father when I was home and then be something totally different when I was on the rig. All I knew was that from the moment I left home I missed them, and it always left a big hole. But I also felt that this was my big chance to better myself at last. I wanted to be an important link in a chain. I knew that I could handle the danger. It was more of a calculated risk now that I could fit all the pieces together.

So far, this seemed the only thing that I knew how to do well in my life. It was almost like it had been tailor-made for me. It had the element of danger and how I could overcome it. I could use my hands and brain to figure stuff out and fix it, or even make it better. I was learning to weld and fix electrical and mechanical machinery. I was now actually qualified for the first time, and became a valued employee and was being paid accordingly. I was also being valued on what I could do and how I performed, and that suited me just fine. But I also wanted to be cherished, loved, and appreciated by my family.

CHAPTER 43
An Unfortunate Accident

I suggest the weak of heart skip this chapter.
I returned to the SEDCO 707 burning with ambition and more than ready to prove my worth. I didn't know what I was in for!

The rig had had a problem with a hatch covering on one of the pontoons. One of the anchor pennant wires had done some damage. There was also a leak in one of the sea chests inside one of the legs. It was decided that the rig should go into the harbour for repairs. The rig was towed and also used its own thrusters to go into Peterhead, Scotland for the repairs.

The massive floating oil rig, now completely ballasted up and showing the tops of the pontoons, was moored alongside at the end of the concrete breakwall. There was a narrow jetty on the inside of the breakwall. There wasn't supposed to be any shore leave. We were still getting our offshore rate. The heavy seas were breaking over the top of the wall, so it was too dangerous down on the pontoons to risk going ashore. Well, we were invincible divers, so that didn't count. We crept down the many metal stairs and scaffolding in the dark of night, dodged the big goffers, and made it ashore. We had a few drinks and some laughs, then dodged the waves getting back on board, many of us getting soaked and risking life and limb.

At two o'clock in the morning, Yorky, the assistant supervisor, woke me up. The supervisor was still ashore. 'Ahem. Kevin, the tool pusher has just informed me that one of the dockyard workers in one of the legs is in trouble and they have asked for our help,' he said with trepidation in his voice.

I dragged myself out of bed. I was still a little foggy in the head from the few beers I had drunk only a few hours previous. 'What's the problem? And why do they need us?' I asked, thinking this had to be a mistake.

It was quickly explained to me that this worker was inside the small sea chest at the bottom inside of the leg. The sea chest was about six feet by six feet, and about five feet high with a small hatchway at the top to gain access. Inside there were various seawater pipelines and valves that could be remotely opened to allow water into the pontoons to affect ballast.

Yorky explained that this young welder was on a night shift doing the important alterations with a cutting torch and welding rod. His mate and firewatcher, who sat above the sea chest, heard an explosion and then saw flames shooting out of the hatch. He legged it up the metal stairway, doing nineteen to the dozen as the flames were licking at his ass. When he arrived at the top of the leg, which was also the main deck level, he ran over to the acetylene and oxygen bottles supplying the welder down below and wisely turned them off. He called for help, which came rapidly because more than one person had heard the explosion. There were huge amounts of black smoke billowing out of the leg hatchway. They then put fire hoses down into the leg to quell the fire. It was quickly assessed that the emergency firefighting breathing equipment was too large to fit down the small hatchway on someone's back.

I asked how much water was down there, if it was still flooded, and if it was still burning. No one seemed to know. If there was a chance this guy was still alive, I had to at least give it a try. I quickly got dressed in to a dive suit and put a KMBM mask on. Yorky was supplying me air through my umbilical hose. Because of all the smoke coming out of the top hatchway, it had been decided that I should enter the leg horizontally through another small inspection port below. Yorky had me on the comm as I crawled through a series of hatchways and over bulkheads to reach the sea chest. The only light I had was a small flashlight. I had no idea how long this guy had been in there. I eventually made it to the top of the sea chest hatchway. It had been burned completely black by the acetylene. There was still smoke everywhere, but the fire was out. I got down on my knees, looked into the black hole, and shone my flashlight around. Apart from about a foot of water, I could not make anything else out. There was certainly nothing moving. I wondered if he had tried to get out and was maybe somewhere in the bottom part of the leg, which was also covered in water.

I told Yorky, 'Okay, I'm going in.'

'Be careful,' he said. Yorky was an ex-Navy CD and had then been a civilian policeman for quite a few years. He was now too old to dive, but was a handy guy to have around in the crew.

I climbed in, and right away I noticed a black form in the far corner curled up in a ball. His clothes were mostly burned off. His hair was burned. His eyelids were missing, and he was black and charred. I told Yorky what I was looking at and that the man was most definitely dead. Right at that moment, somebody in their infinite wisdom decided to turn his ventilation air hose on full blast. The one-inch, open-ended hose that had been dangling through the hatchway took off. The hose was uncontrollably whipping up and down.

'Tell them to turn the fuckin' hose off before it takes my

damn head off!' I told Yorky.

He then informed me, 'They want you to bring him out.'

I looked down at my hands and realized, in my haste, I had forgotten to put gloves on. I put my bare hands on him. He was still relatively hot, and it was an awful feeling because he was caked and greasy. I heard some voices above the hatch. By now most of the smoke had cleared in the bottom part of the leg. They passed me down a rope and I tried to reach under his arms to thread the rope, but he was impossibly crunched up in a ball.

'Okay, tell the lads to pull up on him slowly,' I said to Yorky.

As much as we tried, we could not get him through the hatch. Yorky, obviously having done this sort of thing in the police, said, 'You're going to have to break his arms and try to straighten him out.'

Oh, fuckin' wonderful, I thought. So, I went about this disgusting task and eventually, bit by bit, he started moving through the hatch. I told Yorky to warn everyone that he was not a pretty sight. We managed to push and pull him through the several hatchways. As he was being raised through the last hatchway, his stomach gave way and we were all showered by bits of him. Two guys then ran to the guardrail to retch over the side.

Yorky then said, 'You have to go up onto the jetty. The police want a statement.'

The weather was now unbelievably calm. As I wandered up there, I was thinking about what I had just done. I had been totally fine. I just got on with it. I didn't even have to think, but as I recounted what I had seen and done to the cop in the patrol car, I started to feel very ill. He stopped taking notes, as he must have noticed the awful colour I was turning, and said, 'Hey, mate, why don't you go and get some fresh air? We can do this later.' I walked up and down that jetty for over an hour before I could go back and finish off the statement.

A cold, cloudy dawn was breaking as I breathed in hard trying to freeze the dreadful memory. A chill ran through my body and I started to think about how lucky I was to be alive. This poor kid was only twenty-three. Only a week previous, he had been pinned to a wall by a forklift truck, narrowly missing death. Today, out of the blue, death came for him again. He was halfway through a double shift and had stopped for a smoke. I had found matches and a burnt packet of cigarettes by his foot, which still had the sole of his boot welded to it. He must have mistakenly left his acetylene torch on. It was just a simple lever. The gas must have partially filled the sea chest, so that when he lit his cigarette it sadly became his last.

CHAPTER 44
The First Commercial Deep Bell Dive

A few months later we got the middle of the night wake-up call, at the bewitching hour. Ian Beeton had been promoted to supervisor, and this was his first time as a supervisor during a deep dive. There was a problem down below. They had put the BOP on the wellhead and something wasn't lining up. I was to take some measurements and then attach two tugger wires so they could heave and try to level it out. The bottom depth was over 400 feet. We didn't know yet if we could do this as a bounce dive or if it would take longer and become a saturation dive.

It was my first commercial deep-sea working dive and I did not want to mess up. All eyes were on me. My bell partner was also having his first deep dive, but he had been around a bit and I trusted he knew what he was doing. My training was showing and I felt very confident.

We eventually got the green light. After many hours of contemplation I was feeling almost relieved when we climbed into the bell. We closed the bottom door on our way in and dogged it closed. The scrubber was slowly whining away. However, every now and then we had to give it a quick hit to restart the motor. We were sitting in the dim light, his nose only inches away from mine. Behind us were our cumbersome umbilical hoses. Both of us had checked and rechecked our band mask hats. Our lengthy checklists for the bell and systems, which I had been instrumental in putting together, had been completely checked off at least twice. We had been lowered through the interface and bounced about a bit by waves, but the bellman called out, 'We have a seal.'

He read off every fifty feet of depth from our external gauge to the surface control. When we were getting close to bottom we slowed our descent. I peered through the lower port and eventually saw the BOP through the gloom. I had topside stop the descent at about twenty feet from the seabed. This commenced as a bounce dive, so minimum bottom time was of the essence. Not only did I have to get the job done, I had to do it as quickly as possible so we didn't commit to a more-expensive and time-consuming SAT dive decompression. I set myself up standing on the bottom door; it was now undogged. I was completely dressed in and talking to the supervisor through the mask comm when we started the countdown to blow down. I was really feeling like my hero. *Move over, Neil, this subaquanaut has work to do!*

The supervisor set his stopwatch as the countdown reached zero, then the bellman opened the very noisy blow-down valve. To show our professionalism, we had to blow down to depth at least a hundred feet per minute. Even though there was a nose-clearing device in my mask, I still had my hand underneath, pinching my nose and trying to keep up with clearing my ears. After the first hundred feet the clearing became easier due to the lack of the doubling effect. A simple yawn now seemed to do the trick, so I was able to fix up my Band mask. I was getting used to the metal taste of helium as it started to get really hot with the increase in pressure. I was dumping hot water directly into the bell trunk and not through my suit. I was also watching the internal depth gauge, as I wanted to be ready when the door opened.

The bottom door fell open on its own weight as the pressure inside the bell equalized to the outside pressure. Out I went. Freezing cold water ran down my neck, bringing back memories of past navy dives. I opened the hot water to the suit and was immediately bathed in warmth. *Ah, lovely!* I was a wee bit disorientated, but I quickly got my shit together. I had a job to do. The bellman was looking through the port and giving me the thumbs-up. I gave him a return sign and got my ass out to the job. Now then, what exactly was I supposed to do? *Oh yeah!* I remembered as my head cleared a little more.

I gave them the measurements from the indicator pins and then zipped up to attach the two tugger wires. Topside then told me to return to the bell while they did a pull on the BOP. I stuck my head into the bell trunk and waited over half an hour while they completed their pull. The Scottish bellman was talking to me, and I was having a real hard time understanding what he was saying. I mean, imagine a broad Scottish accent at 400 feet on helium!

I was then instructed to go take the same measurements. It was a success. The BOP flange had aligned and sealed. I zipped back up and released the tugger wires. I think in my determination to not screw up, I must have put my every sense on overdrive. As I was doing these relatively simple tasks, for brief seconds my mind inadvertently started to wander. My first realization had been that no other human being had ever stood where I had stood. I was 400 fucking feet underwater! This whole shooting match, including the bean counter in Houston, was waiting on little old me! All this super technology had been developed just to get a person down here to perform this simple task.

I could hear my breathing, but there were other noises – metal noises – and in the distance I could hear many other faint sounds. Sound travels much faster through water, so sounds from the rig itself or boats close by sounded much closer. It made me feel like I wasn't completely alone down there. Other strange things came to me when I focused closer to my mask visor. In the dim light coming from the bell I could see thousands upon thousands of tiny swimming things darting back and forth. Down there it was another world waiting to be discovered. We might have been to the moon and discovered much about its surface, but our own Earth's seabed was still very much undiscovered and still held many secrets.

I shook my head from my reverie as I was told to return to the bell. I climbed in, bringing up the bottom door with me. We closed the top door and, with the use of the main blow-down valve, we blew the bell down an additional couple of feet to seal the door. 'Top door sealed. Ready to leave bottom,' we informed topside.

Seventy-two minutes on bottom mostly waiting for the rig, Ian had started the bounce dive decompression as soon as we were on deck. He put us on a SSM7 (Sub Sea) bounce table right up to fifty feet, and then we finished off on a USN sat table. We were out of the decompression chamber in forty hours and forty minutes. My bell partner, a bit of a techy, told me that we would always have a small amount of helium in our body for the rest of our lives. *Okay, cool!* I thought.

CHAPTER 45
Construction

It was common knowledge throughout Sub Sea International that the construction diving side of the business was where the big money was being made. It was an American company, so there was a little bit of favouritism going on, but then again, the whole oil drilling business was run by Americans. This was the early, heady days of the North Sea oil and gas bonanza. The Brits and Norwegians were picking up the technology and taking it to a whole new level, but American money would still run the show for many years to come.

The occasional American diver showed up on our crew to gain some experience, and usually after a few months he was whisked off to the dizzying heights of a construction job. Biscuit, being one of the chosen few Brits, had gotten to where he was by excellence alone – that and the fact that he was willing to spend vast amounts of time offshore. Most Americans came for the season. Winter weather in the North Sea sometimes slowed down construction jobs to a standstill. It made no sense for them to be spending time ashore in a hotel. It made much better sense to spend literally months offshore, basically living on the job! The company didn't need to constantly find replacements, so they were quite happy to go along. This was what we had to compete with if you wanted to try for the big dough!

I think we all knew we would also not be able to do this indefinitely. It was a young man's job. The big money was there, as long as you were willing to put the time in – lots of time. For the fortunate few, it was there for the taking.

I didn't see Biscuit very often, but when I did he filled me in on all the extraordinary operations he was performing. It was mindboggling. It was common practice for guys to go into SAT for thirty to forty days, come out for a week or so, and then go back in for a repeat. Biscuit was averaging over six months a year in SAT! To accomplish that, he was spending over 300 days per year offshore!

He was making his supervisor rate per day of somewhere around 180 dollars a day. In SAT, he made another fifteen dollars an hour on top of that, twenty-four hours a day! A rough calculation showed him to be making upwards of $120,000 a year. In 1979, that was a lot of money!

The construction jobs were run usually from specially designed dynamic positioning (DP) vessels or a converted floating oil rig. The sat system sometimes consisted of three six-man chambers, one solely for the use of decompressing. The other two were constantly pressured up year round to whatever the depth of water they were working at. There was one huge transfer chamber and sometimes two independent diving bells. The dive control rooms were huge and the decompression control room below decks looked like something out of a Star Wars movie.

As a construction diver, you had to know how to arc cut underwater with the use of special arc rods known as Broccos, and to do the occasional weld. Installing pipelines, you had to know how to use underwater air power tools and high-pressure water jets. Diver ultrasonic and magnetic particle inspection was a whole different field, but you also had to have those qualifications and many other skills to get anywhere.

I had been asking my boss at the Sub Sea head office if I could go on a construction job. I must have done something good, because while I was at home on my two weeks off I got a call. I was to fly out to the Northern Frigg field. I was immediately made a lead diver. My day rate was now a hundred dollars a day, and whatever diving I could get to add to that. I flew fixed wing to Lerwick in the Shetland Islands and then caught a chopper out to the Frigg oil field. I would be working on a concrete platform for Elf Aquitaine Norge. The standalone platform was massive and had a huge circular concrete wall surrounding it. We were only working at twenty feet or so, but I was using all kinds of underwater tools, including underwater arc cutting tools and air grinders. We were installing huge clamps on the oil and gas risers, and cutting old parts off. I was basically in charge of a team of young Americans, who were desperately trying to get into offshore diving. Most of them were very green. They were almost working for free just to get some experience.

One day, the rig set off the emergency sprinkling system while we were working on the concrete wall down below. Our whole diving set was soaked. They then called for an emergency drill. We had to go to our lifeboat station. I was pretty pissed because my calculator and dive and operation books were now soaked. One kid came up to me in the confusion and asked, 'Why do they put salt in the water? Does it help to put the fire out?' Duh!

After about six weeks, the job was completed and I returned home.

CHAPTER 46
Ocean Kokuei

There was a joke going around the company that the *Ocean Kokuei* submersible oil drilling rig was where they sent the bad boys. I was wondering where I had screwed up on the last job. Why was I going back to being a rig diver? What the heck had I done?

After talking to the supervisor and some of the lads that I knew from other jobs, I got the scuttlebutt. This old tub, the *Kokuei*, was a floating exploratory drilling rig like the SEDCO 707, but it was now working in the successful Argyle oil field. The known satellite wells were being pipelined one at a time into the main production Transworld 58 oil rig close by. This had been the first oil producing field from the UK sector. Oil was sent out to a single buoy mooring (SBM) where a string of lined-up tankers were filled and then shipped ashore. For all intents and purposes, it really was a small diving construction job.

I was still on my construction pay rate, and the two weeks on and off really didn't apply anymore. I learned very quickly that you had to stick out working on deck, as we called it, as long as you could. This meant tending to all the dive operations, from the lowering and raising of the bell to tending the divers in SAT. Plus, there was all the grunt work of passing tools and handling winches for the diver down below. We also completed shifts in the dive shack, helping the SAT tech (if we had one) keep the chamber environment correct, or even decompressing the men when each job was completed.

Once the supervisor was duly impressed with your performance on deck, you might get into SAT too, making the extra cash on top of your day rate. Every dive system needed constant meddling and upgrading, but the *Kokuei* system was one of Sub Sea's first systems offshore. It was a relic, with over ten years' service, and was held together with duct tape and hard graft. It was handy if you could weld, because there was always something that had rusted and come apart.

All in all, you could be offshore anywhere from a month to three months. Whatever shore time you might receive could be cut short after only a few days if there was a shortage of personnel. It seemed to be manned with mostly Brit divers. We were doing very similar work to what the divers were doing on the big jobs, but we only received eleven dollars per hour in SAT. As much as we complained, it was never changed. Because of the nature of the work we were doing, most of the SAT dives lasted between a week and ten days.

The rig itself was also old and rusty. It also seemed to be accident prone, for whatever reason. Just about every trip out on the *Ocean Kokuei,* or Ocean Cock Up as it was commonly nicknamed, there was usually an accident or two. Choppers had to be dispatched seemingly quite regularly to fly maimed workers back to hospital minus a few fingers, or in one case all of his toes. When we weren't busy, for entertainment we headed up to the drill floor and chatted to the driller in his shack. We noticed right away, looking through his window, that our job was definitely not the most dangerous on board.

I remember asking the old Louisiana driller what kind of

chewing tobacco he had chocked in his mouth, and in his drawl he said, 'Well, son, I got some Red Man over here,' pointing to the big lump on one side of his cheek, 'and down here,' pointing under his lip, 'I got some Copenhagen. They calls it a cocktail.' Chewing tobacco was a nasty habit that a lot of divers used, including me from time to time.

When the system was down I went through everything, tracing every line and valve and drawing them into my book. Incredibly, the bell was actually smaller than the one on the SEDCO 707! It was plain to see the various fabrications that had been made to bring it, and the rest of the system, up to par. We had been instructed to make some adjustments with a series of levers on the transfer chamber toilet. This was a very small seat and funnel affair. There was a two-inch line with a large quarter-turn valve before it went to the outside. On the outside of the chamber there was another quarter-turn valve with a two-inch reinforced rubber hose hanging down below the open grid deck plates to the sea below us – very simple, but potentially dangerous! On similar systems worldwide, divers had mistakenly or accidentally opened the valve while still sitting, and due to the huge differential in pressures, had inadvertently lost part of their bowels! With the new makeshift levers we had figured out and installed, it was almost impossible for this to happen.

To use the toilet under pressure you went about your business and then added some water into the funnel from the shower. You then asked topside to flush the toilet. One of the on-deck lads then climbed behind the system, opened the quarter-inch valve, and stood by. He then tapped the transfer chamber or waved in the porthole. The relieved diver then quickly opened and closed the inside valve. At 300 feet inside the chamber, 150 pounds per square inch of pressure acted upon the remains. At that point you would hear a loud *bang* as the now atomized remains were shot out of the end of the hose. The hose, very similar in looks to an elephant's trunk, would rear up and sometimes shoot the mud man's door thirty feet away.

Happy Hapthorpe was our illustrious leader, an ex-navy CD. Although he was quite qualified and knew his stuff, he could be a bit of a mother hen. I remember him following me a few times like a shadow, trying to sort out some problem. He once even followed me into the rig washroom. I was sitting on the toilet, wanting some peace and quiet, and he was talking to me from behind the door. 'Okay, that hose fits over on the O2 line on the chamber,' etc. Other people were walking in and wondering who the hell he was talking to.

First SAT dive on the *Kokuei*

On my first SAT dive on board, I was in with my buddy Dave Asquith. Right away we were getting used to the system's idiosyncrasies. The bell had to be swung back and forth to be successfully trammed over to the moon pool area. Inside the tiny bell, every bang and bump was exaggerated and our hoses and hats were falling all over the place. Dave's nose was about six inches from mine, and we were wondering if this might have been a mistake on this antiquated system. Nonetheless, we didn't complain, and were eventually on bottom at 260 feet. I was going to be the diver. We had blown down to the bottom depth and I locked out.

The job was to oxy arc cut a flange clamp on an eight-inch oil pipeline going from this wellhead to the oil production platform. I had learned to be real careful around open-ended pipelines at depth, especially if they might be empty, i.e. full of air. If you did manage to successfully remove the flange, an empty hose is going to immediately fill up again due to the differential in pressure. It would become a huge vacuum cleaner, sucking up everything in its path, including the odd diver or two. The next problem would be if the hose was still under pressure. A mini blowout could occur and oil pressure from miles underground would then come roaring out.

I asked all the questions before I started cutting the bolts, knowing the tool pusher was in the dive shack. 'Go ahead, Kevin,' the tool pusher said. 'You're good to go. No pressure on the line whatsoever at either end.'

I attached the ground clamp away from me, because I didn't want to be between the ground and the rod when I struck an arc. I would get zapped. The Brocco rod I was using was a small tube with lots of mini mild steel rods and one manganese rod inside. Once you made contact, the supplied DC current caused a spark, and you then pulled the trigger, allowing the pure oxygen to ignite. The whole seabed around you would be lit with a bright white flame. In your hand you would have the vibrating power to cut through six inches of steel. Sometimes, if the cable hadn't been properly insulated, you might get tiny arcs coming from the metal nose-clearing device inside your mask, zapping your nose. If you had fillings in your teeth, you ended up with a bad taste in your mouth, as if you had just chewed on a battery.

I very easily cut through the two bolts, but the clamp holding the flange together did not fall off as I expected. I didn't like this, so I asked again, 'Topside, are you sure there is no pressure on this line?'

'Hang on a mo.' He was obviously asking the tool pusher. 'Nope, he absolutely guarantees no pressure. He called over to the platform and they told him the hose was open-ended there. Go get a big hammer from the bell toolbox and beat off the clamps.'

'Oh, okay,' I said, not wanting to push the issue. I found the big hammer and a-beating I did go. I hammered for a full ten minutes before a spurt of oil came gushing out that looked very much like it was under pressure. I told Happy what was going on, as I was starting to get oil on my mask. Then, all of a sudden, *Bang!* The end of the hose going out to the platform launched itself, and the whole seabed around me started turning a reddish-black. I immediately headed back to the bell, on my way informing Happy what had happened. By the time I had returned to the bell and put my now oily head inside, I was astonished to hear Happy asking Dave if I was telling the truth over the bell speaker. Dave told him that I had just come into the bell, I was covered with oil, and there was a big reddish-black slick coming toward the bell.

'Get in the bell, Kevin, and close the outside door,' Happy said.

We both sat in the cramped bell for almost two hours before Happy told us that someone had made a mistake over on the platform. They had been looking at the wrong hose. 'But it's all sorted now,' he said. I looked out of the ports and the slick was gone. 'We need you to go back out and finish the job.'

Nobody said sorry, just shut the fuck up and get on with your job! I went out to dismantle the hose from the 'Christmas tree' (mini BOP) and a few other items. We spent six hours on bottom, mostly waiting for stuff. We returned to the chamber and waited for a couple of days until they did some checks and lowered a BOP in position. We completed a five-day SAT.

It seemed after that I was getting in on most of the dives with various other divers. Later, I was in with Don Weir and we did an eleven-day SAT. I almost had a repeat situation on one dive when I was asked to remove an inspection plug on a blank flange before taking the flange off. Lo and behold, the hose was under pressure again. I was unscrewing the plug with a wrench and kept telling topside that it was unusually tight. I asked them to double check that they were sure they had the correct hose this time.

Sandy Strachan was now the supervisor. 'No, it's okay. Go ahead take it off,' he said, obviously having no knowledge of my previous experience.

Luckily, when the plug came off I was not standing in front of it, because it shot out like a bullet. My fingers were burning as I returned back to the bell, again covered in oil.

Elmer J. Chickenshit

There was never a dull moment on the job, and if you weren't looking out for yourself, then you were a fool. I was on the *Kokuei* for almost a year and saw a lot of accidents, mainly coming from the drill floor. The diving crew had our moments, but thankfully no one ever got hurt. I was managing to get in SAT a lot, but never more than eleven days at a time. I was used to all the idiosyncrasies of the old dive system. It was amusing to see the faces of new divers coming on board and seeing some of the things we had gotten used to when running a dive.

I had been informed that a big shot American diver was coming on board. He was ex-US Navy, and apparently had done a 1,000-foot experimental dive in a chamber while in the navy. He had heard about all the SAT we were getting out here and wanted some. Head office had instructed the supervisor to have him go into the very next SAT, jumping the queue of the existing divers doing their time on deck. It was going to be a quick job; we expected it to be around six days or so. Within hours of him coming off the chopper, the dive was scheduled for later on that night. I showed him the system, and he gave me a few raised eyebrows at various parts that looked like they had come from the Middle Ages. He seemed an okay guy, but tended to boast a lot, which always made me nervous.

Most of my dives this year had been with John Penny, the guy I had met in Fort William. We made a good team and had earned a reputation for getting the job done, whether it was down below or fixing anything on deck. I swear that sometimes I thought he was almost telepathic. I would come back to the bell for some tool and I would see his hand holding the very tool suspended below the bell trunk. I just knew if anything went wrong out there he would risk his life to save me, and he knew I would do the same for him.

It was decided that because John wasn't too well that the new American guy would be my bellman. I wasn't too excited about diving with an untried stranger, but he had some amazing credentials, so I thought, *Hey, maybe I'll learn something*.

Later that evening we ran the dive. The bell with the stage attached was raised and the moon pool door was opened. The anchor had already been lowered to the bottom – we thought. The anchor was a forty-five gallon oil drum filled with cement. It was lowered to the seabed with one of the deck winches. The bell had a short pennant wire that was attached via a sliding shackle to the anchor weight wire. The reason for this was to stop the dangerous pendulum effect the bell had when going from the deck level to the interface eighty or so feet below. The bell would swing so much we were afraid that it might crash into the rig structure.

The bell was lowered, but at about 200 feet the bell started to tip. We had the bottom door closed, so there was a few tons of pressure holding that door closed. It was definitely not going to open, as we had not blown down yet, so the inside of the bell was still at one atmosphere. I called topside, 'All stop on the bell!' I knew what the problem was. Somebody on deck had not done their job right. The anchor weight was not on bottom. I repeated the instruction, but no one was listening. The supervisor, Sandy Strachan, must be out on deck. The bell was now almost on its side, and our diving umbilicals were falling onto us and we were in a mess of hoses and helmets!

Elmer – I will not give his real name – started to panic. Rule number one in this game: Never, ever panic! In seconds, he had the comm speaker in his hands and was screaming into it. Sandy had returned into the dive shack but couldn't make head nor tail of what was being screamed at him. Inside the bell it was absolute turmoil. The light was flickering on and off, and now Elmer decided to start playing with valves. I had hold of him, trying to drag him away from the speaker, but he was not letting go. I was realizing very fast that if I didn't stop this crazed man soon we might both die. Thankfully, he was smaller than me. I eventually manhandled him away from the speaker and stood on his neck. He was frothing at the mouth with very wild eyes, and we were in very, very close quarters.

The bell was almost on its side before I could get to the speaker. At this point, Elmer could not speak because I was busy choking him. I said as calmly as possible under the circumstances, 'Topside, all stop on the bell. Could you please lower the clump weight to the bottom.'

Sandy gave the order to the deck crew and then proceeded to give us shit. 'You guys are supposed to be professionals. What's with all the screaming? I couldn't understand a fuckin' word you were saying.'

'Okay, Sandy. Sorry, mate, a little misunderstanding,' I replied.

As the anchor weight was lowered and the slack taken out of the main umbilical and lift wire, the bell finally righted itself. I released a little pressure on his neck, and with my hand over the speaker, I quietly informed him, 'In the next few minutes I'm going to be locking out of this bell. If you so much as touch anything or move any valve just a fraction, I will come back and I will kill you! Do you understand what I am saying?' He nodded and I released my foot from his neck.

He was obviously embarrassed, but did exactly as I said. The rest of the SAT went relatively well. We did a few more uneventful bell dives over the next few days and then went into decompression. I never brought up the incident with him again, hoping we could return to surface unscathed.

I had recently learned how to play chess and I had brought a little plastic set into the chamber with us that I had purchased the last time I was ashore. I played game after game, and I beat the shit out of him every single time. After about my sixth win, he astonishingly picked up my chess set and smashed it on the wall. It broke into a thousand pieces. We had two more days of decompression as I sternly warned him, 'One more silly move like that, mate, and you are history.'

I pretty much lay awake watching his every move from then on. I was so glad when we made surface. It had been six very long days.

The scary one

One of the last dives I did on the *Kokuei* happened to be my all-time scariest. There was another young American diver that had been on deck for a couple of months trying to get into SAT. He was an okay guy, very friendly and seemed to be very proficient on deck. He had bided his time and done all the right things, so Sandy Strachan decided it was time to break him out. If he did one SAT with no problems he would then more than likely be transferred to the bigger construction contracts that Sub Sea had offshore.

I showed him the bell and all its workings, and he seemed more than ready. We were committed to do a pretty simple job of connecting a broken guide wire on the BOP and checking on a suspected leak, among other minor issues. I was going to be the diver on this mission, and a later one would be his. The bell was lowered and everything was going to plan, a typical deep-sea dive. This was going to be a good first dive for the chap, and remembering my first dives, I was giving him as much confidence as possible.

We blew down and I locked out. Immediately, I heard this low rumbling noise. It was almost below hearing. I could almost feel it in my chest. I went to do the first job that had been asked of me, attach the new guide wire. *Easy stuff,* I was thinking.

In ten minutes I was ready for the next task. 'Check for a leak out on the yellow pod hydraulic line,' Sandy said.

'Everything's okay there, Sandy,' I said, 'but there is a leak somewhere down below me. There's a whole lot of bubbles coming up.'

Sandy, in his usual distrusting way, said, 'No, can't be. Let's get on with the other jobs.' The tool pusher wanted to get this over with.

'Yeah, but Sandy, I'm telling you, big bubbles, vibration and a lot of noise. I should go down there and check it out.'

Everything went quiet. He was obviously in conversation with the pusher. 'Okay,' he said, 'go check it out.'

I swam down below the BOP where it sat on the wellhead guide base. It was pretty dark, but I had my flashlight with me, and there below the guide base was where the huge bubbles were coming from. It was really noisy and I was afraid to get any closer. I told topside what I was seeing, and again Sandy didn't believe me!

'Okay, we are going to send down the video camera on one of the guide wires. Go video it for us,' he said.

This seemed to take ages, so I kept myself busy completing the rest of the jobs asked of me. All the time, the deep rumbling noise was giving me the willies. The massive BOP was vibrating. Eventually the video camera arrived. I unclipped it from the guide wire and headed down. The bubbling seemed to have gotten worse. I pointed the video as close as I dared, and then in a split second Sandy said, 'Get back to the bell!'

I was asking him what was going on, but he was not replying. I got to the bell and the young bellman literally dragged me in. 'Hey, hold on, mate. What's the rush?' I was saying as he struggled with my mask.

As soon as he got it off, he said, 'We have to get ready to be raised real fast.' I did what I was told.

'Come on, lads, get a move on,' Sandy said. 'Tell me as soon as you have a seal on your top door.'

What the heck is going on? I thought. We sealed the top door, informed topside, and the bell immediately started to be raised. We came pretty much to the interface and then stopped at about twenty feet.

After a few minutes I started to get anxious and called topside. Sandy said, 'Just hang tight, lads. I'll be right with you.'

After another ten minutes, I was getting a little worried. 'Okay, Sandy, what's going on?' I asked adamantly.

'Okay, lads,' Sandy said, 'here's the situation. The gas is blowing from outside of the casing, and that's not supposed to happen. They are calling it a possible bad cement job.'

'Well, okay, just get us out,' I said.

'Hmm, well, they are not sure about that either,' Sandy said nervously. Ten long minutes later he came back on. 'Okay, guys, stand by. We're taking you out of the water.'

About friggin' time! I thought. However, we breached the water, but then halfway up to the deck everything stopped again. We were starting to pendulum back and forth. Our only saving grace was that the anchor pennant wire stopped us short before we got into a bad swing. Sandy came back on the comm. There was obviously a major commotion going on in the dive shack. I looked across at the kid and noticed that he hadn't said a single word since we left bottom. His face was yellow and he looked like he was about to throw up. *Oh, shit, another panic mechanic*, I thought. If he started to throw a wobbly while we were so vulnerable and under pressure, we were done for. I started to throw a couple of comments his way. 'Hey, mate, no problem. They'll have us on deck soon, you'll see.' He had no reply as he aimlessly stared at some inanimate object.

Sandy said, 'Okay, lads, here's the situation. They are not completely sure, but they think this is a blow out, and the rig is being evacuated as we speak. There is only the diving crew, the pusher, and a few essential others left on board. The rest have been crane lifted off onto the emergency supply vessel.'

All rigs at sea have a duty supply vessel that circles the rig for men overboard or other possible emergencies. A few floating oil rigs had sunk because gas from the well had come to the surface. An oil rig does not float on gas bubbles, so it sinks like the proverbial stone, taking everyone on board with her.

'Okay,' I said, 'so get us on deck!'

'Well, no, we are thinking that we might have to have the bell slung under the rig and put onto the supply vessel,' he replied.

I pleaded with Sandy. 'Listen, mate, I have a choice in the matter. Do not do that. Put us on deck and we'll take our chances from there.' We swung under the rig for at least another fifteen minutes before someone came to their senses and brought us on board.

The bell was set on the moon pool door, and no one made an attempt to put the bell on the system to have us decompress. I was starting to get really cold, but was putting on a brave face for my partner, who had still not said a single word and was an ashen white by now. We sat there for what seemed a lifetime, but in reality it was only about half an hour. Although I was now shivering with cold, I tried my best to keep things positive. I really didn't want him passing out on me.

Much to our relief, Sandy finally informed us, 'Okay, lads, we're putting you on the system.'

As soon as we locked into the transfer chamber and sealed the top hatch, Sandy put us on an emergency abort table. We were still too deep to go on oxygen, but I noticed that we were losing depth really fast, and I was thinking that at this rate one of us was going to get a hit (bend) sooner or later.

A few hours later our Sub Sea manager from the office was peering into the porthole. Oh, my God! They had flown out the top brass so soon. He took over the emergency decompression schedule from Sandy. I was just hoping that they knew what they were doing. I then noticed through the porthole, as I was breathing pure oxygen through one of the bib masks, that there was a small tubular emergency recovery chamber about to be fitted to one of our door hatchways.

During the next five-minute break from the O2 bib mask, I asked the big honcho exactly what they thought they were going to do with that. He calmly replied, 'Well, son, if the situation gets any worse, you're going to have to get into that and we'll take you to shore on the chopper where we can finish your decompression.' I asked him if I had a choice in the matter and he flatly replied, 'No!'

We had spent almost four hours on bottom at 248 feet, so we were completely gas saturated. The normal decompression at that depth would be around two and a half days. We were out in thirty hours. By the time we reached the surface they had successfully re-cemented and capped the well. My diver's logbook showed it to be 10 March 1980 on the *Ocean Kokuei* in the Argyle field. I never saw anything in any of the newspapers. The oil company, as always, had kept it very quiet.

The day after we had surfaced they asked me to return to the dive and finish the job I had originally started. I never saw the young kid again. He spent his recommended twenty-four hours on deck after decompression before catching the next chopper ashore. I thought if I didn't go back in, I never would, so I had to get back on the horse. I did the next dive without a problem and was out in three days.

All in all it had been a good year. I had done a lot of SAT. I wasn't there with the big boys yet, but I was doing okay. I had learned so much about the practical side, but mostly I had discovered a lot more about myself.

CHAPTER 47
My Crack at the Big Time

My next job was on the *Bredford Dolphin,* a diving support floating rig that was attached to the massive Ninian field central platform. Biscuit was my supervisor on a short test air dive. I was the bellman for a test on a head-mount video on a heavy, specially designed Kirby Morgan Krasburg helium reclamation full helmet. Later, I spent a whole month on deck while the chamber had four divers in SAT, one of them being Biscuit. I saw right away that even though I had come with good references from my previous *Kokuei* days, I would have to wait a while to get to the front of the queue to get into the pot.

I then thought I'd made it lucky when I was sent to the *Star Canopis*. It was a state-of-the-art diving support vessel, devoted totally to SAT diving. It was a directionally propelled (DP) vessel, in that it had propellers around its hull controlled by two computers (one fail-safe). It used stars and other points on the sea (other platforms) to set its location. It was said that the ship would not vary from a point on the seabed by more than six feet.

The large three-man bell went directly through the hull to reach its destination. On coming up it was then locked onto the huge transfer chamber one deck below. The saturation control room looked like something out of NASA, and the resemblance didn't end there. The three four-man chambers connected to the transfer chamber almost took a whole deck and looked like the space station. Amazing stuff!

The dive supervisor on shift worked from the bell dive shack on the main deck level. All the decompression was handled by a crew of specially trained SAT techs. This was heady stuff, and I wanted in big time. Jack Highly was the superintendent, a very hard man to please. He either liked you, or you were on the next chopper ashore. To get on board the ship, you had to hang on to netting on a cage and then be lifted on board by a crane from up on the platform.

My first meeting with Highly hadn't gone that great, so I did everything on deck to show I knew what I was doing. The big job here was removing the pile guides that were originally used during installation of the platform. The massive jacket platform was floated out and then sunk exactly where they wanted it in the oil or gas field. These big piles were drilled into the seabed, basically to nail the platform in place. Huge pile guides had been originally installed for this purpose, but because of sea currents and various other problems, these obsolete guides needed to be removed. About twenty feet high and three feet in diameter, they were pretty heavy chunks of steel to remove.

When I first came on board, Biscuit was one of the shift supervisors. Although he didn't give me any preferential treatment, I wish he would have been on board weeks later when I was to prove myself.

I had done my spell on deck, and now I was told that I was in next. This was going to be my chance to show my hard-earned talents and maybe join the big boys. They always say never to piss anyone off out on the job, because you might end up in a situation where he will be a supervisor or some big wig that would get his chance to bury you. I was told my bell partner was going to be none other than Elmer. *Oh, my god,* I thought, *not him!* He had somehow made his mark out here with the many Americans who virtually lived offshore.

As much as I complained, it was go with him or don't go in at all. I was a small fish out here and in no position to decide who I would or would not dive with. Nobody knew about the experience I had with him. If I had mentioned it to anyone, and of course if they even believed my story, he would for sure have lost his job.

I had been on board around three weeks when we were put into the bell. Elmer was first out. The depth that we were currently working at was only 160 feet. The seabed would be over 300 feet below us. The ship was in DP mode about fifty or sixty feet away from the main platform on our beam. The deal was to swim out from the bell until you reached the rig, then find the pile guide. Once there, a cutting torch would be passed down from the platform diver deck crew and you would commence cutting each side of this huge guide. A crane wire would be sent down before it was completely cut. The guide would be connected to the crane wire, and once the guide was free, it would be lifted onto the platform.

Elmer returned from his four-hour dive. We changed over and he explained where he was on the job. He gave me a direction to swim toward where the platform was. I locked out and got myself organized. For some reason, I had never noticed that at the bottom of the bell there was a direction numbering system. Although I had been on board three weeks, somehow it had slipped my attention. I swam out in the direction Elmer had originally pointed, which just happened to be the complete opposite. Elmer had obviously wanted to get his own back, so I was now doing a great job of swimming out to sea.

The shift supervisor was giving me sheer hell, because with the weight of the full 180 feet of umbilical Elmer had also kindly dumped out, I was now descending in depth. I was working extremely hard just to stay at the correct depth. Twice I came back to the bell. The supervisor, who doesn't know me from Adam, thinks I'm panicking as I'm hyperventilating. I was totally shattered the third time back. I just knew they were going to pull me. I had been in the water for an hour and half and done nothing except breathe heavy. Elmer then leaned down into the trunk, pointed out the numbering system, and also pointed me in the right direction. He'd obviously had second thoughts. If I got pulled, he might have to come out with me.

Now that I was on the right course, I immediately found the platform. Even though I was friggin' tired after all the swimming, I found the torch and commenced cutting. I had it out with Elmer when I returned. Nobody believed that I had simply not seen the numbering system on deck. Elmer lied to everyone. He knew which way my umbilical was going from inside the bell, and had he told topside, the problem would have been solved immediately.

We did two more dives and then we got pulled. I was immediately sent ashore with my proverbial tail between my legs. I then received a telephone call from Jack Highly. He said, 'I was told you were in pretty bad shape. You need to get fit before you start diving again.'

I was then sent out to an air diving job for the rest of the summer season until further notice. I knew I had completely fucked it. I got right to the top and then screwed up big time. You didn't get second chances in this game.

I had ceased using the train to travel home, as the three- or four-hour journey, usually with friends also travelling south, became a bit of an embarrassment for Marilyn when I was literally poured off the train. Alcohol, after many weeks being dry offshore, hit me very hard. When I once missed my stop and had to catch another train back many hours later, Marilyn ceased to see the funny side of it. With the extra cash I was now earning, I had been flying down from Aberdeen to Manchester on the business class special.

Marilyn was waiting with the kids as the plane taxied to a stop. The steps up to the airplane door were attached and the many businessmen, some with bowler hats and briefcases, filled the steps. There was a slight halt to the rush as a tall, dark shape appeared at the top of the steps. He also held a briefcase as he wavered and then suddenly fell, careening into all of the bowler hats, knocking them over like skittles. There was shortly a rather large heap of bowler hats and briefcases wallowing at the bottom of the steps, as many brollies (umbrellas) were mercilessly beating at this dark, inebriated shape that had done them such mischief. As much as Marilyn was happy to see me, she was trying her best to not let on that she even knew this buffoon.

'Mummy, what's wrong with Daddy?'

'Oh, Daddy's not feeling too well, but he'll be okay once we get home, dear.'

CHAPTER 48
Diving Supervisor

The *Tender Commander* was a supply vessel that was anchored off in the south end of the same platform that the *Canopis* was working in on the north side. We were installing large zinc sacrificial anodes on the many oil risers and structures on the platform. This being one of the early steel jacket platforms, they were concerned about corrosion. Some of the metal support beams were over thirty inches in diameter, so these anodes were big and probably weighed in at half a ton or more.

One nice surprise I received as I arrived on board was that, because of my experience, I was promoted to air supervisor and received a better day rate. I was the night shift supervisor and was now making $120 a day. Surface dives were paid on how many feet you went down, and increased at certain depths. I tried to make up the extra cash, and also to prove to the powers that be that there was nothing wrong with my health. At the end of my shift, I had the day shift supervisor supervise my dive, which was the deepest of the day, usually around 150 feet. After O2 decompression in the air chamber, I then generally finished my shift around three in the afternoon.

An ex-RN officer was the company rep. He would time each dive to see who was the quickest to install their anode. The lads would spend hours on deck rigging up their own anode and planning how they would use the two winches and deck capstan to install it. When I left the job, nobody on board had beaten my record at 150 feet. Competition was rife, as most of these mainly American divers wanted to break into the big money being made on the other side of the platform on the *Canopis*. This was the proving ground.

I saw that some of these young lads were definitely going to be the future superstars. They handled themselves very well. One of the divers said he had seen a shark. We occasionally saw blue sharks, but in this temperature of water they were harmless. On his next dive I wrote on his back with yellow crayon *Diver – Do not Bite*.

Even diving from the stern of this vessel had its challenges. I was below installing my anode when I had an anxious call from the supervisor. 'Get under the brace. They have just dropped something from the platform.'

As much as we told the platform not to work above us, it usually fell on deaf ears. I went under one of the large braces and waited. My umbilical was completely unprotected between me and the stern of the ship. If anything caught my umbilical, it would inevitably drag me to the bottom and certain death. I was given the all clear after five anxious minutes. Apparently they had been moving ninety-foot drill collars. When they had all become loose on deck, one of them went whistling over the side. I didn't see or hear it, but it had passed me by not more than forty feet.

Chapter 49
Dad Leaves Us

Toward the end of the summer I received a call from the office. My dad had just died. I would have a relief supervisor diver sent out on the next chopper the following day. In as much as he had given us all hell when we were growing up, I was beginning to learn forgiveness. For all our idiosyncrasies, there was usually a reason behind our failures. His life had been pathetic compared to the life of adventure I was now living. I was also beginning to see how two people in love could inflict so much pain on each other. One moment you could be blissfully happy, the next the bitterest of enemies.

Mum and Dad were never far apart. Even though divorced for many years, she still surprisingly did his laundry. When he wanted beer money, through all the complaints, she still gave in to his constant pestering. He spent more time at Mum's house than he ever did in his own.

In his mid-sixties he was a sad state. He had shrunk in height considerably, and the large hump on his back made him look deformed. He had recently broken his hip slipping on some ice and had laid on the pavement for hours before anyone thought to help him, thinking he was a drunk, which in all honesty he obviously was. His only mobility was with the aid of his metal walker. With his labored breathing and sad watery eyes, he was indeed a wretched and depressing sight.

After all he had done, he could still con any of us to feel sorry for him and inevitably take him down to his pub, the Legion Club. He would proudly drink from a pewter mug I had given him with my name and the ship I had served on engraved on the front. He would sit on his own, as did other men, usually in a thick cloud of cigarette smoke.

Quietly, and in much somber thought, those sad men drank their lonely and seemingly sorrowful lives away. When they eventually reached that point when thought was just a mixed confusion of sad pictures just before oblivion, when everything thankfully went blank, they would stagger off to some dark, dingy hole, usually a rented room in some back street of a house that had been classed as derelict twenty years ago.

I struck up a conversation with one of those lonely chaps who sat at the next table to Dad. This was *his* seat. They always sat in the same place, and kicked up a fuss if you happened to sit in their seat.

He had told me a few months back that Thwaites, the local beer brewery, had unsuccessfully tried a coup to take the other brewery on and remove them from the club. A tractor-trailer had showed up in the parking lot, a doorway appeared, and steps were installed. A large sign was then erected advertising free beer. For a whole afternoon, much greedy guzzling was had by one and all.

This chap, in between puffing on his very smoky pipe, said in a broad Lancashire accent, 'Aye, lad, tha dad's a rum un, by gum! He can sup sum stuff im. Never seen owt like it. He wus burnin' up bloody carpet back an' forth t' booze lorry. Made imsel sick twice. Didn't put 'im off fer a bloody second. Reight back owt at it agin 'e wus. Aye, lad, he can sup sum stuff 'im. I never seen owt like it.'

Translated into the Queen's English this would read:

Yes sir, your daddy's quite a charmer, by heck! He can sure drink a lot of beer. I have never seen anything quite like it. He was burning up the carpet, back and forth to the beer truck. He made himself vomit twice just to make room for more. It didn't put him off for a damned second. He was right back out and at it again. Yes sir, he can sure drink a lot of beer. I have never seen anything quite like it.

On that last occasion I spent with him, he told me in his deaf fashion that he could now only drink two or three pints before he'd had enough. He would repeatedly say, 'I'm finished,' while aggressively pointing down to the floor, meaning he was ready to be buried – or, what I thought he was trying to tell me, 'I'm going to hell!'

My sister Rita and her husband were visiting Mum, and as usual Dad was behind her so she couldn't see him. He was, as always, charading drinking a pint and anxiously pointing toward the club at the end of the street. With his pleading expression and sad demeanor, he would eventually grind you down, much to Mum's chagrin. Rita eventually gave in, and away they went to the club. She bought him the usual pint of mild beer, as was his want. In conversation with her husband, she absently looked over to check on Dad. He had quietly, and without demonstration, died!

I had long ago forgiven Dad and reconciled my feelings toward him. None of the bad stuff should have ever happened, but it did. He was just a man. We can all easily say he had many chances to take other paths. Although I make no excuses for him and his wrong doings, I am not the one to cast a stone, as no one should. He lived in a period of time when his handicap was not just physical. It was mentally demeaning. He was never allowed to come above his station in life. His life was mapped out to struggle. I think at some point in his life he realized that it would never get any better. He was always put down by people who he knew he could do better, given the chance. That chance would never come. When his health became a problem, it was just another weight added to the scale against him. What little high he may have gained when the alcohol took charge of his life just took him into a downward spiral of despair.

There were those ever-precious moments when I occasionally witnessed something good, like the look of pride in his eyes when he first saw me in a uniform, or whenever I had achieved something special in my life. Whenever I had felt a determination to qualify, when all the odds were against me, I felt him silently guiding me. If there was something risky and perhaps dangerous to do, when I had worked out all the possibilities for success, I wanted to be the first one to do it. They could all then look around and say, 'That crazy motherfucker, he did it.' Dad was in there somewhere guiding me.

When I wanted to be the mucky street kid who did good and showed all those toffs what I was really made of, Dad was there in my mind's eye, with that sly grin, tapping his forehead. The few times in my life when I had to use my hands to make a living, Dad was there showing me the way. I was never afraid of learning something new. Whether it was welding or building a wood cabinet, it didn't matter. I just had a determination to figure it out. Unknowingly, he gave me many gifts that I have used throughout my life.

I went home with a heavy heart to see Mum. She was in a mess. In the last few years, even though he had his own hovel of an apartment, he had become more or less a fixture in Mum's house. Now that he was gone, she was realizing that as much as he was a pain in the butt, he was company and part of her life and her history, the father of her four children.

It came as a surprise to all of us, after everything he had done, how much we were saddened by his death. Mum was in too bad of a state to be at the actual crematorium, which was probably a good thing. We were all a bit spooked as he went through the curtains. The sky turned black, and in minutes there was a violent thunderstorm. The church felt like it was vibrating with the loud thunder and lightning. I later tried to bring Mum's spirits up by telling her about the spooky thundering and lightning.

I said, 'Do you know why it did that?' As she looked up at me with her ever-so-sad eyes, I told her, 'Because he never finished his pint. He left a full untouched pint when he passed away.' We both had a laugh. I could always make her laugh, even then, when she must have felt so alone. She was never the same again and missed him terribly.

Misbegotten Life

He was a careless man
He let it all go
He was a fearless man
Bring it on

(Chorus)
Ooh, ooh, misbegotten life
I said ooh, ooh, never had a chance
Well, he'll take another drink
Then he don't have to think

He was a loving man
Didn't know how to care
He was a deaf man

But he could figure things out

(Repeat Chorus)

He was a workin' man
Filthy dirty work
He was a thinkin' man
They thought he was dumb

(Repeat Chorus)

He was a sad man
Had a broken heart
He was a drinkin' man
When he took his last breath in the bar

But when he left us
Whoa -- when he left us
He left us -- a full glass

—Kevin Firth, April 2012

Visits with my mum

Over the last few years Mum and I had not been seeing eye to eye. She had never really forgiven me for the secret wedding. As much as I tried to explain my reasons, had she been a bit more receptive to my future wife it might not have happened that way. Mum never seemed to have a good thing to say about my wife. It was always negative. When I returned home I would hear the same negative judgments about my mother. The two women in my life were constantly at war. My visits to Mum became less and less frequent. I simply could not handle the arguments.

I eventually found a little success in secretly visiting my

mum and keeping all conversations about my spouse out of bounds. We could now have fun and be silly. Mum always loved that. I could be myself and cuddle her, show her my affection. For a few short, wonderful hours, I was a boy in her arms again, that invisible bond between mother and son. I would come away recharged, literally brimming with love, but I will always remember the ache in my heart every time I had to leave and see the sadness in her eyes. She never *really* knew what I did for a living. I never wanted her to worry about me. I know she always did. I had made up some story or other that I was never really sure she believed.

CHAPTER 50
There Has to Be Something More

Life at home was changing. I was making more money than I ever thought possible. Even though my special diver accountant saved me lots, at the end of the year I was still annoyed at the amount of my hard-earned cash that was still being deducted. I worked with many divers that had never paid a dime in taxes, especially the foreign nationals. This was a risky business and it was pretty obvious, like professional footballers, you only had a short window of youth to make your fortune.

I could be away for a month to six weeks and then only be home for a few days before I got the call. Marilyn understood that this was probably only going to be for a few years. I was twenty-nine, and unless I was promoted to deep-sea diver supervisor, which wasn't likely to happen after my screw up, my days were numbered.

We had holidayed in Majorca, which would have only been a dream years earlier. We rented scooters and toured the island. Little Michaella sat on the front of my seat and Dominic sat behind his mother. Life was indeed good, and for a time things could not have been better. I knew I couldn't have it all, to have the finances to enjoy life and still be at home with my loved ones.

I looked around at where we lived. As much as I had always loved Haslingden, there really was nothing there. Almost everyone you talked to was unemployed and living on the dole. It seemed the local economy was heading further into the doldrums.

In my travels meeting lots of Americans and Canadians, I was starting to see that there could be a better life out there. Dominic was getting older, and I was starting to wonder what was going to be there for him when the time came for him to go out on his own.

O, Canada

Marilyn had an older sister who had moved to the US and then finally settled in Canada. This had happened quite a few years before I met Marilyn. I had met her and her two kids when they were on holiday in the UK visiting her mum. I had spoken to her husband, a Dutchman, over the phone many times. He constantly asked us to come visit them in Canada. As a special treat, because I had been working away so much, I agreed to take three weeks off and we would visit her sister.

From the moment I got off the plane in Toronto I fell in love with the place. Everything was so clean, for starters. Everyone seemed so proud of where they lived. The license plates on the cars said 'Keep Ontario Clean.' After a meal at a fast food outlet, everyone would take their own rubbish and put it in the bin, which was unheard of in the UK at the time. I also noticed that there was every nationality under the sun living seemingly in harmony. Black, white, and yellow, nobody seem to care. There didn't seem to be a class system. Everyone was valued on what they produced. Meanwhile, in the UK we were having race riots in Birmingham and London.

It seemed to us that everyone in Canada worked hard to keep their nice houses and cars. Margaret, Marilyn's sister, even had a swimming pool. Frank, her husband, had left England where he was a welder and also had to work as a taxi driver on the side to make up his wage. In Canada, he started a small metal fabricating company that had since expanded many times. He now had a crew of fabricators and welders, including his son, working for him.

Living in the UK, we could only dream about their life – and it wasn't just in material values. At least once a week, someone in their neighbourhood had a basement or pool party. It seemed everyone you met was an immigrant who still obviously missed their original home, but had now made long-lasting and trusting relationships. Drinking beer at barbecues in the backyards while the kids splashed in the pool just seemed to be a normal way of life there, nothing special.

In England, we had gone through a decade of major union strikes. Whole towns and cities were out of work for months. The white and blue collars of England just weren't on speaking terms. It was a mess of unprecedented proportions. Margaret Thatcher, the Iron Lady, was in power, and whatever good she might have done for England, it was far overshadowed by the sheer destruction of the working class families, mainly in the North. Like many conservatives before her, it was always the working class that had to tighten their belts.

Meanwhile, for the people that could work or had spent years getting their qualifications, they were seeing a dismal future of having to pay for this lack of understanding. English talent was leaving the shores of the UK in droves. We had a joke in England at the time: 'Would the next businessman leaving England please turn off the lights.'

It wasn't long before Marilyn and I were busy talking about emigrating. We loved everything about Canada. Frank and Margaret agreed that they would gladly sponsor us for the two years that was required by the emigration rules.

As so many people were coming to Canada and a better life, immigration was starting to get picky about who they let in. Only special trades that were needed in Canada were welcomed. I had met Cory, one of the guys who worked for Frank. He was also Dutch and was Frank's best friend from Holland. He told me one night of how he came to Canada and had to live in a rooming house until he found work. He was now one of Frank's most respected workers. He was also married to an English lady named Elsie, who was a riot! They had a beautiful wood cottage surrounded by huge, mature trees. I loved visiting them, and right away Cory and Elsie, who were much older than us, were becoming close friends. We left Canada, and on returning to England, started the emigration process in earnest.

Not the Kokuei again

I got the call almost immediately after we arrived home: I was to go back to the *Ocean Kokuei*. *Ah, the bad boy's rig again*, I thought. No problem. Right now I would rather be a big fish in a small pond.

The *Kokuei* had moved to the Tartan fields and was in much deeper water, almost 500 feet. I met up with my old buddies again. John Penny was to be my bell partner on the next dives we did in SAT in the coming months. The system was old and dilapidated, but I knew it, and I also knew the crew. With lots of duct tape and imagination, we kept that system alive and kicking. John and I kept up our reputation for getting the job done below. We weren't slouches on deck either.

We had talked about other jobs that were going on with other companies. I told him about my 'foopahh' on the can of piss (*Star Canopis*), and that I probably wasn't going to be going anywhere fast with Mr. Highly in charge. I wasn't about to get any second chances. He had his team of favourites and that was it! But we also knew that Sub Sea had an excellent reputation for safety. Neither of us had been witness to any serious accidents, though John had been burned and suffered some face injuries in an accident with another company. Even so, we still talked about possibly making a move, and we were confident in our experience and knowing what not to look for.

I was sent out to the *Buchan Alpha*, a production platform where I went into SAT for seventeen days at 380 feet. For me, it had been another successful year.

CHAPTER 51
Balder Davis

I stayed in contact with John, and we later met up in Aberdeen. I think we had both become a little fed up with playing second fiddle and having to work on a system that really should have been scrapped. We had heard that there was a gold bullion salvage operation on the go. Two W Diving Company had been talked into it by a charismatic Keith Jessop, an ex-Royal Marine. This would be the second year they were going to try and find the gold bullion that sank with *HMS Edinburgh* in the Second World War. It was estimated at forty-five million pounds sterling. After visiting Two W Diving, we were told that the ship was at 800 feet. This would be a record SAT dive – that is, if everyone made it back! We were also told that, as it was a salvage operation, if you found the gold you got paid. If you didn't, well, tough! John and I were both married men with children, and as much as it sounded like a real adventure, we sensibly declined.

I knew one of the divers named Scouse Cooper, who had decided to take the chance. I had served with him on the *Brereton* years ago in the navy when he was a baby diver. We later heard on the national news that they had found the treasure. He was in SAT for six weeks at 800 feet and was the diver who dangerously cut through into the bomb room where the gold was found.

There is a brilliant book that was written called *Stalin's Gold* about the whole adventure. Scouse walked away with $30,000 for his six weeks of work.[11]

John and I had heard there was some work over at Oceaneering, also a branch of an American company. They hired us once they saw our log books that proved we were seasoned SAT divers.

We joined the *Balder Davis*, a DP diving support vessel that looked like a converted supply boat. The whole system sat on the outside deck. It had the usual transfer chamber and two decompression chambers. The unusual element was the roll over bell, which took a bit of getting used to. Once the bell came up through the hull of the boat, it rolled over onto its side and was then hydraulically pushed toward the vertical sealing ring on the transfer chamber. Being inside the bell, this was a weird sensation. You had to ensure that everything was securely fastened back. It almost felt like being a mouse in a circle treadmill.

We explained to their head office that until we got to know the crew, we would only dive together. We came as a team. They didn't seem to have a problem with that.

The ship was alongside in Aberdeen. We were told that in order for the dive system to be certified, with all the new rules coming out, we had to have an emergency escape capsule installed. The capsule looked like a large diving bell and would be installed on the other side of the transfer chamber. John and I were given the job of installing it! We had to figure out how it could be launched and what kind of automatic device would set it free. We installed a rail system that would slide the whole thing over the side, and through some handmade linkages, the system could be unlatched once the divers were safe inside. On the first test launch it sank to bottom of the harbour, but we had lines tied to it, so it was easily lifted back on board. Much more

---

11. http://www.hmsedinburgh.co.uk/salvage7.php

floatation was added, and then we had a christening.

Some bigwigs from the company came, as well as the diving regulation board and some newspaper reporters, to witness this launching. John and I were getting real nervous. We had never expected this. The capsule was launched and, much to our pleasure, it actually floated – until someone suggested that there was no one inside yet! No one wanted to test it from the inside, so we each climbed down the ship's side and stood on top of it. After every diver made it and stood on top, a huge cheer came from the crowd – until the sixth person, when it slowly started to sink. At that point, six divers were seen to scramble over each other to climb up the lift wire to a now-laughing crowd. Needless to say, we finally got it to pass the regs, and John and I became the proud fathers of the capsule that no one in their right mind would ever use!

The superintendent was an ex-Royal Marine SBS who was really good to get along with. He had handpicked his crew from most of his diver friends in Cornwall. We, and a few others, were fill-ins. Ashore, this guy was an animal. John and I got into some sad states drinking with him. Offshore, this was the only vessel or rig I had ever been on that actually allowed booze, but no one ever overindulged. We did spend the New Year in 1982 having a crazy party miles out to sea, but I don't think any one of us saw twelve o' clock. The skipper told us to drink what you wanted, because tomorrow the booze cabinet would be locked.

Just give divers alcohol

I was settling in very well. The crew proved to be a good bunch of guys who seemed to know their stuff. Unless we were in the pot, we were on the regular schedule of three weeks on and three off. The money was also better. I had sat for a written test for saturation dive supervisor in the office of an old chief

RN CD who was part of training and regulations. I had duly impressed him with my knowledge. Not to blow my own trumpet, but I was finding that some of the older guys that had been in the RN, or even in commercial diving, were way behind when it came to all the new advances in our business.

I always tried to keep up to date whenever I could from the SAT techs I met or whatever I found to read. For example, there was the test on High Pressure Nervous Syndrome (HPNS). This symptom occurs when the blow down is too quick, usually over 400 feet. The fat around your nerve endings, the myelin sheath, gets compressed, sometimes causing severe jitters. It had been previously thought to have something to do with O2 poisoning, because of the similar effects. So, they blew some guys down to a thousand feet in a chamber at KD Marine Diving (another company I would work for in future) and gave them alcohol. It worked a treat – no more jitters. So why, I ask, do they not just give us divers alcohol?

My day rate increased again and at the next available opening I would be a mixed gas dive supervisor. The move to another company had been very successful – I was on my way!

CHAPTER 52
Canadian Immigration

We received a letter from Canadian Immigration. We had been refused. Frank had come up with a plan – he would offer me a job as a metal fabricator. While in Canada previously, I had applied for diving work. Bill Duncan from KD Marine Canada said he would take me on immediately if he could. The problem was that, at the time, they didn't want foreigners coming in and taking jobs from Canadians. In this case it was even worse. All of the diving work was being done off Newfoundland in the Hibernia fields, and Newfoundland wanted a minimum of 30 percent Newfoundlanders on the rigs. He would be getting himself into big trouble by offering a job to a Brit. He told me he was in need of a saturation diving gas supervisor, and if ever I was to make it over there I had a job, but I had to make it there on my own steam.

Frank offered me a job, but he had to advertise it for three months. If no one took the job, I was okay. He advertised it three times and it was taken every time. We were beginning to lose hope. I sent off all my papers yet again with an updated resume.

I had recently finished a course on non-destructive testing. A lot of the SAT jobs were asking for this, as most of the aging rigs needed to be inspected for corrosion. The *Alexander Kei-*

land floating oil exploration rig had just sunk, killing 123 men. One of its five legs had sheared off due to a faulty weld during a storm, and it had completely flipped over in a matter of minutes. On the course, we learned magnetic particle and ultrasonic inspection, which was basically a tool that would tell you if there were corrosion, or worse, a crack in a weld through a reading on the front.

It didn't seem very long before we had a reply letter stating that I was to appear at a Canadian Immigration office. Lo and behold, the immigration officer was delighted that I had applied, and the ultrasonic testing certificate I had was indeed worth its weight in gold. I could get a job anywhere and name my pay. I went along with him, thinking, *Does he really know what this is? Is this all going to come crashing down around my ears any moment?* Well, I guess it was enough, because we succeeded in the emigration process. I came out of the office doing a jig.

Back on the *Balder Davis,* things were getting interesting and John and I were getting our fair share of SAT. Both of us liked using the Oceaneering RAT hats.[12] I found these helmets were much more comfortable to wear. You didn't have to bite on a tit. You just needed a slight breath in and the hat supplied you with breathing gas. The ship was working the Argyll field. We were checking all of the satellite well Christmas trees (BOPs) and the pipelines going to the main platform. It was January, and the weather was quite often bad. Because we were diving from a small ship, the weather didn't have to be that bad before diving was stopped. We spent a lot of time in SAT waiting for conditions to improve, which was okay with us. We got paid the same if we were working or not, twenty-four hours a day.

We had to do some spring-cleaning on one of the wellheads that had been there for quite some years. It was a mini-micro-

---

12. http://www.divescrap.com/DiveScrap INDEX/Oceaneering.html

cosm of life, totally overgrown with barnacles and various crustaceans, and of course almost the complete food chain of sea life thereafter. The well was only at 250 feet, so during the day quite a lot of light still filtered down that added photosynthesis to feed the hungry.

We noticed that quite a few wolf eels had made their home in and around the well. These are pretty ugly eels. A large one can have a head the size of a football, with nasty, gnarly looking teeth, and have a short eel-like body roughly two feet long. The male guarded the green jewel-like eggs, while the female went off to forage for food (sounded like a good plan to me). During this breeding and rearing time they were very territorial, and unlike most other aquatic life we came across, they would sometimes threaten you, which at times, especially in the dark, could be a bit disquieting. We had a spear in the bell stage toolbox to ward them off if we had to work around their nests.

With its computer-controlled directionally propelled (DP) system, the ship boasted that it would only move a minimum of six feet in any direction. What a load of bullshit! It is so easy when you're on deck. You really don't have any indication if the boat had moved during DP operations, because you're surrounded with ocean. Down below, however, it was a different story. Exiting out of the bell, the first thing you had to get used to was a moving target. As the ship heaved up and down with the swell, so did the bell, even though it was supposed to be compensated. Add to this that, for no apparent reason, the bell would occasionally take off across the seabed – not good if you were inside the protective cage over the wellhead! Being dragged through the cage with your umbilical was quite unnerving at times. You also had to time your entry into the bell trunk so as to not get 'clunked' when it was heaving up and down. After a while you got used to these idiosyncrasies. You always had to make sure that your umbilical was free all the way back to the bell.

We had a Canadian diver on board, and I had been picking his brains about Canada and told him I would be immigrating there that year. I was intrigued that it was feasible to commute to the North Sea and still live in Canada, as he was doing. I was enjoying being on the boat, and knew that in the not too distant future I would be supervising. I really felt like I had finally landed on my feet.

Killer wolf eel

The Canadian was on bottom and I was in the dive shack as assistant supervisor. I had developed a cold, so had missed out on the SAT. John was in with the Canadian guy. He was having a problem with the wolf eels. The company rep was breathing down my neck, so I was telling the diver to just ignore them. If you have a problem, go get the spear. I spoke to John in the bell and asked if he had had any problems during his dive. He said that he hadn't. There were lots of eels, but they hadn't really bothered him. When the guy started to tell me that they were ganging up on him, I thought it was getting a little out of hand. Luckily, even though the comm set had the standard helium unscrambler circuit, the rep really couldn't understand what the diver was saying. I put the headphones on and quietly let the diver know that this was becoming embarrassing and he really should try to ignore them.

Things went quiet for a while, so I took off the phones and put the radio back on the speaker. In the next instant we heard a bloodcurdling scream. 'It's got me and I can't get it off!'

I called John and told him the diver was coming back to the bell and he should take up the slack on his umbilical. I was trying to console the diver and get more information, but he just kept yelling. I could not make any sense of what he was saying.

He eventually made his way into the bell and John inspected his heel. Sure as hell, he had two punctures through his heel!

We all had a laugh. Even the rep saw the funny side. John locked out to finish the dive. We had a tugger wire rigged up for the dive for sending tools down. One of the lads brought an umbrella, the type that opens up with the press of a button. We tied a big rubber glove on the end pointing a finger and sent it down the wire for John. He laughed himself silly when he saw it by the bell. One of the lads had made a cardboard picture of a shark's mouth open and ready to bite. He taped it to the inside of the transfer hatch, so when they had equalized and opened the bell door to the transfer lock it was gaping at him. He took a lot of ribbing. Had it happened to any of us, we would have been just as shocked.

Drinkypoos in Paris

The main pipeline on the seabed going into Scotland from the offshore oil fields had been damaged, probably from fishing boats. It was mentioned on national TV, and for a while it was a major panic. The ship was hired to do some work with a remotely operated vehicle (ROV) to video the pipeline and the damage. Most of the large diving operations over the last few years had to have an ROV with their own tech crew on board for safety reasons. The first ones we saw usually didn't last very long. It was an expensive piece of complicated equipment that was sometimes lost down below and never seen again. They were quickly improved upon and became very valuable tools. The later models were also equipped with small manipulator claws.

The tech crew had done the videoing and the company rep had spoken to the powers that be ashore. Within hours there was a chopper hovering over our back deck, lowering some bigwigs down a line. The weather wasn't that great and the ship was bouncing from side to side as they were being lowered. We were callously taking bets on who was going to get killed first. Through sheer luck no one was hurt. These guys must have been paid well. They did their ROV inspection of the pipeline for the bigwigs, and a few days later we went alongside a platform to disembark them by crane.

A few weeks later the ship was sent to France to pick up a huge wheel of special six-inch coflexip pipeline. The whole thing was welded down to the back deck, ready for deployment once we returned to the oil fields. We had a great run ashore for the one night. Most of us took the train to Paris for a session and we all had a ball. It was so comforting to sit in a bar in Paris knowing that we were still collecting our offshore day rate.

We returned to the platform, where I was taken off by the crane cage to take my three weeks off. I said cheerio to the lads and that I would see them shortly.

I never went offshore in the North Sea again!

CHAPTER 53

The Big Move

We had our house on the market for a few months and attracted a buyer right away. It was hard to believe the day was coming when we would leave England and everything we had known for good. We both knew to get any further ahead we had to leave. A bright future lay before us if we were brave enough to leave.

All of this reminded me of when I first left home and walked down the street waving goodbye. It would be heartbreaking. But as I had proved to myself more than once, if you don't take those chances in life you tend to stagnate. The pubs in town were full of stagnating people that seemed to know no better. For Marilyn, it was particularly hard, as her mother was starting to become very sick. My grandmother was also very ill, recovering from an operation.

I had not mentioned any of my emigration plans to my mother or siblings yet. I was leaving it to the last, because I knew if I didn't I might be swayed to stay. I had worked hard for this, and deep inside I knew it was the right thing to do for all of us. Dominic was thirteen; he would find it particularly hard, as he now had close friends and was doing well at school. But his prospects would be increased tenfold where we were heading. I saw a future for him in a profession of sorts, a doctor or an architect. Michaella was happy wherever she was, the least of our worries, but she would also have a bright future with more prospects than Marilyn or I had ever had. I think Marilyn saw her future being close to her sister in Canada, having a nice home and being happy. Our marriage had not been going too well over the last months, mainly because I was away so much and she was living a single mother's life. She was more than capable of handling a home and kids, but she was probably lonely a lot. We both saw that the move might also improve our marriage and life in general.

I was watching the news on TV one night when I heard about an oil rig that had sunk off Newfoundland. I knew there were only three rigs working offshore there at the time, and I was wondering if the KD Marine divers had been on board. Apparently, nobody survived the disaster. Eighty-four men were lost. Bad weather was shown to be the cause, but more investigation would be needed in the coming months to see if there were any other reasons. The now sunken rig was the Ocean Ranger, one of the largest floating oil rigs in the world. I was shocked and feeling a bit perturbed. *What kind of weather would turn over a rig of that size?* And I had been considering working there! The news kind of blew the wind out of my sails a little, but I was way too far into this to think of changing my mind. I decided it would probably make sense not to advertise this fact to my wife or family, for obvious reasons.

An awful day

When the awful day came to tell my mother, she wept and pleaded with me for hours. I had broken her heart when I left for the navy. I had done it again when I decided to have a secret wedding. She had been upset for months when she found out what I was doing on the oil rigs. I was now putting the final touches to her demise and leaving England and my home forever.

I tried to underplay the event by explaining, 'It's not like that nowadays, Mum. The world is a much smaller place. People emigrate and come back on holidays. I'm not going to disappear!'

Seeing her like that, weeping and full of hurt with all the pain and anguish I had inadvertently inflicted upon her over the years, broke *my* heart! But I had to be strong. I knew if I started to weep not only would I lose control, it would also show that everything I had said was a lie. I promised that I would come and see her a few more times before we left, as she was in such a state. I kept this nonchalant facade while I was with her, trying to have her believe this wasn't such a big deal. 'I'll come back next year to see you and we'll have some fun.' However, as soon as I was in my car driving home, the tears came and I had to stop the car somewhere over the Grane to try and come to grips before arriving home.

Making Mum laugh was an art that I thought I had mastered. Growing up, Freda, Mum, and me were addicted to slapstick humour. We watched many Charlie Chaplin silent movies and fell about laughing at his antics. When she got going, Mum would literally howl with laughter. By now, Freda and I would be on the floor in hysterical laughter. If she seemed miserable and needed cheering up, funny faces was my all-time favourite, and if that didn't work, well, I'd just pick her up, swing her around a few times, and then tickle her. I had accidentally cracked one of her ribs one day with that stunt. She didn't tell me until months later. It might sound pretty basic to an outsider, but it was simple, good fun, nothing more and nothing less. She was just different from the norm. We felt and understood her. It was our indelible connection to our mum.

She had become quite eccentric in her older years. She was

in her mid-sixties and wore very colourful odd socks and Deerstalker hats with feathers and a plastic eyeball at the front. She had her two large dogs that were never leashed. They never left her side. She would take the long walk into town, stopping here and there to buy her bits and pieces. Everyone loved her because she was such a character. She was even written about in the local papers and had her photo taken with the dogs in the local market.

A few months prior to me leaving, I was driving her into town when she asked me to stop the car. I could plainly see she obviously had something on her mind. She had recently been speaking to our grandmother, who had wanted to give her some information before the operation she was due to have. Grandma had told her about her first husband, whom none of us had known. She had left him just after our mum and her brother, our uncle Fred, had been born. He was one of the lucky few that had returned from France during the First World War. Our grandfather on our dad's side, Wilfred Firth, didn't make it back. He died from a gas bomb. Her husband unknowingly returned with a venereal disease. Apparently, this was rife during that period of time with men returning from France.

They had two children in quick succession, Fred and then our mum. Fred was born with a kind of epilepsy that came and went for most of his life. Our mother lost her hearing when she was twelve, and that was when they found that they had both been born with the disease. Mum had suffered a kind of meningitis that had left her deaf. She had told us when we were young that she had to have a lot of medicine after the meningitis. This was, in fact, heavy medicines to cure her of the disease she was unknowingly carrying.

Grandma had carried this awful news all of her life until now, but all she had told our mother was that she had had a venereal disease. We found out all the other facts much later. She was understandably upset as she was telling me this. I was trying to console her by explaining that I was a man of the world and had travelled a bit. In the rest of the world, venereal diseases were so common it was almost as rife as the common cold. Only we Brits had to deal with the stigma of it. Shit happens. We are all human, and it doesn't matter who or what you were, if you had unprotected sex you were at risk – period. I seemed to have quelled her fears. She, like our grandma, wanted to let us know some facts about the skeletons in our closet, just in case they passed away without telling us.

A burning mishap

The weekend before we left for Canada, Biscuit and Lynne came up from Bristol to say their farewells. Of course, we all went out to the Commercial Pub. John, the owner, was particularly upset that we were leaving. John and I would miss our many Monday evening wine tasting sessions together after he'd closed the pub. He had been the only one that actually enjoyed listening to my adventures, and I in turn enjoyed his stories from his youth.

Biscuit and I were sat at the bar while the ladies drank their sherries close by. He looked at me menacingly and said, 'Kevin, we have to do something special. This is your last night. We need to do something really big to be remembered by. Wot say we do the dance of the flaming assholes?'

'What a good idea,' I replied, while thinking soberly that this was a pretty busy night if Marilyn was about to witness me momentarily screaming across the pub naked with a flaming newspaper stuck up my butt. I don't think she would be particularly amused, and she would more than likely come after me with a carving knife. A lot of her friends where there, and I didn't think I could have gotten away with it. She had seen me do some pretty silly things, especially with Biscuit, but this would probably be a bit much.

On a previous occasion, Biscuit and I had challenged the whole pub to a spooning competition. We had made a big fuss at the bar about who the reigning champion was, to gain the attention of the brawny guys at the pub. We then sat facing each other with the spoon handles in our mouths, and proceeded in turn to violently clunk each other over the head. After much acting, one of us would give in and throw the spoon, giving the other the championship. We would offer one of the lads at the bar a pint if he could beat the winner. We had previously decided that I would be the loser, and I had asked John for the largest soup ladle that he had in his kitchen. I would feign being the lad's coach, whispering to him the tender parts of Biscuit's head to aim for. When it was Biscuit's turn, and the lad's head was looking down waiting for the hit, I would time Biscuit's hit with me smacking him with the noisy soup ladle. It usually brought huge laughter from the bar, even from the lad's best friends. After a couple of rounds with the guy surprised and sorely rubbing his head, we would conveniently show him the soup ladle. Amazingly, we had done this many times for a laugh, and it was always taken in good humour.

I knew our wives would not take this navy joke well, but I decided for the moment to go along with it. We quietly disappeared into the kitchen behind a pair of swinging doors to the pub. I think that Biscuit had a little more alcohol than me as he prepared himself. I told him to go first and I would follow. We had decided that being totally naked probably wasn't a good idea in our inebriated state. So Biscuit still had on his underwear as he fiddled around trying to get a good hold of the tight end of the newspaper up his butt. I set it on fire and away he went, blasting through the swinging doors into the busy pub and all the surprised onlookers. I was literally on my knees laughing as he zipped by a surprisingly unfazed Lynne.

She apparently said to Marilyn, in a very nonchalant voice, 'Oh, that's just Biscuit being silly again.' In her WREN days she had probably seen a lot worse, and she was also used to Biscuit's many other crazy diver friends showing up out of the blue. He came back and slid through the doors on his back in much distress, madly slapping his ass. The newspaper had set his nylon underwear on fire. I managed, between laughing, to put him out with a towel. Marilyn immediately came into the kitchen and gave me that look: *Don't even think about it or you are dead meat.*

The following morning I called his mum to see how he was doing. She told me in her melodic Geordie accent, 'Oh, he's had a terrible night, Kevin. I'll get him to tell you about it when he gets up.' He much later called and told me of his nightmare of events in the twilight hours.

He was in a lot of pain when they arrived home, so Mrs. Mac (Elsie), who was an ex-nurse, found some cream and applied it to his now badly burned bum. Shortly thereafter he started to have an allergic reaction to the cream. I had recalled that when we were young he was allergic to certain things. When he started to feel like he was going to pass out, they wisely decided to call the ambulance. On the way to the hospital, all he could think about was how they would write up the cause if he died: 'Man dies from freak flaming asshole accident.' By the time he arrived at the hospital he was having hallucinations and couldn't walk. He honestly thought his time had come. All the dangerous diving he had done in the navy and the North Sea would come to this calamitous and ridiculous end.

My partner in dominoes

Marilyn's father came to our house the day before we left. I wanted to leave some stuff behind that I probably would never use, but being the hoarder that I was, I just couldn't throw it away. The very last time I saw that lovely man, he was walking up our street with my old navy kitbag poignantly slung over his shoulder. He had promised to look after it for me. I would never play dominoes again with him on Sunday afternoons at the pub. We never said much to each other when playing dominoes, as it was a deadly serious game to win. God help me if I played the wrong domino. He might take his pipe out and say, 'Tha' follers me, not me thee.' I never saw him again!

It must have been doubly painful for Marilyn to leave, as her mother had taken a turn for the worse. She had been Marilyn's rock over the years and had always been there for her in her times of need – including the times when I probably was not the husband I should have been. She was now sleeping in a makeshift bed in the small living room. It was painfully obvious that her days were numbered. My memories of her are all good. She was tough and fiery, but she never said a bad word to me. It seemed I was always in her good books. I was blessed to have had such a wonderful mother-in-law.

Canada, our new home

It seemed everything was against us right from the start. Frank, Marilyn's brother-in-law in Canada, had a heart attack and died on holiday, only weeks prior to us coming to live with them.

Leaving England and our family and friends was the most difficult thing I had ever done. It was by far the most heart-wrenching experience of my life. I constantly asked myself if I was doing the right thing. Was it worth all the tears and sadness? My brother and sisters didn't really know what to make of it. Why should I want to leave England? This is all we had ever known. How much pain had I inflicted on the loved ones I had left behind? Was it *really* worth it?

We arrived in Toronto to more sadness. The whole house was like a morgue. Margaret was obviously devastated and wasn't sure where to go or what to do next. Getting Frank's body back from the US had been a major hurdle. Julie and Stephen, her kids, were still in shock and understandably needed constant consoling. Dominic was inconsolable. He missed his friends so much that many nights he cried like a baby until sleep came to him.

Two weeks later my dear old grandmother died. Over the last very busy years, I had seen less and less of her, to the point I was probably only visiting her two to three times a year. We would write to each other often. She was always concerned about my safety and always let me know how much she loved me. She knew her son Fred was one of my heroes and how much I cared for Aunt Ena, so she kept me abreast of where they were in the world and what they were doing – and when are you going to come visit me again? I was ravaged by guilt because I knew I could not even take the time to grieve for her. I had a sleepless night thinking about her and what she meant to me, then I took an early morning walk to say goodbye. It would be a lonely and teary grieving walk, because at home I had to be the consoler.

Marilyn was getting more upset by the day, as news from her now-dying mother, who was diagnosed with cancer only weeks before we left, was sadly being relayed across the many miles. I think if someone had handed us a ticket to return back home we would have gladly gone. From all of this bedlam, as the days became weeks and weeks became months, it started to gradually get a little better. Six weeks later we had found our house, the one we had dreamed about. House prices had increased so much since our holiday two years prior. We purchased a fixer-upper. A builder stonemason had divorced and the house, as usual, became a pawn. Her lawyer made the deal, and I had a contract that the guy would return to finish the stonework. It was a detached custom-built home with a large backyard backing onto a forest.

I loved the area, which was just outside the town of Pickering, northeast of the sprawling city of Toronto. We could go on many lovely walks through the forest to rivers and streams, and the drive to Margaret's would only be twenty minutes or so away.

When we were settled I called Bill Duncan. 'Okay, I'm here. Is that job offer still on?'

I told him I might still commute to the North Sea if things didn't work out. He sounded very keen to have me, and sent me a ticket to fly out to St John's, Newfoundland.

CHAPTER 54
Zapata Ugland

I arrived in St John's in March of 1982, just prior to my thirty-first birthday. A girl from the office had been sent to pick me up in a van. The snow in Toronto had mostly gone, but here there were piles of snow almost six feet high that had been ploughed to each side of the road. Even the main roads had a covering of snow. This tough-looking gal, who had obviously had a few drinks prior to picking me up, was talking in a real broad Irish accent. I only caught every other word. She seemed to be driving awfully fast on the snow and ice for my comfort. I must have asked her a couple times to slow down, to which she looked at me strangely and laughed like I'd cracked a funny or something. By the time we had reached the hotel, which was out on the highway miles from anywhere, it was snowing pretty hard.

'This is where I'm going to be staying?' I asked. It was like a series of log cabins, with one restaurant/bar/office area. It was late in the evening, so I had a quick bite and found my cabin. I called Bill, and he said he would be around in the morning to pick me up around seven.

Halfway through the night the power went off and it started to get a bit cold. I tried to call reception, but the phone wasn't working. *Idiot, the power's off*, I thought. I decided to get dressed and go over to the office, when I realized the door, which opened out, was now blocked with a huge snowdrift that had formed outside the door. I found as many blankets as I could, wrapped up as best as I could, and started to wonder just what the fuck I was doing there. I had to be stark, staring, friggin' crazy. I had a great job. I was happy! Everybody was happy! Now my wandering had gotten me in a log cabin in the middle of fucking nowhere freezing my ass off. The power was off for about an hour and a half before I managed to get some sleep.

I had done a lot of soul searching in that hour and a half, and I was almost ready to explain to this Bill Duncan guy, thanks, but no thanks. Please take me back out to the airport. This has been a huge mistake. He arrived and spoke to me through the door, because I still could not get out of my room. He had a guy from the reception shovel me out.

He seemed to be a nice enough kind of chap and was very friendly, an obvious Scot by the accent, and he was having a laugh as I told him of my experience. 'Ah, ye got tae get used to it 'ere, laddy.'

In the car on the way to his office he explained that he had a team of divers out on one of the rigs basically doing three weeks on and three off. One shift supervisor had already returned to the UK, so he had an immediate opening. He also had more deep-sea contracts coming up and there would be a need for another complete two shifts. He also looked after some air diving contracts off Halifax, Nova Scotia. The future was looking pretty bright with lots of work.

I explained that I was willing to give it a go, but I still had a job in the North Sea if things didn't work out. What seemed a big plus for me was that I would now have my chance at being a deep-sea diving supervisor. At my old job with Oceaneering, I might have to wait for a few months for someone to quit or a new job to start. I was more than confident that I could do the job – and Marilyn would sure be happy with the three-on and three-off routine.

The afternoon chopper out to the rig had been cancelled due to bad weather, so I decided to go and check out the town of St John's. I caught a cab from the motel and then walked up and down the main street. There were lots of people, but I didn't notice too many bars and was starting to think what a boring place it must be. I walked down to the docks. There were two fishing boats alongside the docks selling seal meat and flippers. They were surrounded by placard-holding, Greenpeace marchers. I went closer to see elderly women grabbing big chunks of bloody seal flippers and putting them into plastic bags. News reporters were filming all the action. Again, I wondered just how far I was from home. No one would possibly believe me if I told them what I was seeing here. I might just as well be on the moon!

Everyone seemed to come from Ireland, by the accent I was hearing. The following day I flew offshore and landed on the *Zapata Ugland,* a floating exploratory drilling rig, not any different from the ones I had been on in the North Sea. *Ah, familiarity at last,* I thought.

Peter Davies, the dive supervisor, met me. He was a Welshman and had been working out of St John's for a couple of years. On the way down to the living quarters, I enquired why there were so many Irish people there.

He said, 'No, no, they're Newfies. That's their accent.'

I wanted to go and look at the dive system real quick to see what I had gotten myself into. I was disappointed. It was a mess, and I was wondering if it was even dive able. Peter said it probably needed some work, but he had run some successful bounce dives in the past. Just one glance told me that it was an accident waiting to happen, and not what I was used to at all. The last thing that I wanted was to be on a system where somebody had died or been hurt. My record was clean, and so far in my years in the business I had never even seen an accident. I had witnessed some minor bends, but nothing serious. News traveled fast in this business. If you had anything remotely connected to a death, your chances of work diminished greatly.

I called Bill and gave him the bad news. *I wanted off. Thanks very much for the offer, but no.* He then asked me what I thought it needed to be workable. I gave him a few examples, the major one being the need for a complete new umbilical winch.

He said, 'Okay, I'll tell you what. Do your three weeks with Peter and bring me a complete list of all the things you think it needs to become safe and workable.'

I decided I had nothing to lose, so I went ahead and made up the list. It was going to cost a small fortune to get this rusting heap up to par. I faxed the list to Bill. I doubted very much that KD Marine was going to cough up the dough for it. Lo and behold, when I went ashore after my three-week spell, Bill told me that most of my requisition had been granted and in the next few months I would see all the items on the rig. I think I was more surprised that he had listened to me, a complete unknown, and I felt he had put a lot of trust in me. With that, I decided to stay a bit longer.

The following trip out I was the dive supervisor. In a roundabout way I had achieved what I had been working for these past few years. Bill ended up being a great person to work for. He trusted my judgment, and when we eventually did have our first dives with the system, there were no accidents and we performed them in a professional manner.

Peter later told me that I must have been blind if I hadn't seen all the bars on Water and Duckworth streets. He had made Newfoundland his home, and he was loving it.

Trying to make it work

Home life had started to get a little better – for a while. I installed new kitchen cabinets, we had the stonework completed, and most of the renovations were starting to get completed. After quite a while Dominic was even settling down. He found right away that school in Canada was a lot more lackadaisical than what he had been used to in the UK, of which he took complete advantage. His teachers all said the same thing. He was a very bright kid, but he didn't want to show it. Michaella wasn't doing quite as well. She, like her dad, was a late learner in life.

Michaella was seven years old when we were called to talk to her teacher during a parent day. The inquisitive teacher asked me some weird questions. 'Mr. Firth, what exactly is it that you do for a living?' When I asked why she was inquiring, she said curiously, 'Well, Michaella told us that you made sandwiches underwater, or that is the nearest thing we can come up with.'

When I told them what I did and what I thought she had got confused with, we all had a laugh. When I was away on the rig, if a TV program came on showing divers, Marilyn would say, 'Kila, that's what your dad does when he's away.'

When I was home, Kila would ask, 'Daddy, why do you always have to go away?' I would say 'To make jam butties,' meaning I had to work to feed us all. I guess you have to be so careful what you say, because children take things quite literally.

Kila was settling in quite well, and we both noticed very quickly that her Lancashire accent was changing. Our little sweetie was starting to sound very much Canadian.

Marilyn was a different story altogether. In our first year in Canada, her mother deteriorated quickly, and understandably she was taking it very hard not being there with her during her time of need. It seemed that every other day she got more and more sad information. Offshore, I would look forward so much to coming home. Things were going very well for me, and I couldn't wait to come home and tell her all the positive things going on in Newfoundland. I don't know whether she resented the fact that I was getting all the glory, or felt guilty about her mum and that I had inadvertently taken her away from her in her time of need. Either way, our arguments quickly turned ballistic in the blink of an eye.

When I was offshore I missed my family terribly. I never ever got used to the feeling that my kids were growing up without me. This was my job. I was successful in what I was doing and becoming a respected person in the office. When I came home we might have that honeymoon thing go on for a few days, but then it pretty much always faltered and we were back at one another's throats. The excitement and build-up of coming home was sometimes such an anticlimax, and I would inevitably end up going on long, lonely walks, trying to bring some sense into what was going on. When her mother died things went from bad to worse. Marilyn wanted to go back to England for good. I knew now that she blamed me for her not being with her mother when she was ill.

Friendly Newfies

I made lots of friends on the rig. Newfoundland people, I found, were the friendliest people you could find. Many times the chopper couldn't fly out to the rig for a couple of days because of fog. There were other rare occurrences when the weather was so bad that all rig personnel were evacuated ashore. It didn't happen very often, but when it did we got to sample St John's. Peter introduced me to his favourite haunts, and there were many. The whole street was a labyrinth of bars. In one building there might be three separate bars on different levels. The music was fantastic and was right up my street. I found bars and clubs that were playing folk music and others with amazing blues bands. Sometimes I played harmonica with the local bands. The whole place buzzed. I had never been in a place quite like it. You could be in a bar on your own and within a couple of hours you could easily make friends and end up at two different parties before dawn. Big oil had come to St John's, and like Aberdeen, this was quickly becoming the gold rush.

Marilyn had met some Newfies in Toronto and had mentioned how friendly they were. I said many times that we should sell up and move to St John's. I know she would have loved it, with her Irish background. Whenever the weather was bad I would be home more and see more of the kids. She flatly refused. She already felt very lonely with only her sister and a few friends that she had met, and didn't want to be uprooted again. Thinking back now, that was probably our biggest mistake.

Workin' Away Blues

Come and get your love here
Come and get your love right here
I'm on a sinkin' boat
An' I can't float
I got a year's worth of cryin'
I'm drownin' in my tears

(Chorus)
I got the work away blues
I got the work away blues, honey
One of these late nights
I'll come home
And keep you warm

Come and get your love here
Come and get your love right here
You say you're lonely
And been so sad
I got your letter
Now I'm feelin' bad

(Repeat Chorus)

Come and get your love here
Come and get your love right here
If I can ever
Get outta this can
I could take some leave
Would be my plan
I gotta invest some time
To be your man

(Repeat Chorus)

—K. Firth, May 31, 2011

CHAPTER 55
Mantis Duplus Submarines

Bill was busy finding new contracts. At the same time, a rich businessman purchased the Canadian division of KD Marine. Our company was now called Wolf Sub Ocean. Out of the three rigs working in the Hibernia field offshore, Bill had contracts for the diving support on two of them. But we were having difficulties manning them; a lot of the young divers just weren't making the cut. Peter and I were the only qualified supervisors, so quite often I wasn't getting my three weeks off, as I was sent elsewhere to fill in. The company was also investing heavily in underwater manned submarines, as that seemed to be where future underwater work was heading throughout the world.

Bill had given me some material to read up on. I had never seen this level of technology, even in the North Sea, which was undoubtedly number one in the world for all underwater work. One of the new partners in Wolf asked me how I would compare first, the risk factor, and secondly, the ability to perform underwater tasks between a sub with manipulators and a diver. On the upside, you could go down to over a thousand feet in one of those babies, perform some simple tasks, then return to the surface and just open the door. This was a one-atmosphere system; therefore, there was no expensive and potentially dangerous decompression to deal with.

However, I stopped him short and said, 'Oh, yeah, I can see that, but they haven't yet replaced the human hand.' There is nothing yet that can replace what a human diver can do at depth. However, it still got my attention, and months later the company purchased two state-of-the-art Mantis Duplus one-man submarines with their complicated topside control systems. They also hired an experienced sub pilot named Richard Chittleborough (Chits). This was cutting-edge technology, and I dearly wanted to be involved. It looked so futuristic and interesting. It brought back memories of my favourite sci-fi movie, *2001: A Space Odyssey,* when the astronaut was in his craft outside the mother ship. It also had two manipulators.

Bill had mentioned that I might be a bit too tall for one of these things, but I still pressed him to keep me involved. A few weeks later I received a call from Bill that he had hired some electronic techies straight from college and a couple of young divers. He was going to send them with Chits, the hired pilot, to Leicester, England for training. It would be a three-week training course at Osel Ltd., where the subs were made. Interestingly, he also wanted me to go and do the course. We would cram in as much as possible, including manned dives.

Chits, a fellow Brit, had been around subs for a while working in the oil and gas fields mainly around Thailand and the Far East. He had been pretty much living in Thailand for the last few years on his time off and had some interesting stories. Like most people in this line of work, he was a bit of a wild man too.

He and I boarded the plane in Halifax, Nova Scotia with the six very excited young men bound for the UK. On the way I had been talking to Chits and mentioned we had better hit the bank first thing and get some beer coupons (money). One of the young lads overheard this and came up to us later and said,

'What's all this about beer coupons?' Right away Chits and I knew we could have some fun with this, so we came up with an elaborate story about the pubs in the UK being particularly dangerous. Bars were rife with robberies, so instead of money you used beer coupons, which you could buy at any bank. They were all amazed at this and totally believed us.

I fell asleep shortly thereafter. It was a red eye flight. The next thing I knew we were landing a little early. I looked out the window, still not quite awake, and noticed we were landing in Halifax. I was thinking, *We were supposed to land in Manchester, England, not Halifax. Ah, well, the airport must be weathered in.* The plane had lost an engine over the Atlantic and had returned to Halifax, Nova Scotia. Four hours later we boarded another plane and eventually made it to the UK.

It was pretty funny watching the lads in the lineup at the bank waiting to exchange their money for beer coupons. And typical for British snotty banks, we heard the teller say to these obviously non-Brits, 'Sorry, sir, but we don't do that sort of thing over here.' When they turned around and saw me and Chits laughing our socks off, they realized what they were up against for the rest of the course.

I sat in on most of the techy stuff in the factory, even though some of it was above me and more for the electronic buffs. All the well-placed controls inside just made sense, and most of us got to grips with that quickly. We were all then transported to an old flooded quarry outside Leicester with the training inspectors. We would learn how to pilot or fly these subs and all of the complicated topside apparatus that came with it. The famous scientist Graham Hawks had designed these subs that could work manned or remotely operated unmanned up to 2,300 feet.

The one-man sub was basically a narrow tube with a thick clear dome at the front. Entry was from the rear. You slid in and laid on your stomach and the domed hatchway was closed behind you. In my case, I had to cross my legs so the door could be closed. We soon all realized spending a lot of time resting on your elbows got quite painful, so we each developed sponges or towels to keep our elbows from going to sleep. We had levers for thruster controls for forward, reverse, up, and down. On the left were button controls for the left five-function arm and manipulator. On the right was a pistol grip with triggers and swivel to control the more advanced seven-function arm that even had a telescoping manipulator. Directly in front was a monitor that displayed video from two low-light cameras, one above the front dome looking over a compass and the other on the five-function arm. In seemingly complete darkness down below, as you looked through the dome it was still possible to see quite clearly ahead through the video screen.

We had a steady trickle of O2 coming into the sub and a small Sodasorb scrubber taking out the CO2. Readings had to be taken every so often to check the levels for crucial life support. The reading material we were given said that you could live up to 100 hours inside the sub. My calculations from my diving experience showed much less. And at that, the cold would probably get to you first anyway. We all wore warm woolly bears (designed for dry suit diving), as it would get chilly after three or four hours in the sub, even in the shallow quarry around sixty feet.

Once in the sub we did all of the checks with the supervisor topside over the comms. He then had the sub lifted with the overhead winch, swung out over the water, and then lowered. Once in the water we checked for leaks and that all the controls were working correctly. When all of the checks had been done from the inside, we opened a valve that allowed water into the ballast tanks. At sea, we did this on deck so that we would be heavy going through the interface. The sub would then be negatively buoyant and sink. Once on bottom again, we went through a series of checks, and even checked emergency sonar through water communications in case of a tethered umbilical loss. The tether (lift wire) that also supplied power and communications would be slacked. Then you opened a valve inside the sub, allowing air into the ballast tanks and displacing the water until the sub was slightly positively buoyant. One quick thrust up would get you off bottom, and then you adjusted until you arrived at neutral buoyancy. In an emergency, the lift wire could be disconnected from the inside and the sub could operate on battery power for a limited time.

A working frame had been placed on the quarry bottom that had a sonar pinger. Inside the sub we had a sonar receiver, so you basically followed where the sound became louder to find the job.

Mostly we had to get used to using the manipulators. We had to learn how to fix a shackle and pin through an eyebolt. A very simple task like this could take literally hours of frustration. If you dropped either the pin or the shackle, it was a royal pain trying to find it in the silt. If you used any of the thrusters for movement, then you were covered in silt for the next ten minutes until the water cleared.

For about a week we worked a twenty-four-hour shift system so that we could all spend a maximum amount of time in the sub or learning the topside controls. When we were off shift, there were a couple of pretty good pubs just a wee walk down the road that evened out the frustration – well, that was our excuse. Most of the techies really didn't like being in the sub. The few divers took to it very well. For me, to come out dry and with no decompression to do was a no-brainer. I could see many advantages for the mundane offshore work of underwater videoing or very basic tasks, but as far as doing any real serious work, they had a long way to go. The last week was basically for the techies, so I stuck around for a few days and Chits and I introduced the lads to the many interesting English pubs.

Just for a laugh, I taught them a little ditty called 'Snow White and the Seven Dwarves' that I had learned in the navy and that was sure to get a few free beers. I would go into a busy bar and ask for one pint of beer and seven halves. Usually the bar staff would be kind of confused. My excuse was that I was in training for a speed-drinking contest, which usually brought a few smiles. I would then line them all up evenly along the bar and then sing out loudly, 'Hi ho, hi ho, hi ho.' By now, the whole pub would be looking over at this nut case and wondering what he was going to do next. They were probably contemplating calling the local constabulary. At that moment, the boys would all come marching in through the pub main doors on their knees singing, 'Hi ho, hi ho, it's off to work we go . . .', going all around the pub and finally stopping at the bar, where I would nonchalantly hand them all their beers.

It worked a treat a couple of times, and we did get a few free beers to perform at other pubs in the area – until one night the boys decided it was time to get their own back! I had set up the beers and done the loud 'Hi hos,' and was looking around the pub at the usual blank what-the-fuck-is-he-doing faces, but nobody came in. So I repeated, and still no one came. Everyone was now looking at me, like maybe they should be calling the local loony bin. I had to embarrassingly drink all the beers, and once outside the pub I came across Chits and all the lads by a window. They were all on the floor in painful laughter. They had got me back, as I sat on the curb totally bloated with beer!

CHAPTER 56
A Surprise Visit

I called Bill and he allowed me to take a few days off, as it was mainly heavy techy electronics stuff, way beyond my scope. I rented a car and drove north to visit my mum. It had been almost two years since I had seen her last. She was totally surprised to see me. We spent a few very precious days together. I walked downtown with her and the two dogs in and out of all the little shops she frequented, where she proudly introduced her son 'who worked on the oil rigs.' We went to the market and visited every stall. Everyone knew her. We drank homemade sarsaparilla and had a wonderful spud pie dinner in the market's upstairs café. I was royally introduced to the waitresses, kitchen staff, and other people in the busy café. She was so proud of her son. Most of them wanted to comment on what a character my mum was. She was always cheerful. Her dogs never wandered too far from her side.

I didn't care that she had one of her crazy hats on, a black beret over her long, dyed black hair. Not a single item of clothing actually matched, right down to her socks. She was my mum and I was proud, simply because she was content to just be herself.

Grandma had forced her to wear a hat when we were growing up, a modest prerequisite from a bygone age, and she hated them with a passion. She would only wear them when Grandma came to visit. At this time it seemed to me that this was her rebellion on hats. If she had to wear a hat, well, it was going to be something special and make a statement of her individuality. She was free to do as she pleased, and they could just take her as they found her – or not at all. She didn't give a hoot!

I sadly noticed in the two years since seeing her last that she had aged a lot. She had cataracts and her precious eyesight was going. She was terrified of going blind, which was understandable with her deafness. We all thought Mum was otherwise in good shape. She walked a lot and most people would not think she was in her mid-sixties.

I was so relieved that Freda lived next door with her husband and their two daughters, but it didn't help my guilt when it was time to leave. I promised when things were more settled at home that I would be back to visit again. Mum and I always wrote letters to each other, as we had done all through my navy days. She would never know how much they had become such a comfort for me in times of loneliness and doubt, though I couldn't tell her how unhappy I was at home. I didn't want her to worry, and she never really got on with Marilyn anyway. That was something I had to keep to myself. I had made my bed, as it were. I was now travelling a somewhat bumpy and unfamiliar road of my own making, and I had no idea where it would take me. Again through many tears, I dragged myself away back to Canada and whatever awaited me there.

CHAPTER 57
Bowdrill One and Two

Bill had managed to purloin two more contracts on two Bowdrill exploratory floating rigs being built in St. John, Nova Scotia. These would be working off Nova Scotia using the Mantis Duplus sub systems and not diver support. He had ordered two subs to be installed with the system on *Bowdrill Two* when it was out of the dockyard.

At about the same time he also got the contract to raise the *Ocean Ranger* that had sank back in 1982. The rig had completely flipped, and as the water depth was around 260 feet, the bottom of the floating pontoons were close enough to the surface that some of the large tankers could be in danger of hitting her. It was fairly obvious that I was going to have more work than I could have ever hoped for – too much.

It didn't seem very long before we were installing the sub system on *Bowdrill One*. Both of the Bowdrill rigs were way behind schedule and had become an embarrassment for Canadian shipbuilding on the east coast. My first trip on board was dotted by a few scary moments. We had a fire on board and some of the emergency systems didn't work as they were supposed to. We then had a serious list that almost necessitated evacuating the rig. Rig construction was actually still in progress as it was being towed out to location and for the first few months of drilling!

The main rig control room that was responsible for the important task of keeping the vessel upright and sufficiently buoyant looked like a disaster. One of the two American rig control operators had just quit in despair. He said it was just too dangerous and he didn't want to be on board. It was not very reassuring that not more than a couple of years had passed since the disaster with the *Ocean Ranger*. All eighty-four men had been lost, and now it seemed that the lesson had not been learned. No one seemed to care in the least that it could very easily happen again. Big oil was number one and safety did not seem to be of primary concern. After a few hiccups, we finally had our sub system up and running and successfully ran some test dives.

Bill had managed to hire a couple of experienced Norwegian technicians who had worked on the same Mantis Duplus sub system. I was very glad that he had, because without them we might have been in serious trouble. The new techies that had taken the training had a long way to go before they would be ready to fully understand the mechanisms of this highly sophisticated technology.

Luckily we had a couple of divers on the crew, as the rig had problems with its anchor lines. I had to run a series of surface dives to get them sorted out.

One of the lads in the crew was an ex-Canadian navy submariner, so he was a natural in the sub and wasn't as fidgety and nervous as some of the other men. Of course, being ex-navy, we both hit it off and had many laughs recounting sillier times while serving in the military. We had both changed crew at the same time and hit the airport bar in Halifax for a few. He lived in Halifax, so he didn't have far to go. Not having had alcohol in the weeks I had been offshore, the drinks he seemed to be loading into me were hitting their mark. I remembered him helping me with my bag as I boarded the plane.

I awoke later as I landed in Saint Pierre Miquelon, an island just off the south coast of Newfoundland. *What the hell am I doing here?* I asked myself as I realized the big joke he had successfully made at my expense. There were no flights out, so I had to stay the night and leave first thing in the morning. When the Visa bill came in later that month showing the cost of the additional flight and hotel, I had to hastily ensure all evidence was immediately destroyed before Marilyn saw it.

CHAPTER 58

Raising and Sinking the *Ocean Ranger*

I had heard about the *Ocean Ranger* job, and it had never occurred to me that I might not be part of the crew involved in the salvage operation. This was going to be a huge task that would be heard throughout the world, especially in the diving community. I was fortunate to be here working for the same company that was probably going to make history.

Bill had previously hired a supervisor diver named Dutch Ritter. He was from Holland (obviously). He and I hadn't seen eye to eye on a previous rig where I was the supervisor and he was part of the crew. We had had a power struggle, and Bill very wisely took him off the rig. Offshore, I was a different animal. When it came to work and safety, I wasn't there to make friends – the job always came first.

When I heard that Dutch was going to be running the job as dive superintendent, I knew right away that I would not be included in the crew. I couldn't believe my luck. I had worked so hard and spent so much time offshore for this company to be pushed aside like this. I pleaded with Bill, but he had made up his mind. By learning the sub system and keeping the other two diving rig jobs going, I had somehow maneuvered myself out of the big one.

I spent a very busy summer hopping from one job to another. Peter was on the *Ocean Ranger* job, so Bill had to scurry around trying to find suitable personnel to relieve me offshore, only to then send me down to Halifax to supervise the sub jobs. I spent very little time at home, and what time I did was difficult, to say the least. Marilyn was becoming increasingly dissatisfied and wanted to return to the UK. It was feast or famine. Here I was supervising three rig jobs, and even though I had been passed aside for the job I really wanted, I knew I was still an important link.

I couldn't even think about returning to the UK and what I had left behind workwise. I had come so far and achieved more than I ever expected. Here I was, a big fish in a small pond. I also loved everything about Canada – you worked hard and you played hard. That had always been my motto. I saw so much opportunity. It was almost a frontier for the taking. Canadians, especially the Newfies, seemed to be hard working. 'Okay, let's get the job done, but let's not forget to enjoy ourselves while were doing it.' It was that kind of attitude. The only class system I found was the amount of money in your pocket, and in most cases, even that was hard to justify. Most of the people I had met who had money were still very much down to earth.

There was no question that there were many things I missed about my life in England, and I always would. This, I knew, was where my future lay, where I could flourish and widen my horizons. I could always return to England and the bosom of my family whenever I liked. But now I could also return successful, not to show off, but to feel their pride in me. Our strange upbringing had brought my siblings and me closer together. We may not have called each other as often as we should, but I knew that they would always be there for me.

I had not totally given up on the fact that I still might get on the Ranger job. I was keeping a close ear on most of the information coming from the lads coming out to the rigs. They had installed a deep-dive system on board a massive ship. The bell was launched over the ship's side. The company had the contract to install large valves on the lowest part of the ballast pontoons. They were used to pump air to displace the water in the pontoons to help float the rig. It would then be towed out to deeper water where she would be sunk again out of harm's way.

There was a Dutch air diving company on board that had the contract to install the same valves on the shallower part of the ballast pontoons, which were obviously closer to surface since the rig had flipped upside down. Earlier on in the work, an English diver working for the Dutch company was accidentally dragged to the bottom by one of the heavy valves. By the time they returned him to the surface he was pronounced dead. A little while later, two of the Dutch divers were working together using a tool that shot threaded bolts directly into the hull where the valves could later be attached. Pockets of gas must have built up in the top part of the pontoons over the three years it had been underwater, because the first hot bolt ignited the gas, ripping a fifteen-meter hole in the thick steel hull. Both divers were instantly killed. The death toll for the Ocean Ranger now totaled eighty-seven.

For most of the lads working on this contract, this would be their first saturation dive, and they did well. The job was done with few problems and no accidents from our company. One evening, the rig surprised everyone by floating to the surface unexpectedly. It was then towed out, but it sank again before reaching the intended destination. However, it was in enough depth to be of no concern, so it was left at its new gravesite.

CHAPTER 59
Hangover at Eight Hundred Feet

The night before flying out to the rig, Chits and I had a particularly heavy drinking night ashore with the lads in Halifax. I had just returned ashore from being out off St. John's on the rig with the diving crew for six straight weeks. I now had to go offshore again, having had just two days ashore and not enough time to fly home. I was fried in more ways than one. Even though things were bad at home, I still missed my family and desperately wanted to go home. Bill promised he would get a relief supervisor out as soon as possible. Booze seemed to be the antidote to freeze all the crazy thoughts going on in my head.

The following day we arrived on board, and all I wanted to do was sleep off my nasty hangover. It wasn't going to happen. They had a problem on bottom, which was at 800 feet. Chits wanted me in the sub, as the other lads on board weren't too experienced. I was really out there as Chit's night shift supervisor. Okay, no problem. Let's just get on with it. Thankfully, by the time the rig had got themselves sorted out, it was a few hours later and I had time to recover a bit.

I slid into the sub and crossed my legs, as I was unceremoniously squashed in and the sub was launched after we finished all the checks. On bottom we did all the checks, including the through-water sonar comms. Everything was in working order. We slacked off the lift wire and I went neutral and motored over to find the wellhead. They were trying to pass a drill collar into a small hole in the guide base to pump down cement. They had been at this for a while, judging by all the scraping and dints in the guide base. As I videoed the damage, they decided that they should change the tool, so I had a serious wait on my hands while they took up 800 feet of drill collar. I cleared well away from the area in case they dropped something, then I went heavy on bottom.

Every time I turned on my outside lights during the videoing, a million or so tiny shrimp converged on my dome, so all I could see was red. If I used my thruster it sucked up a few thousand, and now it was really red with all the smashed up shrimp now plastered on my viewing dome. So I kept the lights off while I waited. The only light inside was from the various control panel switches. My elbows and knees were getting sore, so I managed to turn over on my back. It was pretty tight in there, and I laid my head on one of my elbow pads laid on the TV monitor. It was so peaceful there at 800 feet. It was totally black but with lots of swimmy things around the dome.

My headache was throbbing a bit. I thought, *I'll just close my eyes for a second*. I woke with a stir. How long had I been sleeping? I looked at my watch. Oh, maybe ten minutes or so, no big deal, but it had been awfully quiet on the comms. Then I noticed that some of the breakers on the panel at the top part of the sub were off. Oops! I must have accidentally turned them off when I turned over on my back. *Shit*.

I flicked them back on and immediately heard a very concerned voice on the comms. 'Kevin, you okay, over?'

'Oh, yes, no problem, Chits. I . . . um . . . accidentally turned off the comms breaker. Sorry, mate.'

I was used to waiting. Even as a diver, you do an awful lot of waiting for tools to be passed down or for the rig or ship to do some test or other. After quite a wait, the tool was back and I motored back over to the wellhead and grabbed the pipe in my seven-function arm manipulator. There was quite a strong current, so I was having difficulty staying on station and holding the pipe all at the same time, so I gave control of the arm to Chits. He had the exact replica of my controls in the sub control room topside and could remotely work all the same functions that I could down there, and with the two video screens he could also see what was going on. Between the two of us, he had the arm and I worked the thrusters to push the pipe over the hole. We missed two or three times because, by the time we had relayed the message to the driller to come down, we missed and, *doink*, the full force of the rig came down on the pipe and bent it all out of shape. On the third attempt it threaded into the hole nicely – job done.

In the couple of years I had worked with those amazing machines, we never had a serious problem or a situation that was too dangerous. I was mainly a supervisor, but when Chits was on board I got to dive them myself, which I found quite rewarding.

Flying home always seemed to be an adventure for me, maybe because I had looked forward to it so much. We were constantly tested. When the day came when I was told that I had a relief ready to fly out after a long shift offshore, and then be told that the weather was too bad to fly, the disappointment was hard to take. Sometimes this went on for days; being fogged in, the frustration level was almost unbearable. Then the heavenly day came and away you went with a light heart.

On one memorable flight, I had arrived at the international airport in St. John's, Newfoundland and was awaiting the direct flight to Toronto. Peter was also ashore, so we had a few drinks – just to be sociable. It was an unusual occurrence to have us both ashore at the same time. Eventually, as I was lining up to board the plane feeling quite merry, I remembered that Marilyn had asked me to bring home lobsters. I had told her in a letter that they sold them at the airport quite inexpensively. I immediately rushed off and purchased a dozen lobsters that I personally chose from a big tank. They were packed in a cardboard box surrounded by ice. I then hastily ran to the plane and boarded.

My seat was at the very front of the plane on the aisle. I introduced myself to the two teachers in the two seats to my right. Across the aisle, I also introduced myself to an attractive business lady wearing glasses who was looking at some papers. I had the box of lobsters on my knee and my briefcase under the seat. In front of me was the wall, so there was no place to put the lobsters. The stewardess shortly came and explained that the lobsters would have to go into the hold because there was no room under the seats. In my happy state, I had some fun with her, which in those days you could get away with. I told her that if they went into the hold they would die, and I had promised my wife they would arrive home alive. There were a few sniggers around me. The hostess was smiling as we had some silly banter back and forth. I leaned over and asked the lady across the aisle if she would kindly look after my lobsters, as she had room under her seat. She also saw the funny side of it and agreed.

Twenty minutes into the flight I was missing all the sniggering. It had got me going, so I leaned over to the business lady. 'Excuse me, ma'am.' She looked up smiling. 'I thought you said you were going to look after my lobsters.'

'They're fine,' she said. 'Leave them alone.'

'But you haven't checked on them in over twenty minutes,' I protested.

She pulled out the box and opened the lid to show me that everything was in order. The sniggering had now spread to a few seats behind us. After the third time of asking roughly fifteen minutes apart, she was starting to get a little exasperated, but still smiling because of all the laughing.

I said, 'Okay, I need to see my lobsters. Give them to me.' She handed over the box and I opened it. 'Oh, no, they are dying!' I cried out loud enough so that the whole front of the plane could hear. The stewardess, who had been listening in on most of the banter going back and forth and had joined in the laughter once or twice, knew I was at least a happy drunk!

'These lobsters need some exercise. They are dying!' I cried again quite loudly. I immediately removed the elastic bands that held their claws together and let all twelve of them loose on the plane. If you have ever seen a lobster move once it has seen freedom, well, needless to say they can move pretty fast. The whole front of the plane was in laughter by now.

Then the stewardess, who was trying to keep a straight face, came up to me and said, 'Sir, can you collect your lobsters? They are annoying the passengers!'

Everyone fell about laughing as I walked back in the aisle collecting my lobsters. One lady was standing on her seat with a lobster firmly gripped on her handbag. If that had happened today the RCMP would have been waiting for me in Toronto to lock me up! There were many other situations that I inadvertently got myself into travelling home after long and sometimes dangerous hauls offshore. Some, as above, were funny, some not so funny!

CHAPTER 60

My Kids

As I write this, I know I am cherry picking all the interesting bits. However, for the most part while offshore, I spent many long periods of time with nothing to do but think. During the short busy periods time went by quickly, full of interests and adventure. There were more times when all I could think about was my kids. I missed them so much. Dominic and I were growing distant.

Dominic couldn't have been more than seven or eight years old back in England when the social workers were telling us it was time to inform him that I wasn't his biological father. I knew it had to come from me, so I took him on a car drive over the Grane to my favourite spot. We went for a little walk. He never knew the wall he eventually sat on was where my dog Jake was buried, and it was also where I had buried all of the letters I had collected from Angela. The wall overlooked the three reservoirs in the valley, with Haslingden in the distance. Haslingden, the only place I had found some happiness in my youth.

I had been explaining to him on the way over in the car how, 'When I came along, you were already a tiny baby, a little treasure, and I loved you and your mummy so much that we became a family.'

He didn't ask many questions, but I had a feeling he knew what I was saying. Weeks later while I was away, Marilyn spoke to him to see if he had understood. Apparently, he just said, 'I don't care. My dad's my dad and that's it.'

Over the following years, I don't know if it played on his mind or not. We never spoke of it again, but he was never quite the same. Now that I was constantly away and he had been taken from all he knew in England, I knew he felt resentment. He also saw that his mum and I seemed to be constantly arguing. My heavy drinking wasn't making too much ground with him either. I had nightmares thinking I was turning out just like my ill-fated dad.

Break the Chain

Leave this man be
Let him drink to oblivion
Till sweet thoughtless sleep
Slumbers him on
This port's like any other
You'll find 'em by the score
Propping up the bar
Sailors from a different shore

These husbands of the sea
Escape reality
To court the widow maker
The cruel sea mistress
She'll grip you and hold you
Till you drown in her distress
The story's like many others
You'll find 'em by the score

Hearts riven . . . homes broken
Souls rotting to the core

(Chorus)
Break the chain to change the course
Stop the pain and ease the force
Find the wound and heal the source
History repeating over and over again

Long since memories burnt
The father who found his reason
At the bottom of his glass
This child who took the burden
Of the crashes and the screams
From the hands that would lash
Days without beginning
Nights without end
Did he start the chain
Or does the story go back further
Did he feel that childhood pain

(Break)

This legacy of shame still festers and burns
It hides in the soul and tosses and turns
Hold back the tears
It'll heal with the years
Hide all the memories
And paint out the good
This body has no room for
A little girl's hug
The curse that he holds

You must not inherit

(Repeat Chorus)

—K. Firth, June 1998

    Kila was different. She was close to me, no matter what happened. We would go on long walks together, her little hand in mine, and she would plead with me not to go away again. It was all I could do to wrench myself away, making promises that I knew I couldn't keep that I would be home again soon and try to bribe her with promises of a wonderful holiday.

    I received letters from Kila inside her mother's letters while I was on the rig that, in just a few lines that I read over and over again, would literally break me in two for days at a time. I would take them into the bell or chamber with me, and at some ungodly depth at the bottom of the North Sea in a flickering dim light I would read them again. When I was home I loved to sit by her bed and watch her sleep. She looked like a little angel. I almost knew that it was too much to ask to have her with me always. Sooner or later, I had the feeling she would somehow be taken from me.

CHAPTER 61
My Transgressions

For the remainder of the year after the raising of the *Ocean Ranger*, the rest of the lads came back to the rigs to tell of all their interesting adventures that I'm sure will be passed on to their respective grandchildren. I was getting a little more time off, even though I was still working from three rigs. My life seemed to be in a complete quandary, the Jekyll-and-Hyde life all over again. I was having a lot of success at work, and there were all kinds of future prospects, but then I went home to depressive arguments. It wasn't long before temptation ashore brought me in contact with other women.

The few days going from one job to another or weathered off, if I was allowed and there was enough time to go home, I always made that choice. What I wanted was my wife. I loved her and I wanted her love – and I sorely needed her affection. I wanted to make her happy and for her to be proud of me. I remembered how she used to look at me. All of that was now a distant memory and completely out of my grasp. I knew this job had a lot to do with it. She must have spent many lonely days contemplating her life. I know she wanted the same material things that I did – the nice home and nice car. Neither one of us wanted to go back to worrying if we could pay the rent or if we could send our kids to school wearing the right clothes.

I had taken this road and I had found success. The job, apart from the being away bit, was all me! Could I walk away from it now? What else could I possibly do? I had learned enough in my life so far that going back was *not* an option.

Women ashore, especially in Newfoundland, were very friendly. This was like the gold rush in the Klondike. Not only were we in the oil business, we were deep-sea divers, and everyone knew that we must be making a fortune (if they only really knew). I must have looked like the catch of the century being a deep-sea diving supervisor. I knew it was wrong, and I always felt very guilty. I could come up with umpteen excuses why I thought it was okay, but deep down I knew this was the beginning of the end of my marriage. While I was home I swore to myself that when the temptation came again I would resist. Somehow through all of this I still loved my wife. If only we could work it out or, better still, move our family out to Newfoundland, just maybe she could get used to this country. I found Scarborough or Pickering in Ontario cold as regards to making friends. They were more the outskirts, almost bedroom communities of greater Toronto.

It seemed that there was nothing I could do to make things better. Too much water had run under the bridge. Happiness in Canada for us as a family just wasn't meant to be! She very soon found out about my indiscretions, and I fully expected her to leave me. I had let her down terribly. By some miracle we made it through. Things were never quite the same, but I thought there was a small hope that things would change in time.

CHAPTER 62
Ocean Ranger Seabed Clearance

The following year, Bill got the contract for the seabed clearance of the remains of the *Ocean Ranger*. When the rig had flipped over, just about everything came off the main superstructure. In the following years, it had been beaten around with currents and the atrocious weather we experienced on the Grand Banks off Newfoundland, so there wasn't much still attached to the superstructure. Everything from the main deck upwards was now scattered over the seabed. The fisheries were kicking up a fuss, as it was disturbing their main fishing grounds, a major contentious issue in later years. Mobil Oil was about to spend millions of dollars to do a cleanup. I wasn't going to miss out on this one, and made sure that Bill knew it!

The second largest ship in the world, the *Mighty Servant 2*, slowly came into St. John's Harbour. Coming through the narrows, it was stirring up mud from the bottom. We were up on signal hill where Marconi had made the very first radio transmission to Cornwall, England in 1901. Together with TV news crews and hundreds of people watching, this massive vessel squeezed through the narrows. After this monster had tied up alongside the docks, there didn't seem much room left over for anything else. The huge ship was 130 feet from side to side and 625 feet long. It was basically all flat deck, with a seemingly small bridge and living quarters at the forward end. It was designed to flood its massive empty void of a hold with water to sink almost to the bridge, then it would back up under a type of oil rig called a 'jack up.' It would then pump the water out, raising the complete oil rig to move it to its next location.

The far aft part of this huge deck had already been refitted with a diving moon pool, a long tunnel from the deck to an opening in the ship's hull way down below. It was also fitted with a huge crane with a lift capacity of 350 tons. It had a deck crawler crane that looked like a dinky toy on its deck.

We now had the job of installing our deep-sea saturation diving system on board. We were split up into two shifts, and as usual I got the night shift. The system was one that we had previously taken off one of the rigs that had recently left the Hibernia field.

We had a large transfer chamber, a two-man decompression chamber, and a larger six-man living chamber. Because of a miscalculation of bolting on the living chamber flange, it had to be installed slightly sideways, so the table and beds inside the chamber were all off kilter. We had a team of British technicians that had come out from the North Sea KD Marine operation to help install the system. Of course I knew a few of them, and we had a good talk about Biscuit, who they had just left on a job. It was indeed a small world!

Peter would come on board at noon, and I would catch a few hours' sleep and then head off ashore not to be seen until midnight. All of the bars were a short walk up the road. A few weeks later the system was completed and tested. It was ready for action. By now, Peter and I were suffering badly from 'alcoholicatisis' and needed to go offshore to do some serious drying out.

The ship pulled out with our system completely installed, our living containers, and pods upon pods of helium gas quads and various other support containers. We also had an ROV team with their own operations shack to one side of our dive shack. As the ship exited through the narrows, we were being filmed by Canadian National TV, among many other news teams. Signal Hill was lined with hundreds of people. It was a lovely sunny spring afternoon, and it didn't take long before the whole diving team decided to line up on deck and moon everyone. It was on national TV throughout Canada.

About five miles out of harbour we stopped to allow a small boat to unload the explosives on board needed for the job. We had all done a course on explosives a few weeks prior to leaving.

This wasn't a DP vessel, so anchors had to be set before any diving could commence. Normally, the ROV would be deployed to find the debris. Once it was located, we would set up the dive. The bell would be launched through the long moon pool tunnel. Arriving on bottom, the ROV would meet the diver coming out of the bell and take him to the job, also supplying the diver with light to work in. We had various winches on deck that we used to pass down working wire tugger lines for the diver to use to haul long, heavy strop wires.

For example, the *Ocean Ranger* rig anchor capstans weighed in at over twenty tons each. The first job was to ensure everything attaching it to the seabed was cut, including the anchor wire, which was two inches thick. A heavy two-inch strop wire had to be wrapped around the capstan winch, and the eye of the strop lifted to where the huge crane hook hung with a heavy shackle attached. The pin for this shackle probably weighed in at four or five pounds. If you could attain a lift of one of these anchor winches on deck in your four- to six-hour dive you were doing good. There were eight of these anchor winches and eight wildcat anchor chain winches to be brought up.

Some of the divers picked up pretty quick and got the idea, but I was getting very frustrated supervising some guys that shouldn't have been there in the first place. It was obviously dangerous work, and some of the new guys just didn't seem to get it. One new diver flatly refused to leave the bell one night. The Mobil rep in the dive shack was not amused as I spent hours trying to talk him into it. The lad was absolutely terrified. Embarrassingly, we had to abort the whole dive. We couldn't send the other diver out, because we knew if he got in trouble the other diver was too scared to go and rescue him. The whole thing was a costly experience when we had to decompress him out of SAT.

The Brit tech crew had left and we were already having hot water problems. I was spending way too much time trying to fix stuff on my 'sleep' off time. Dennis Barrington had worked as assistant supervisor for a little while. I thought that he was ready to jump into a full supervisor position.

Dutch Ritter was the dive superintendent and was berthed with the other Dutch crew below the bridge superstructure way forward of us. At any time of day we had six divers in SAT, and usually a pair of them down below in the bell. Nobody had thought about how we were to be fed. That fact had slipped everyone's attention. Bill and the powers that be at Wolf Sub Ocean thought that the Dutch company, Wijsmuller, who had this whole contract, was going to supply cooked food. We really were just the hired diving company. The first day on board I took my crew up for breakfast to their canteen, and the chef gave us raw bacon.

'Ahem, excuse me. Could you please cook it?' I asked.

'No, we eat bacon raw,' was my answer.

Lunch was raw mincemeat with a raw egg on top. I complained, and from that day on we were banned from their quarters. They then supplied us with buns and sliced ham, which they called *boligges*, two or three times a day. After a few weeks of this everyone was ready to mutiny, especially the divers in SAT. Bill flew out on a chopper and saved the day by bringing McDonald's for everyone and some cooking facilities with boxes of food. We now had to cook for ourselves.

Once I thought I had the dreaded hot water machine fixed, I asked to go into SAT. Dennis would take my position as supervisor of the night shift. Peter thought I had completely lost my marbles, as he advised, 'You do know I hope, if you fuck up just once, do you think you're going to be able to supervise again? And besides that, don't you think you're getting a bit old for this at thirty-three?'

The average diver in SAT in those days was in their early twenties. Nonetheless, whether I had a death wish or just wanted to prove it to myself again that I could do it, I pushed the issue and was eventually put in with Derek St. Clair Golding, whose nickname was Critical Mass Golding because he had almost blown his hand off as a kid making bombs. He was a bit on the crazy side. But hey, who wasn't in this business? I had been working with him for a few years and trusted his ability. He was the kind of guy you could trust if you got in trouble.

On one of our first dives, I had locked out and returned to a very bad smell in the bell. He had been bored and had caught some of the tiny shrimp flitting around in the bell trunk and decided to cook them with the hot water from his umbilical. Another time, I came back for some tool or other and looked through one of the ports to see him juggling with a pair of dive knives.

On my first dive, we stopped the bell around thirty feet off bottom, as I could see wreckage close by through the ports and didn't want the bell to get snarled up in it. We generally didn't wear fins. They mostly got in the way. We would normally put a few weights in the suit leg pockets and went heavy. Once on the seabed, you would put the heavy and cumbersome umbilical over your shoulder and drag it to wherever the job was. You would then set yourself up with the arc Brocco cutting torch, another set of cables to deal with, and start arc cutting wires and huge chunks of steel. The ROV was out of service for our first few dives, so on this daytime dive at 260 feet, a fair bit of dark-blue light was still diffusing down, showing me what we were up against.

It is hard to explain the feeling of seeing mounds of bent and tortured containers, pieces of deck and cables of every description. There was even a lifeboat crushed upside down mangled up in the wreckage. I was being lowered down by Derek in the bell, giving me slack on my umbilical. Everywhere I looked there was wreckage. It was all around me. Before I realized it, I was being dropped into a dark hole in amongst the wreckage. I had to ask topside to tell Derek to 'all stop' on my umbilical and 'take up slack' while I found a solid purchase to climb out. The whole area looked like a scrap yard that had been dropped from a great height. Insanely disfigured objects had dealt with years of nature at its worst! Above me I saw that there were huge bent steel girders covered in loose cables, looking like they were just waiting for that moment in time to come crashing down. I got out of there real quick and returned to the bell. We had them move the ship over so that we could start at an edge and work our way into the wreckage.

Between the two of us, we were doing quite well bringing up the anchor winches. We then had the job of bringing up the living compartments, so it was a bit eerie to say the least. Every time we tried a lift something else was attached. We brought the bell up above the lift, just in case anything fell on us, so we were in and out of the bell for over twelve hours. It was already hooked on the crane and the weather was starting to get bad, so we had to keep at it. Thankfully, it eventually broke loose. All we could see from the ports was a huge dark shape through the daylight murk coming up past the bell. When we tried to raise the bell we found that the bell winch had cut out. Some of the guys up top were trying to find out what the problem was and thought it had just overheated. Meanwhile, this dark shape, which we had both nicknamed the killer wall, was coming closer and closer to the bell. The current was pushing it toward us like a big sail. When it almost seemed like it was on top of us, the bell winch fired up and we were thankfully brought up.

Having the ROV on the bottom was definitely a luxury – well, when it was actually working! It would sit by the bell like an obedient dog and wait for the diver. Once you locked out it would turn, almost wag its tail (not really), and you would follow it. The little ROV looked like a large football. It also had a little manipulator arm, camera, and a light. These operators sure knew their stuff, and on many occasions made a difficult task just a little easier and somewhat safer. As a supervisor, being able to see the diver at all times and how he was rigging his job made controlling the diving operation much easier.

When we were out cutting wires and steel in amongst that scrapyard, it was easy to get your umbilical tangled up. We were using a special Kirby Morgan helmet fitted with a Krasburg helium reclaim, which meant another thick exhaust hose in an already heavy umbilical that had to be dragged around the seabed wherever you went.[13] Our exhaust gasses were returned via the umbilical to the surface reclaim unit. The gas was then sanitized, the CO_2 removed, and the correct mixture of O_2 added for the depth we were working at. The gas was then resupplied to the diver – a huge saving on the expensive helium gas.

---

13. http://www.divescrap.com/DiveScrap INDEX/History Krasberg.html

The experienced ROV operators went back to check our hoses and reported if they saw a problem. If we were busy and didn't really need the ROV, the operator would sometimes ask the supervisor if it was okay to go off exploring. The supervisor would ask the diver and would usually give the okay. He came back once and gave me a full nylon bag with his manipulator. Ominously, I later found that it was the emergency chamber heating blankets for the diving system on the sunken rig. On a previous dive weeks earlier, a pair of divers had brought up the decompression chamber from the sunken rig, which kind of put the willies into everyone.

Peter had sent me out looking for a large piece of debris. Again the ROV was not working, so once away from the bell lights I had to rely on my flashlight. It was night, so there was no light coming down from the surface. I think they had found something large on their sonar and had given me a heading. We were using 180-foot hoses, which were kind of naughty. In the UK, anything over 120 feet was illegal. I was half walking and half crawling on the seabed, dragging my umbilical over my shoulder, looking every which way, when all of a sudden, *boink*, my helmet hit a steel plate. I felt with my hands, and yep, whatever it was, it was big. I turned on my flashlight and looked up. It was a flat piece of steel plate, and I couldn't see where it ended. Whichever way I looked, it just went on and on. It reminded me of the monolith in Arthur C. Clarke's *2001: A Space Odyssey*. Okay, so bite me – I have an imagination!

Peter said, 'Hey, mate, you might have found the helideck.'

I eventually found an end and went behind to find a good lift point. They sent down the crane wire with the heavy strop, and after an hour or so of rigging, we successfully brought it on deck. It was the largest piece of the structure still in one piece. Peter said over the comm how he and the others were impressed at such a huge load coming on deck.

We later found the drill floor, which was a solid four-inch steel plate. Even the 350-ton crane couldn't budge it. We used explosives twice, and even in pieces it wasn't going anywhere, so today it is one of the few pieces still remaining on the seabed.

Life in the chamber with the five other divers was dull. When the weather was okay, we would dive around the clock, eight- to twelve-hour shifts each. The light was constantly off, as sleep and a bit of food is all that was needed. When the weather was bad, we got to rest and recuperate and play cards or dominoes. A Sony Walkman was my favourite friend. I had three or four cassette tapes that I must have heard a hundred times.

Some of the new guys on deck hadn't yet figured out what the pressure differences were about when passing in food through the medical lock. If you stacked plastic glasses on top of each other, it was impossible to part them once pressured up in the chamber. Anything with bubbles, as in soft drinks or even lemon meringue pie, did not arrive in the chamber the same as it was on the surface. Passing in Styrofoam cups of coffee ended up a big mess in the med lock, as the cup shrunk to about two inches tall. And lastly, it's always nice to have knives and forks to eat with, thank you! Had you made any of those embarrassing mistakes on some of the big jobs in the North Sea off Scotland, you might never get in SAT.

Another side effect under pressure was that you kind of lost most of your taste buds, which under the circumstances on this job was probably a good thing. After a few days lying around in your bunk in the cramped quarters, it was almost a relief to lock out of the bell and stretch for a while. For a few days the hot water machine gave us some trouble, and as I was unable to fix it, being in the pot we had to grin and bear it, becoming very cold at times. Then I figured, why complain? That's why we got paid the big bucks!

One of the divers said he thought he might have seen a body down below, which obviously freaked him out a bit. When he mentioned this fact topside, everything came to a grinding halt. Even three years later, the sad parting of the eighty-four men was still being mourned as if it had happened only yesterday. It had been a catastrophe that had affected so many people living around the St. John's area. The close community was devastated. Everyone knew someone or was related to someone who had perished. We had been warned when coming out on this job to be very careful what you said or who you talked to. Anything out of the ordinary had to be dealt with the utmost of discretion and at the sole permission of our head office. Feelings were understandably much frayed, and this was a gravesite.

A disgruntled Dutch crane driver flew ashore on the chopper, and apparently after a few drinks in a bar, told what he had heard from the divers. He had been blamed on board for dropping the six-ton sister block twice during our dives, once narrowly missing a diver. He was immediately dismissed by the company, as the following day it was in all the newspapers. They were now calling for an immediate halt to all diving. Dutch informed us later that same day that the salvage job was now halted. We were now to go and look for bodies!

In the chamber, we were totally dumbfounded. This had only been a maybe. The diver confirmed he had seen a red pair of overalls and it looked like maybe some remains. We all had seen the destruction down there, and agreed it would be impossible for any remains, or red overalls for that matter, to still be there after three years. Maybe someone had dumped some overalls over the side during this or last year's operation. None of us was too keen on rummaging around inside the crumpled containers looking for bodies that would not be there after all these years.

They were asking us to risk lives again for no sensible purpose.

Bill was sent out to talk to us. It wasn't that we refused; it just didn't make any sense. Thankfully, after a few days, the powers that be realized that this had been completely blown out of proportion and that it made no sense. We did later discover the pair of red overalls in question, and indeed they were definitely not from the Ocean Ranger, nor were there any remains to be found. You only had to look at a piece of metal that had been on the seabed for a few years to see that life eventually takes over. Anything that is not metal would be completely consumed in a very short period of time.

The Dutch deck crew spent most of their time cutting up all the material that was brought on deck. The deck crawler crane picked up the pieces and put them into the cavernous hollow hold below. The hold was probably two football fields long, and probably as wide as a football field, and maybe forty feet deep. At the end of the job we had pretty much filled it all. One of the lifts that came on deck was the crumpled drilling derrick tower with the *Ocean Ranger* sign still ominously intact. Bent and torn, it still managed to remind everyone of the horror that must have happened in sending it into the deep grave below.

Ocean Ranger

> *She was named Ocean Ranger*
> *With a nickname the danger*
> *Where men from the land*
> *Took oil from the sea*
> *Their fatal demise*
> *Was taking for granted*
> *The fury of the cruel sea*

This angry sea took the hearts of these men
Pulverized by fear in this nature gone wild
This mightiest of rigs couldn't
Tame this rabid beast
Made a grave in this watery hole

(Chorus)
Black is the night that pours in your eyes
Green is the water so furious and cold
Your body is screaming
But your voice makes no sound

Eighty-four men lost their lives to this wreck
This mountain of steel
Laid here in the depths
Husbands and brothers, sons and
Your kin
All loved ones – close to your heart

There's twisted metal is all that remains
This once fine example of man's expertise
Is crushed like paper
From a great mighty hand

(Repeat Chorus)

There's boats overturned
Where few dared to leave
But sadly were smashed
And dragged to this depth
Now mixed with this nightmare
All crumbled and torn

Made a grave in this watery hole

Our job is to salvage
This vessel of death
Now three more brave lives
Have been lost to the sea
As divers struggled to set her free

It's three in the morning
My shift almost done
The living quarters – we're taking this long night
Through the darkness I hear
The ripping and the groans
As the crane takes the weight
And rips it from her womb

In this deep darkened water
My thoughts start to wander
       —K. Firth, December 1995

Excerpt from the CD Reunion

"As a deep-sea diver for many years working on the oil fields off Scotland and Newfoundland, I had many a memorable experience but nothing came close or was as demanding as the salvage of the Ocean Ranger. This floating oil rig, the largest in the world and probably the most technologically advanced of its time, capsized and sank off the tumultuous coast of Newfoundland. There are many similarities between this and the Titanic, excepting one – no one survived! During the first part of the salvage, three divers were killed in two separate incidents. At 260 feet, saturation diving techniques have to be used, with six divers living in pressure chambers working in shifts around the clock for thirty-four days! It is hard to express in words the feeling of being amongst this huge mangled piece of destruction. In respect to the families of the deceased mostly living in St. John's, Newfoundland, I would like to devote this song to their memory, in hope that a catastrophe of this dimension will never be allowed to happen again."

Derek and I were eventually decompressed, having spent thirty-four long days in SAT. We were a few pounds lighter and looked very pale and emaciated. Breathing the fresh sea air made me feel a wee bit high for a few minutes, but ever so happy to be out of the cramped conditions inside. I wandered over to where all of the huge capstan winches were stored on deck. They seemed smaller and more organized than what I had remembered.

I had been away from home for more than four months and was looking forward to getting off the boat and returning to my family. I was very tired!

CHAPTER 63

Oops!

I had sent home many letters and even some voice tapes. Things were going to be different. I had promised Dominic I would take him camping in Algonquin Park. Little did I know, because I had either been lying in a bunk or diving, my legs were giving me a lot of trouble. Barring the few weeks it took to install the system, it had been the longest time I had ever been away, not counting my navy days. With the saying that absence makes the heart grow fonder, I might have come home to a warm welcome, but something else was in the air.

I fulfilled my promise to Dominic to take a three-day camping and canoeing trip to Algonquin Park. We had a wonderful time portaging through many lakes into the quiet outback. My shins gave me hell for the first few days as my legs got used to walking again, but we spent a lot of time in a canoe so it wasn't too bad. Steven, my nephew, came along. Dominic seemed a bit testy with me at times, but overall it was a good father-and-son holiday. I put off the testiness because he was in fact a teenager, and of course my lack of being around. Sadly, it was the last time we ever had anything closely resembling a meaningful father and son relationship.

I even camped in our backyard one night with Kila to keep

her happy. She was nine years old and was a joy to be around. We would cuddle and watch TV together, and she was my constant companion on walks through the forest down to the river. Like my mother, she loved to be picked up and whizzed around and tickled. She was the ultimate daredevil when tobogganing down the snow hills, and often forced me to go with her. I remember bouncing off the sled and going face first into a snow bank. She was laughing her face off, while I was ready to puke since my head had frozen.

Dominic had stopped sitting on my knee when watching TV a year or so earlier. He too could be quite affectionate. A tickle would often end up in rough-and-tumble play fighting. Now that he was going through his difficult teens and obviously feeling a disquiet between his mum and me, he was going through a difficult time, and from time to time he got into trouble and Marilyn would ask me to scold him. I knew he resented every moment I was talking to him by the look in his eyes. I had never laid a hand on either one of my kids, apart from a mild spanking when they were small. Grounding him just brought on even more resentment.

After the first week of seemingly good times, Marilyn and I settled down to our usual bickering. Things were pretty much the same, except she seemed a little more distant.

While I had been working on the *Ocean Ranger* job for most of the summer of 1984, international oil prices had plummeted. Production of oil offshore in Hibernia, Newfoundland would be expensive, so the oil rigs were leaving in droves. It would be a few years before it would make financial sense to put money into producing oil there. There was only one rig remaining, and it was working off Halifax, one of the Bowdrill rigs with our sub system still on board. After my few weeks at home, Bill sent me out to supervise. I would spend pretty much the rest of the year crew changing from the Bowdrill rig.

I had had a bit of a run in with one of the company reps. I had told him on more than one occasion that when we had the sub in the water all work above must be halted. It was standard procedure and he should have known better. We had the sub on bottom, manned, doing some videoing for the drill floor, when they dropped a length of drill collar. It missed the sub, but it could have been a serious situation. I ran up to the drill floor and gave the rep a piece of my mind in front of all his cohorts. He was not pleased!

On one of the crew changes going out to the rig, we had been sent back to the hotel because of bad weather. The boys and I had a heavy night of drinking. The following morning we had taken the taxi out to the heliport. We were told the weather was still bad but that we should stay around the area, as it was marginal and there may be a flight later. We hit the nearest bar for the hair of the dog and then headed back out to the heliport. We had donned survival suits, as the flight was now a go. Lining up for the security check, I noticed one of the lads had stolen a bottle of scotch from the bar and was busy trying to hide it in his suit. I took it off him. If he was caught with it he would be immediately dismissed. I then put it behind my back and discreetly put it on a table close by. My attempt failed, as the bottle then fell off the table and broke. The security people saw it and came to the conclusion that, because of the vicinity and where we were standing, it had to be one of the diving crew.

When we arrived on board the rig, the rep immediately called me to his office. He had no concrete evidence, but explained because I was in charge of the crew, I would have to take the can, and the following day I was sent ashore. I was dismissed! The rep was glowing with a smile from ear to ear as I boarded the chopper.

I couldn't believe this was happening to me. Six weeks later I was still at home and calling Bill every other day. He told me that all I could do was write letters and basically grovel, which I pathetically had to do. It was to no avail, and as this was the only job remaining, I was royally fucked! I fessed up and told Marilyn what had happened. It was just something else to add to the long list of her disappointments. My savings were running out at an alarming rate. I had to do something soon.

CHAPTER 64
Is This Really Happening?

I was taking Kila out for a walk in the forest. She had a little doll with her. I innocently said, 'What a cute dolly. Who got you that?'

She said, 'Oh, Mummy's friend Joe. He took us to the fair and got it for me.'

My legs went weak, but then I thought, *Ah, she's just mixed up*. On returning, I bided my time and eventually asked Marilyn the question. To my absolute horror, she confessed that, yes, she had been seeing someone. Although I couldn't exactly blame her, what with my track record over the last couple of years, it still came as a huge blow. Deep inside, I had known this day was coming. Neither one of us had been happy. Sure, I could blame it on me being away so much or even my infidelities. In reality, we had just grown apart. Her thoughts of the future and mine didn't coincide. I tried so hard to win her back, but it just wasn't happening. I still felt that I loved her, and the thought of losing her was unbearable.

I had been dealing with this nightmare for over a week on October 12, 1984, wondering if things could get any worse, when out of my turmoil Marilyn answered our phone. She looked at me with what looked to be pity in her eyes and told me, 'Kevin, your mum has just died!'

'NO, no, no, that can't be right,' I said, and I picked up the phone. To this day I cannot remember who out of my family told me the sad news. I can't even remember what I did or how I dealt with it. The whole aftermath was just a blur. Somehow, with Marilyn's help, I booked an emergency bereavement flight to the UK for the following day.

My sister Rita and her husband picked me up from the airport and gave me the bewildering events of the last few days. My mother had died of a massive stroke. They had gone to see her doctor, who had given them the autopsy report.

Rita had previously told our story about Mum's deafness to Geoffrey, her husband. He had thought there was something not quite right, so he checked a little more deeply. He had found what medication she had taken when she was young from her doctor. When Geoffrey pushed the doctor for more information, he reluctantly told him what had been a secret even to our mother. Our mother and her brother Fred had, in fact, been born with syphilis. The disease had not been diagnosed until they were almost in their teens. They had been treated and completely cured of the disease, but the damage that had been done to their nervous systems by that time was immense. It was the cause of her deafness and of our Uncle Fred's seizures. She would still be able to have completely healthy children, so the facts had been denied all of her adult life. The doctor then added that he was surprised that our mother had lived so long. She was sixty-six.

My head was whirring. Just what was going on in my life? Was I being punished for the life I had been leading?

I was with my brother and sisters. We were all together again, a rare occasion in the latter part of our lives. This time we were trying so hard to help each other in our bereavement. It seemed a culmination of the very different life we had been brought up with. We each shared the feeling of being very different through our adolescence. None of us knew another family like ours. It was always like stepping into a time warp coming home. We never knew what events were coming our way. Would anyone actually believe us if we told of our experiences? Now, all of this new information just added to the strangeness and helplessness of it all. As always, though, our love for each other shone through. I have always known that while I have my three siblings walking around in this world, I will never be truly alone.

We consoled each other through our sadness. A huge character had left us that day. Her simple but absolute love for each of us was immeasurable. Sure, we had all been damaged somewhat. At the time, every single one of us was having marital issues that would shortly end in divorce.

Peggy's Dream

> *She could see beauty in a face*
> *We couldn't see*
> *Painted with fingers on old paper*
> *She didn't care*
> *Purple skies and yellow houses*
> *In her dreams escape*
>
> *(Chorus)*
> *Listen with your heart*
> *Hear with your eyes*
> *Feel the sound*
> *In her silent world*
> *She dreams in colour*
> *Voices sounding in her head*
> *She dreams and dreams*

Looking out of the window
Watch her children play
Laughing faces in their game
Touch a mother's heart
All the prayers she ever made
To hear a simple voice

(Repeat Chorus)

Look at the painting now
See a little more
A lifetime of silence and denial
Screams the colour
Eccentric lady in her time
So different from the rest

(Repeat Chorus)

—K. Firth, June 1997

Excerpt from the CD Reunion

"That song was written for a lady who lost her hearing at an early age, who struggled through life with a handicap in an era when deaf people were considered dummies. Nonetheless, she challenged life to bring up four healthy children. One of the few comforts she had was her gift of drawing, and later painting with her fingers, which she did on the back of old wallpaper. In the latter part of her life, she became quite eccentric, painting beautiful murals on her walls (amongst other eccentricities), but she was loved by all that came in contact with her. She was a very colourful lady.

I am very proud to have called her my mother."

After the sad funeral, I decided to head up to Aberdeen and try my luck at finding diving work. The oil problem was worldwide – too many divers, not enough work! I went to Sub Sea Offshore, the first company I had worked for, and met one of my old cohorts now working in the office. He told me that Dave Asquith, my old pal and bell diving partner, the guy that had drowned and miraculously come back, the lifetime confirmed bachelor, had in fact finally fallen madly in love. His lady got pregnant, but she then aborted the baby and left him. He had committed suicide! I left there quickly. I didn't need any more bad news. It was following me around like the plague!

CHAPTER 65
The Final Curtain Call

On returning home, nothing had changed. In fact, if anything, it had actually taken a turn for the worse. I eventually took a job as a commission-only kitchen cabinet salesman, pretty nondescript really. For Marilyn, that seemed to be the last straw. Weeks later, I still wasn't making enough to pay for the gas I was using. Marilyn finally left me for the other guy, and rightly so. I had absolutely nothing to offer. And with my track record, why the hell shouldn't she? I was going down fast and furious.

Cory and Elsie came to the rescue and let me stay with them. For a while their home was like an oasis in a barren, dry desert. They treated me like their very own son. I will forever be in their debt for the kindness in being there for me in my hour of need.

I had previously stopped eating and sleeping, and sometimes found myself driving disoriented in the middle of heavy traffic in downtown Toronto. Occasionally I would have to stop the car because I was hallucinating. A doctor had prescribed some pills to help me relax. I was taking them by the handful.

One evening, in complete despair I checked into a hospital. I was so low and scared that I couldn't spend another night alone. I felt suicidal. I ended up on the top floor of the hospital with the hard cases! I was put into a room where some of the patients were lashed into their beds. All night there was screaming and yelling. It was indeed a scary place. I laid awake wondering how I had gotten myself into this state. In the morning I joined the steady procession of glaze-eyed people walking around the circular corridor. I passed people strapped into chairs pooping and puking at the same time. I started to come to the conclusion that I really didn't belong there. The cold light of day had somehow brought me to my senses.

I found a nurse and asked if I could see the doctor. She was very busy and mumbled something about Monday. It was Saturday morning. I panicked! If I had to stay there for another night, I would for sure be bats in the belfry by morning. I pestered and pestered her until I was allowed to see a doctor. I was straightening out very quickly. The doctor also told me that I should stay until Monday. I pleaded with him and went on a lengthy explanation of my situation. I gave him the whole scuttlebutt – until I noticed he had quietly nodded off.

When I walked out of that hospital one hour later, I could have kissed the pavement. I was a new man. Inadvertently, the one evening in the nut house had put me on the straight and narrow. It was my turnaround moment. I had hit rock bottom, and I knew if I didn't start to come to grips with my situation, I would end up walking around that endless corridor on the top floor for an eternity. Even though I knew I had some huge hurdles to jump in the near future, and some of them would always remain unsurmountable, I had to allow myself to accept the situation. And right there I saw a small light at the end of the tunnel.

I later met Cindy at work. A fellow salesperson designer, she became my sounding board. I desperately needed someone to talk to and make sense out of the insanity that seemed to surround me. We quickly became an item. She had put up with me in some of my worst moments, which she really didn't deserve. For some strange reason, she was then blamed for my marriage break up. I could not understand how my kids could not figure out for themselves that this was such an obvious lie. The whole thing became a circus, as she was drawn into the fiasco. We moved in together, and from there matters just got worse. There were times when my kids told me that they were not allowed to eat at the same table as Cindy.

Bill called me out of the blue about a year later. I met Peter in St. John's and we mobilized a dive system on a rig. The work was to cap all of the available wells in the Hibernia oil field. There was talk that one of the deep dives was going to be over 800 feet, a record in Newfoundland. For a brief moment I thought, very recklessly, *Hmm, what a nice way to go!*

After the last cap, Peter and I knew it was over. *Hasta luego,* my friends, the final curtain call on diving offshore. It would be quite a few years before production of oil came back to the Grand Banks.

I returned home to the same uphill battle that I had left. I was living in hope that sooner or later the hurt would subside and I would be allowed to live a normal life with my kids. It wasn't to be. Cindy knew my kids always came first. She could not understand, any more than I, why there was so much animosity. She tried in her way to give me comfort in my low days, and her parents were also a godsend. My guilt was bad enough under the situation, but now I was also dragging this innocent, caring soul down to my level. I sure was not ready to make another commitment either with my track record, so we eventually came to a sad parting.

I saw the kids some weekends until they got bored. They had changed so much, and almost despised me as much as their mother did. I will never forget the feeling as I watched my little girl run away from me once when I was picking her up from school – the fearful look in her eyes as she looked back at me. How could she possibly think that I would ever be capable of doing her any harm? What kind of sheer wickedness had been inflicted on her mind to try and change her love for me into this defiled hatred? I was completely helpless to change any of this. I was the one out in the cold. Whatever means I tried to make amends were turned around in the most awful way. I could not believe how another human being whom I had loved so dearly could inflict so much pain to gain so little.

No Tears Left

Does a memory from a time
Jog the thoughts of a daughter and a son
Who for a while had the love
And the trust
That was never less than won

(Chorus)
Has the love been lost
When the tears cease to fall
Will the pain and the years
Around a heart build a wall

The photos fade with age
The folds turn to tears
Through the shreds I see their faces
Burn through my inner soul
But their love my heart still shares

(Repeat Chorus)

Where are you now, what do you think
Am I a product of your hate?
Or has the poison of another one
Filled your heart with the shame
Is that my fate?

(Repeat Chorus)

A father's love is no less
The caring is no more
Than when you were in my arms
Innocent and true as the day is long
The blinding trust that could
Take your heart away

(Break)

Look at me now, though the years
Have come and gone
Am I a stranger – I couldn't hurt you
It's only me, only me

— K. Firth, October 1993

I eventually put it down to my one big crime – not being there when they needed me the most. I had failed miserably as a father in the most important way. I eventually found, as I suppose many other divorced fathers do, that the more you try to be with them, trying to remind them that you are still the same old dad, the more the opposing faction tries to destroy whatever small relationship is remaining. The child inevitably becomes a pawn in the ensuing battle.

I came to the heart-wrenching conclusion that I loved my

children very much, so the best thing I could do for their peace of mind and happiness was to let them go. This was going to be my final cruel punishment. I had to be a man and try to roll all of that wonderful and special love into a ball and bury it deep in my heart. I had lost the battle. Now it was time to shed a lifetime of tears and try to live with myself.

Marilyn disappeared shortly thereafter with the kids and her Joe. I didn't see my Michaella for eleven long years. And Dominic, well, just once in the last twenty-five years.

Not knowing where they were anymore on their birthdays, I found myself wandering up and down the birthday card displays in the stores looking for the right card and reading the words I daydreamed my kids would read from me. I watched the other people picking their cards with envy. Sometimes I even read the cards 'To Dad,' trying to make believe I'd just received the card from them. Their birthdays have always been hard on me. I would try and envision what they would look like at their new age and what they might be doing.

Child of Mine

A great sorrow came over him
As he lay his weary head
Grief and sorrow are his only friends
Companions he cannot shed

He remembers braiding hair
Kiss his daughter off to school
Now she looks the other way
Treats him like a simple fool

Oh, what happened

Oh, where to go

How can that precious love so dear
Be turned around and locked away in fear
Why did you use that simple soul
As a pawn now that you've made your goal

In the early mornin' hour
In that time 'tween sleep and wake
I met you in my dream
You were sleepin' on my shoulder
Sweet little innocence
Child of mine

You opened your eyes
Like a doorway to my soul
Can this be real
Please don't wake me

I promised you
With your little hand in mine
I'd never ever leave you
This is the only place
We can ever meet

In my dream – dream – dream – dream
— K. Firth, November 1998

I don't celebrate Christmas anymore. In fact, it has become a dread. I remember happier days when it was a celebration. Nowadays, I want it to be over as quickly as possible.

My Michaella eventually got married. A friend back in

Haslingden sent me a newspaper cutting. I was very happy for her, my grownup girl looking ever so pretty. It read that her father Joe had given her away. She would never know how much that had hurt me to the core.

You see, I didn't get killed in a diving bell. I wasn't maimed by the bends, and I didn't even suffer aseptic bone necrosis, the diver disease that rots your bones. No, none of them. I suffered the other, more common diver's disease called divorce.

After all these years, it is only now that I am able to tell this story. Age, it seems, has taken off the sharp edges. I am certainly not looking for pity. On the contrary, I wouldn't change any of my adventure. If I pop my clogs tomorrow, I know I've had a pretty damn good innings. I might at times have pushed the envelope, but I'm still here telling this tale. Sure, it came to an abrupt end, and I'm just an old geezer with some fancy tales to tell, but it was never my plan to hurt anyone. Life just takes you on its merry little way. You live one day at a time. You never know which one might be your last!

I don't feel hate for anyone. I don't think I deserved to lose the love of my two kids. But as far as I am concerned, I have forgiven. I am happy just to know that I have loved with gusto, with all of my heart. There is still a secret place deep inside where I have a rolled up bundle of special love that will always be a part of me.

I would rather remember the good times. My wife gave me two beautiful children. Whether they care for me or not is immaterial. It is how I feel about them that matters. I could not imagine my life having not shared my time with them. Nobody can take away what is in my heart for my kids and for the few wonderful ladies in my life that I have loved dearly. Affairs of the heart, for me as a young man, were always fraught with disappointment. I sometimes wonder if I brought that on intentionally. Either way, in later years I think I have found some peace.

I have always missed the camaraderie of a bunch of hand-picked trained professionals out on a semi-dangerous operation. The characters in my story are all real and not Hollywood action heroes. They were not full of brawn and muscles, all tanned with a manicured appearance. No, these men were all pretty much rough around the edges. Most of them rode their lives hard, right down to the metal. Tomorrow was always just another day. There were more divers killed in fast sports cars than there ever was on the job. Biscuit, my dear friend, almost bit the bullet on many occasions crashing fast cars.

I have never met or known a diver that has stayed in a marital relationship. They all have one thing in common: disastrous and usually costly divorces. We worked hard and threw in a bit of danger, but we played hard too. We always looked out for each other, on or off the job. Some of them aren't around anymore. It seems every year I lose a couple, and thankfully it has nothing to do with the diving.

I still miss my kids like I did then, and that is the price I have had to pay. I live in hope that one day they will find it in their hearts to forgive me.

Time

Fallin' down is not so bad
Gettin' up is terribly hard
Those days wakin' up
Dark, dark grey skies

Mistakes we can make
Years gone by river of tears
Turn back the time is what we ask

Regrets, regrets disappear

(Chorus)
The past is a beast you can never ever change
And the future is what's comin', simply let it be
Focus on what's good and live

Look outside of your head
Beauty abounds, just open your eyes
And take the time to treasure love
'Cos love can come, oh, but love, love can go

(Repeat Chorus)
— K. Firth, July 2, 2009

A companion CD, *Reunion*, can be purchased from my website, http://kevinfirth.ca/

Most of the songs in this book are on the CD. Various photographs pertaining to this book may also be viewed at the above website.

If you loved this book, would you please submit a review at Amazon.com?

CPSIA information can be obtained at www.ICGtesting.com
Printed in the USA
LVOW11s0726061015

456913LV00003B/2/P